# CUTTING EDGE

## UPPER INTERMEDIATE

Book + 1 CD

*Please do not write in the pages.*

Longman

**STUDENTS' BOOK**

sarah cunningham    peter moor

## Part A **Task**

## Part A **Task**

# Part B **Language**

# Part B  Language

| Language focus | Writing | Further skills and vocabulary |
|---|---|---|
| 1) **Relative clauses**<br>*Pronunciation:* intonation<br><br>2) **Quantifiers, and *some* and *any***<br>(*some, enough, plenty, a little, little,* etc.) | **Follow-up task:** write an eye-witness account of an important event | **Real life:** awkward social situations<br>*Pronunciation:* polite intonation<br><br>**Reading and vocabulary:** history in the making<br><br>Do you remember? |
| 1) **Infinitive forms**<br><br>2) **Infinitive or gerund (*-ing* form)?**<br>*Pronunciation:* stressed and weak forms (reading aloud) | **Writing skills:** linking ideas and arguments (using *however, inspite of,* etc.) | **Follow-up task:** list the pros and cons of being rich and famous, etc.<br><br>**Wordspot:** *about* |
| 1) **Modal and related verbs - present forms** (*can, may, might, must, should*)<br><br>2) **Past modals** (*could, could have, had to, may have, must have*) | **Writing skills:** formal letters and formal language | **Follow-up task:** A real life whodunit<br><br>**Reading and speaking:** *It's all a conspiracy!*<br><br>**Real life:** saying what's wrong with things<br><br>Do you remember? |
| 1) **Review of basic future forms** (*going to, will,* Present Continuous and Present Simple)<br><br>2) **Future Continuous and Future Perfect**<br>*Pronunciation:* weak forms of auxiliary verbs | **Writing skills:** formal and informal messages | **Follow-up task:** arrange an excursion<br><br>**Listening and speaking:** an interview with a communications expert<br><br>**Real life:** dealing with problems when telephoning<br><br>Do you remember? |
| 1) **Talking about hypothetical situations** (*wish, if* + past tense, *if only, imagine, suppose*)<br><br>2) **Talking about hypothetical situations in the past** (*wish, if* + Past Perfect, etc.) | **Follow-up task:** write about an imaginary situation | **Real life:** giving and reporting opinions<br>*Pronunciation:* Stress and emphasis with opinions<br>**Wordspot:** *have*<br><br>Do you remember? |
| 1) **Reporting people's exact words** (basic reported speech)<br><br>2) **Verbs that summarise what people say** (*deny, refuse, insist,* etc.) | | **Follow-up task:** tell a 'human interest' story<br><br>**Wordspot:** *speak* and *talk* |

( **Language summary** (pages 147 – 161) )  ( **Irregular verbs** (page 162) )  ( **Tapescripts** (pages 163 – 176) )

# module 1
# Past, present and future

## Part A Task

Speaking and reading: *The people's century*

Vocabulary: past, present and future time phrases

Preparation for task: three generations of a family talk about their lives

Task: talk about your past, present and future

## Speaking and reading

**1** **a)** The extracts on pages 6-7 come from a book called *The People's Century*. Look at the photographs, and read the captions. What kind of people do they show? Where did they live?

**b)** Read extracts from interviews with these people, and match them with the photographs. Which words and phrases gave you clues as to who was talking?

**2** **a)** Look at the words and phrases in the box. If necessary, check the meaning in your mini-dictionary or with your teacher.

| full of hardship    exciting, good fun |
| secure and conventional |
| unconventional    horrific |
| carefree    irresponsible    tedious |
| pointless    appealing    tragic |
| materialistic    heroic    admirable |

**b)** Which of these words or phrases apply to each person's life? Can you think of any other words to describe their lives? Explain your answers in groups.

① Ernst Weckerling was a German infantryman during World War I, when nearly nine million men died.

② Yvonne Mouffe grew up in a coal producing area of Belgium in the 1930s, a decade of economic depression and industrial unrest.

③ Luigi Cavaliere was a cinema projectionist in Rome during World War II.

④ Suezo Uchida worked in a factory in Japan in the 1950s, a time when the Japanese economy grew very fast.

⑤ Ron Thelin was a hippy who dropped out of college in San Francisco in the late 1960s.

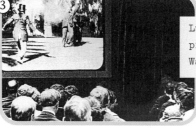

⑥ Jaqui Ceballos was a feminist in the United States in the 1960s and 1970s.

**3** Discuss the following questions.

a   Would you like to have taken part in any of these events?

b   Imagine you had a time machine. Which other centuries would you choose to visit? Explain why.

c   How do you think our present age will be remembered?

> *I would love to know what it was / will be like in ...*

### The people's century

*The story of the 20th century told through the lives of ordinary people.*

**A**

'Everybody wanted to have some fun, and the only thing available was the cinema. Television was not yet available. Everybody would eagerly wait for a new and beautiful film to watch. In these theatres, even if they were not well equipped, people would queue up anxiously waiting to watch the show ... Kids brought pans full of food from home while waiting for the theatre to open. Going to the movies was a party ... everybody wished to forget about the ugliness of the war.'

**B**

'I usually went to the company at eight o'clock. I continued working until nine in the evening. That was the usual day. On one day only – Wednesday – I came home at four o'clock. That was the working situation then. I was a workaholic, I worked almost all Sundays, too. I had no time to talk to my wife.'

**C**

'It seemed like anything was possible … Every kind of character … seemed to appear on the street, because you could dress however you wanted … I opened a shop selling books, crafts, drugs, records. There was even room for meditation and art shows in the shop. We put 'free' in front of everything we sold ... We were exploring what freedom and a free society was.'

**D**

'The air was full of smoke and fumes from the constant firing of the French guns. The crater I was in was so deep that the breeze couldn't blow the fumes away. The air was so bad that we were parched with thirst and breathing was very difficult.'

**E**

'At protest marches we threw our garments and cosmetics into the trash can ... We threw bras, stockings, high-heeled shoes, and false eyelashes – they were oppressive items for women. It was a feeling of power, that we all wanted to change society and that we could do it. And it was a worldwide movement – Britain, France, Italy – there were movements all over the world.'

**F**

'I can remember there being only one room. We used to cuddle up to each other to keep warm, it is much warmer that way if you are on the ground. There were nine children, and we slept on the floor. … Father worked in the mines but during the strike they received nothing at all, so we had nothing but potatoes to eat and from time to time some bread, but apart from that nothing.'

# Vocabulary

## Past, present and future time phrases

**1** Mark the phrases in the box P (past), N (present/now) or F (future). Use your mini-dictionary where necessary. In some cases, more than one answer is possible.

over the <u>last few decades</u> [P]  in those days ☐
these days ☐  nowadays ☐  <u>not long</u> ago ☐
at one time ☐  in the <u>long</u> term ☐  current ☐
in the <u>weeks</u> leading up to ☐  the latest ☐
in <u>100 years'</u> time ☐  during <u>the Cold War era</u> ☐

**2 a)** Use one of the words or phrases from the box to replace those in **bold** below.

*In the past ...*                                    *in those days*
1 Working conditions tended to be much harder ~~then~~.
2 Attitudes towards young people's freedom have changed a great deal **since the 1950s**.
3 **Once**, it was very uncommon for women to go out on their own in the evening.
4 Until **quite recently**, only well-off people could afford to travel abroad.

*Now ...*
5 People are generally more prosperous **now**.
6 However, the **present** rate of unemployment is a lot higher than it was in the 1950s.
7 Technology is changing so fast it can be hard to keep up with **the most recent** developments.

*In the future ...*
8 There will be a lot of demonstrations **in the weeks before** the election.
9 We all hope that unemployment will get better **for a long time in the future**.
10 Will people still be worried about the same problems **100 years from now**?

**b)** What other words and phrases could replace the ones underlined?

**3** Work in pairs. Student A looks at the card on page 141, and Student B looks at the card on page 145. Read out the first question on your card, and give your partner a few seconds to think. Then he / she talks about that topic for one minute or more using at least one of the time phrases in Exercise 2 in the answer. Do the same with each question on the cards.

## Personal vocabulary

# Task: talk about your past, present and future

**Useful language**

**Talking about your life map**

"... is the place where / the person who ..."

"The reason I put this down was that ..."

"Let me explain about ..."

"... is / was important to me because ..."

**Useful verbs**

"I was born in ..."

"I grew up in ..."

"I moved to ..."

"I started / left school / university, etc."

"I became interested in ..."

"I'm thinking of ..."

"I'm hoping to ..."

"I'd like to ..."

**Asking about someone else's life map**

"What exactly is the importance of ...?"

"Can you tell me a bit more about ...?"

"Who / what / where exactly is ...?"

## Preparation for task

1 You are going to hear extracts from interviews with three generations of the Robinson family: Eric (68), his daughter Debbie (40), and his grandson Joel (16). What can you guess about them from the photographs and the key words in their 'life maps' on the left?

2 [1.1] Listen and make further notes about each key topic in the diagrams on the left. Compare answers with a partner.

## Task

1 **a)** Copy the diagram below onto a larger sheet of paper and prepare a life map for yourself. Include key words about the following topics:

- childhood ambitions    • your home / places where you've lived
- when / where you were born    • education / studies / jobs (where / when)
- significant recent events    • hopes / ambitions for the long-term future
- parents / family background    • memorable journeys / holidays, etc.
- plans for the short-term future    • interests and hobbies
- the people closest to you in the past and the present

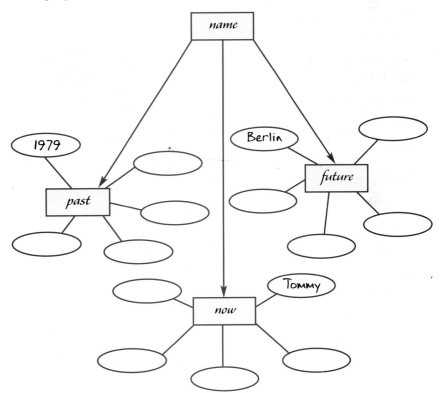

**b)** You are going to explain your life map in the same way as Eric, Debbie and Joel. Ask your teacher about any important words or phrases you need, and write them in your *Personal vocabulary* box. Think about how you will explain your life map to other students. Look at the phrases in the *Useful language* box to help you.

2 **a)** Work in pairs. Explain your life maps to each other, answering any questions your partner has.

**b)** Present your partner's life map to the other students in your group or class. You have a maximum of two minutes, so choose only the most important points.

# Part B Language

Ten things you should know about English verbs (revision)
Different uses of auxiliary verbs
Wordspot: *get*
Writing skills: drafting a piece of writing
Real life: starting, maintaining and ending conversations

## Language focus 1

How good is your knowledge of English verb forms? This quiz is designed to test what you know. Work through it with a partner, then check your answers on page 141 and find out your 'Grammar Genius' rating on page 11.

*1* **a** Which job does the man on the left see as his permanent job? *(1 mark)*
**b** Which does he see as a temporary job? *(1 mark)*
**c** How do the verb forms help to show this? *(1 mark)*

*2* The verbs in the four examples below are not normally found in the continuous (-*ing*) form. Why not? *(2 marks)*
Do you know any other verbs like this? *(2 marks)*
**a** *I know the answer to that question!*
**b** *Her brother's very unfriendly.*
**c** *Do you like this soup?*
**d** *What do you think?*

*3* Two sentences above can be changed to the continuous form. Which? How does this change the meaning? *(2 marks)*

'Of course I really drive Formula 1 cars. I'm only driving a taxi to earn a bit of extra money.'

## Ten things you should know about English verbs!

*4* Read the two sentences below.
*Hannah **broke** her leg while she **was ice-skating**.*
*We **were sitting** watching the television happily and suddenly all the lights **went** off!*
**a** Which of the two actions started first in each of the sentences? *(1 mark)*
**b** Did Hannah continue ice-skating?
Yes. / No. / Maybe. *(1 mark)*
**c** Did they continue watching television?
Yes. / No. / Maybe. *(1 mark)*

*5* You meet a friend in the street and notice she has a new hairstyle. Which of the following do you say? Why? *(2 marks)*
**a** *You're changing you hair – it looks really nice!*
**b** *You've changed your hair – it looks really nice!*
**c** *You changed your hair – it looks really nice!*

*6* Which diagram represents each sentence most accurately? *(2 marks)*
*She's **worked** in television for three years.*
*She **worked** in television for three years.*

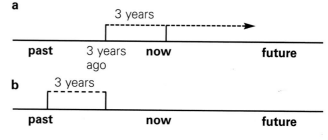

*7* Underline the most logical way to complete each sentence. Give reasons for your choice.
**a** *They'd known each other for a long time*
*... before they started going out.*
*... and they're really good friends. (1 mark)*
**b** *They've known each other for a long time*
*... before they realised they didn't get on.*
*... but they don't get on very well. (1 mark)*

f  She *had worn / was wearing* a new hat which she *was designing / had designed* herself.

g  Their cousin, Alan, *has just started / had just started* working for an international bank.

h  He *trained / was training* to become an accountant.

*8* Underline the most likely sentence for each situation. Can you explain why?

**a** The phone rings.

*I'll answer it. / I'm going to answer it. (2 marks)*

**b** A: *Have you got any plans for this weekend?*

B: *Yes, I'll have / I'm having a party on Saturday. Would you like to come? (2 marks)*

*9* Complete the following sentences in a logical way. Which tense do you use?

**a** *Please call me as soon as you ...*

**b** *I can't tell you anything more until I ... (2 marks)*

*10* All the verbs in **bold** are in the Past Simple, but which of them really refer to the past? *(2 marks)*

**a** *If only I **had** enough time to do all the things I'd like to!*

**b** *As a child, he always **had** plenty of friends.*

**c** *If I **knew** what you wanted me to do, I could help you!*

**d** *I **knew** at once that she was lying.*

Why are the other verbs in the Past Simple?

*(2 marks)*

What is your Grammar Genius rating?

**21–28** You have a good knowledge of English verbs, but it's still probably worth checking in the Language summary on page 147.

**11–20** There are still quite a few gaps in your knowledge. Have a look in the Language summary on page 147.

**0–10** You definitely need to check in the Language summary on page 147.

## Practice

*1* The pictures on the right show two wedding photos: Suzanne's wedding to Sergio in 1991, and her sister Sophie's wedding to Paul, today. In both pictures you can also see their cousin, Alan. Circle the correct verb form in the sentences about Suzanne's wedding.

*In 1991 ...*

a  Suzanne *had got married to / was getting married to* Sergio, a Brazilian businessman.

b  Suzanne *had only known / only knew* Sergio for a couple of months.

c  After the wedding, they *went / have gone* to live in Brazil.

d  Suzanne's younger sister, Sophie, *has still been / was still* at school then.

e  She *wanted / was wanting* to be a hairdresser when she *left / was leaving* school.

*2* Use the information in brackets to complete the sentences about Sophie, Suzanne and Alan's lives **today**. Add any extra words such as articles, prepositions, etc.

a  Sophie ......... (*not become hairdresser / instead / work fashion magazine*).

*Sophie didn't become a hairdresser – instead she works for a fashion magazine.*

b  She ......... (*marry Paul / who / design clothes*).

c  The happy couple ......... (*spend / honeymoon / Barbados*).

d  Suzanne ......... (*not stay married to Sergio / very long*), but she ......... (*stay / Brazil / a few years*).

e  She ......... (*be married / second husband, Dominic, / for about four years*).

f  Unfortunately, Alan ......... (*lose / job / with bank / two years ago*).

g  These days, he ......... (*run / own business from home*).

*3* Work in pairs. Find six more differences between Sophie, Suzanne and Alan now, and in 1991. Discuss which are the best tenses to express this in English.

1991

Suzanne's wedding

today

Sophie's wedding

**11**

# Language focus 2

## Different uses of auxiliary verbs

**1** Read the conversation and complete the gaps with phrases using auxiliaries.

LIZ: I suppose you've heard the latest ... about Ian and Patsy?

KATE: No, what happened?

LIZ: Oh, didn't you hear? They've split up.

KATE: (a) *Have they*?

LIZ: Yeah, I thought everybody knew.

KATE: Hmm, well, I suppose it's not really surprising, (b) ...............? I mean, they never really seemed to have that much in common.

LIZ: How do you mean?

KATE: Well, their interests for a start: he's really into his computers and computer games and all that kind of stuff, but she (c) ............... . She prefers something a bit livelier, going out to clubs and things, having a good time.

LIZ: Yes, she (d) ............... like going out more than him, that's true.

KATE: Has she told you anything about it?

LIZ: Yes, (e) ............... . She phoned me on Friday. It seems that it all came to a bit of a crisis when ...

**2** [1.2] Listen and check your answers.

## Analysis

Where is the auxiliary verb used:
a to add emphasis?
b to form a tag question?
c to show interest?
d to form a short answer to a question?
e to avoid repeating words or phrases?

*Now read Language summary B on page 147.*

# Practice

**1 a)** [1.3] Listen to ten short conversations. Underline the phrase which would complete each conversation logically.

1 (a) I do believe you.
  (b) I did believe you.
  (c) I will believe you.

2 (a) Yes, I am!
  (b) Yes, I will!
  (c) Yes, I do!

3 (a) don't they?
  (b) haven't they?
  (c) weren't they?

4 (a) I won't.
  (b) I don't.
  (c) I'm not.

5 (a) I did tell you!
  (b) I am telling you!
  (c) I will tell you!

6 (a) Do you?
  (b) Are you?
  (c) Did you?

7 (a) Of course I will!
  (b) Of course I do!
  (c) Of course I am!

8 (a) Have they?
  (b) Do they?
  (c) Are they?

9 (a) I'm not.
  (b) I wasn't.
  (c) I was.

10 (a) wasn't it, darling?
   (b) isn't it, darling?
   (c) hasn't it, darling?

**b)** [1.4] Listen to check.

## Pronunciation

1 [1.5]
a Auxiliary verbs can have a strong or a weak pronunciation. Listen and mark the auxiliaries underlined **S** if they sound strong and **W** if they sound weak.

  1 Things <u>have</u> changed a lot since you <u>were</u> a child, <u>haven't</u> they?
  2 We're going to Iceland for our holiday this year. – <u>Are</u> you?
  3 <u>Do</u> you want any ice cream or not? – Of course I <u>do</u>!
  4 Carmen and Roger <u>are</u> going to have another baby. – <u>Are</u> they?

b When do the auxiliary verbs sound weak? When do they sound strong?

2 Listen again and practise the sentences, paying attention to the strong and weak pronunciation of the auxiliaries. Then practise the conversations using Recording 5 on page 163.

2 **a)** Work in pairs. Prepare similar short conversations based on some of these situations. Include at least three examples of auxiliaries.

- A man is trying to persuade a woman that he seriously wants to marry her. She's not so sure.
- Two people are having an argument after getting lost.
- A mother is talking to one of her children who is about to go on holiday without her for the first time.
- A really good piece of gossip about your friend's love life.
- An employer is accusing an employee of stealing some money.

**b)** Practise your conversations, then act out some of them for the rest of the class.

# Wordspot

*get*

1 *Get* is one of the most common verbs in English, and has a number of different meanings. Here are some of the main uses. Check that you understand the examples.

2 Here are some more phrases that are often used with *get*. Check the meaning and write them into the correct place on the diagram.

get stuck    get in touch with someone    get broken    get away
get a shock    get pneumonia    get to work late    get on with something
get it right / wrong    get ready    get your car mended    get into trouble
get a good impression of someone    get a present for someone

3 Work in pairs. Student A reads out the first part of a sentence from card A on page 142. Student B completes the sentence using a phrase with *get* and then looks at card B on page 145.

For example:

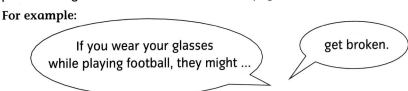

4 Copy the diagram in Exercise 1 to make a poster for your classroom wall.

**13**

# Writing skills

## Drafting a piece of writing

**1** **a)** When you write a composition or an important letter, do you plan it before you write the final draft? What do you do? Compare answers with other students.

**b)** Read *Four stages to better writing*. Do you normally use this kind of approach when you write in English? How do you think it could improve your writing?

---

# Four stages to better writing

### 1 Preparing and gathering information

Give yourself a time limit to brainstorm all the topics you might include, and to check information. Make brief notes by topic. Get as much information as you can on paper – don't worry about organisation or grammatical accuracy at this stage – you can always change things later. See A.

### 2 Structuring

Think about the order in which you will present the information. If possible, check with another student / your teacher to see if they think it is clear and logical. See B.

### 3 First draft and feedback

Write a first draft, giving yourself a time limit to complete the text. Show your first draft to another student / your teacher. Ask them to point out any things that are unclear, or if there are any important mistakes. See C.

### 4 Final draft

Use the feedback from your reader to prepare a final draft. When you've finished, quickly 'proof-read' your work (check it through for simple errors, spelling mistakes, etc.). If you're happy with what you've written, you've finished!

---

**2** **a)** Look at the notes (A) and the personal profile (C) written by a student. What is the title of the profile?

- My sporting hero
- My grandfather who fought in the war
- My oldest and dearest friend
- A rock-and-roll legend
- My favourite film star
- The most eccentric person I know

**b)** Important names in the profile have been blacked out. Can you guess who it is about? (For the answer see page 142.)

**3** Look at the notes and the profile again and answer the following questions.

a What other ideas and topics would you put in your notes if you were writing about one of the other titles?

b Which of the ideas in A would you include in each paragraph outlined in B? Read the first draft of the profile in C to check your answers.

c There are nine spelling mistakes in the first draft of the profile. Find and correct them. Use your mini-dictionary to check.

**A**
- lifestyle now (married with four children)
- now a grandfather
- symbol of rebellion in sixties
- still touring – huge audiences at concerts
- well-educated – went to university
- born 1943 in London
- secure middle class background – father a teacher
- physical appearance (long hair / big lips )
- behaviour on stage
- first hit – 1963
- most famous hits in sixties and seventies
- lifestyle in sixties – wild, lots of beautiful girlfriends
- these days – fitness and health fanatic

**B**
1 what he's most famous for
2 early life and career
3 life in sixties
4 his lifestyle today
5 his career today

c

To many people, ████████ will always be a symbol of sixties rebelion, with his long hair, pouting lips and outragous stage act.

His upbringing, however, was surprisingly conventional and middle class. He was born near London in July 1943, the son of a teacher. He did well at school and went on to study at the London School of Economics. It was while he was studying at university that he met up with his old friend from primary school ████████ Together with a number of other musicans they formed a band, ████████ and had their first hit 'Come On' in 1963.

This was followed by a string of hits in Britain and the US throughout the sixties and seventies including 'Satisfaction', 'Brown Sugar' and 'Honky Tonk Women' to name just a few. But he was eqally famous for his wild rock-and-roll lifestyle; and a succession of relationships with beautiful models and actresses meant that he was never out of the news for long.

However, as time passed, even Mr Rock and Roll himself felt the need to settle down, meeting and eventualy marrying the Texan model ████████ with whom he now has four children. These days he i's more interested in fitness and health – he jogs or works out in the gym every day.

Not everything has changed, though. Today more than thirty-five years after the ████████ formed, he still has no plans to retir. The band still produces albums and plays together, performing to huge audiances all over the world. And despite the fact that he is now a grandfather, his stage act is said to be as wild as ever!

*Follow-up task*

**1** Either in pairs or individually, write a personal profile. Use one of the titles in Writing skills, Exercise 2 or invent a title of your own. Follow the *Four stages to better writing*. You can also look at the time phrases on page 7.

**2** If you have written about someone that other students in your class know, put your profile up on the wall for them to read. Black out any names that reveal the person's identity, and see if your classmates can guess who you wrote about.

# Real life

Starting, maintaining and ending conversations

**1** 🖭 [1.6] Sean and Fiona are meeting for the first time at the reception desk of a hotel. Listen to their conversation.

a   What do they talk about?
b   Do you notice any difference in the attitude of the two speakers?

**2** Listen again and answer the questions. Ask your teacher to stop the cassette when you hear the answers to the questions.

a   How does Sean begin the conversation?
b   What questions does Sean ask Fiona?
c   What kinds of answer does Fiona give?
d   What words / phrases do you hear that show that Fiona wants to finish the conversation? Do you think she was rude?

## 3

**a)** Mark the phrases **S** if they are useful for starting a conversation and **E** if they are useful for ending a conversation.

**b)** Which of the phrases sound:

• polite?   • casual but friendly?   • rude?

**c)** Which would be appropriate in the situations in the pictures?

a) Nice to meet you. Did you have a comfortable flight? ☐

b) Leave me alone, will you? ☐

c) Hi! What are you doing here! ☐

d) OK, I'll let you get on. ☐

e) Well, I'd better be off. ☐

f) Excuse me, I wonder if you could help me ... ☐

g) Anyway, it's been nice seeing you again ... ☐

h) Sorry to disturb you, but ... ☐

i) Welcome to Toronto. Is this your first visit to Canada? ☐

j) Right, I'd better get back to work. ☐

k) Hello! What a surprise to see you here! ☐

## 4

One of the best ways of maintaining a conversation is by asking questions. This means the other person always has something to talk about! Imagine someone said the following to you, think of at least two questions you could ask.

**For example:**

I come from Latvia.

Oh, that's interesting. Isn't that on the Baltic Sea?

Do you? Whereabouts in Latvia exactly? Riga?

Really? So what language do you speak then?

a   I only got here yesterday.
b   I'm a teacher.
c   I'm from a place called San Lorenzo.
d   My name's Amazon.
e   We're just about to go out to the cinema.

## 5

Work in pairs. Choose a situation and relationship from the list. Spend a few minutes preparing your roles then act out the conversation. You have to keep the conversation going for at least five minutes. Use some of the phrases in Exercise 3 to start and end the conversation.

| Situation | Relationship |
|---|---|
| • at an airport | • old friends who haven't met each other for a long time |
| • in a hotel lounge | |
| • in someone's office | • neighbours / colleagues who don't know each other very well who meet unexpectedly |
| • in a cafe or bar | |
| • at a famous tourist attraction / art gallery in your country | • someone's first day in a new job |
| | • complete strangers |
| | • good friends |

# Do you remember?

 **a) The words in the box are used to describe peoples' lives. Put them in the appropriate columns, as in the examples. Compare answers in pairs, explaining your reasons if necessary.**

| | |
|---|---|
| carefree conventional ~~exciting~~ | |
| full of hardship heroic | |
| irresponsible materialistic | |
| secure tedious ~~tragic~~ | |
| unconventional workaholic | |

| positive | negative | not sure / neither |
|---|---|---|
| *exciting* | *tragic* | |

**b) Which syllable is stressed in each word or phrase? Mark it like this:**

*exciting*

**Which time words are correct? If more than one possibility is correct, explain the difference, if any.**

a) My sister's *present / current* boyfriend is from Finland.

b) It's better *in the long-term / in the short-term* to avoid over-spending and getting into debt.

c) We don't go out in the evening very much *these days / nowadays*.

d) *These days / in those days / at one time*, most women gave up work once they got married.

e) Have you heard *the latest / the last* news about Carl and Helen?

f) Kate has been quite ill *over the last month / in a month's time*.

 **There are mistakes in three of these sentences. Find the sentences and correct the mistakes.**

a) My dad's being very bad-tempered at the moment.

b) My grandparents have last visited us just before Christmas.

c) Rosa and Tony have had a really difficult time over the last couple of years: they've just had their second baby when he lost his job.

d) I've been thinking, perhaps we should buy a new car.

e) Hannah's going to phone us as soon as she's got any news.

f) I would help you if I would have time.

 **Put the phrases into six groups. Each group has three phrases with a similar use of *get*. What does *get* mean in each case?**

**For example:** get a bus
get a taxi   get a train
(*get = catch / take*)

| |
|---|
| get flu   get a letter |
| get on badly with someone |
| get angry   get a bus   get cold |
| get cancer   get a suit made |
| get a present   get a surprise |
| get on well with someone |
| get a taxi   get tired   get a virus |
| get your car fixed   get a train |
| get your hair cut |
| get on okay with someone |

 **a) Match the sentences in A with responses in B (not all the responses in B can be used).**

| A |
|---|
| 1 Has anyone got change for a pound? |
| 2 I'm sorry, I was a bit rude yesterday. |
| 3 I haven't seen my cousins for ages. |
| 4 You never agree with anything I say! |
| 5 I think he'd had too much to drink. |
| 6 Are the people you work with friendly, on the whole? |
| 7 My brother used to be a professional football player. |
| 8 You forgot to post that letter I gave you. |

| B |
|---|
| Have I?   Did he?   Was he? |
| No, I don't.   You weren't! |
| Most of them do.   You didn't! |
| Yes, I am!   Had he?   Would he? |
| Most of them are.   Haven't you? |
| No, I didn't.   Yes, I do!   I have. |
| Didn't I? |

**b) Practise the conversations in pairs, adding any extra words to make them sound more natural.**

> Has anyone got change for a pound?

> I have, here you are.

# module 2
# Life's ups and downs

## Part A **Task**

Reading and speaking: *Are you on top of the world?*
Vocabulary: word building with abstract nouns, verbs and adjectives
Preparation for task: people talk about what annoys them, etc.
Task: devise a list of what makes you happy, angry, etc.

## Reading and speaking

**1** You are going to read an article about things that are good and bad for you physically and psychologically. First make lists of your own. Compare your lists in groups.

For example:

| Good for you | Bad for you |
|---|---|
| *regular exercise* | *stress* |

**2 a)** Check the meaning of the words in the box in your mini-dictionary or with your teacher. Then put them in the following categories, according to whether they might relate to:

a your physical health
b your psychological state
c both

---

feelings of aggression and hostility    feelings of anxiety    backache
your genes    companionship and social support    depression
having high / low self-esteem    high blood pressure    a low-fat diet
stress    your life expectancy    having a positive outlook
feeling undervalued    feeling out of control    feelings of guilt

---

**b)** Compare and explain your answers in groups.

**3** The article is divided into two sections 'Some things that can make you feel better' and '... some that make you feel worse'. Work in two groups. Group A read the first part of the article and Group B read the second part.

• Scan your part of the article quickly, and compare the topics it mentions with the ideas that you listed in Exercise 1 above.
• Did the article mention anything that you didn't?

4 Working in the same groups as Exercise 3, and looking at the same part of the article, discuss the answers to the questions below.

Questions for group A
1  What is the value of physical exercise for your mental health?
2  Give two pieces of evidence that show that companionship and social support can be important for your physical health.
3  Why do psychologists believe that watching soap operas on TV can make people feel better?
4  What happens to old people who are given a cocktail every evening? What is the explanation for this according to the text?

# Are you on top of the world?

These days most doctors and scientists agree that our physical health is closely related to our psychological well-being. But just what have the experts discovered about what makes us feel good?

## Some things that can make you feel better ...

### Getting moving
As well as being important to your physical health, regular exercise is now believed to improve your psychological state by releasing endorphins or 'happy chemicals' into the brain. Some researchers consider it can be just as valuable as psychotherapy in helping depression, and engendering a more positive outlook. Even a brisk ten-minute walk every day can help according to researchers. In one project, unemployed urban youths who undertook intensive sports training for several months, not only became involved in that sport, but also in other activities such as study, politics, and voluntary work.

### A lively social life
According to experts, companionship and social support are vital to both our psychological and physical well-being – one reason, perhaps, why married people tend to live longer than unmarried ones. Modern researchers emphasise the value of group social activities in this respect. 'Relationships we form at church or in clubs tend to be more supportive and uncritical than those we form at work or in the family,' says Professor Michael Argyle, of Oxford Brookes University, 'and these positive relationships improve our self-esteem, which is vital to our physical and mental health.' This is backed up by recent research which shows, perhaps surprisingly, that people who spend more time with others actually get fewer colds and viruses than those who stay at home on their own. In fact social support is so important to our mental and physical well-being that it may even increase our life expectancy! Another piece of research found that people who belong to strong church groups, not only claim to be happier than those who don't, they suffer from less than half the number of heart attacks than the rest of the population, and live up to four years longer!

### Watching soap operas on TV
One rather surprising piece of research found that on average, people who regularly watch soaps on television are significantly happier than those who don't! Psychologists believe that this is because such programmes provide viewers with an imaginary set of friends, and a sense of belonging to a community, in the same way that a club or a church might.

### Self-indulgence
Many scientists these days believe that indulging in life's little pleasures – a bar of chocolate, a glass of wine, a shopping trip, even a cigarette – can actually improve your health, because of the psychological lift it gives you. 'There is evidence, for example,' says Professor David Warburton of Reading University, 'that old people living in residential homes who have a cocktail hour each day actually live longer! Indulging – in moderation – in the small pleasures of life can make people calmer, alleviate stress and provide positive health benefits. There is a lot of truth in the old saying that "a little of what you fancy does you good."'

**Questions for group B**
1 What is the connection between backache and 'feeling like an underdog'?
2 Give two examples of groups of people affected by SAD. What is it, and what can be done to help sufferers?
3 From the research described, why do you think people on low-fat diets might be more likely to meet a violent death?
4 Give three possible ill effects of drinking coffee.
5 Can your genes affect how happy or miserable you are?

# ... and some that can make you feel worse

## Low self-esteem

Feeling like an underdog, it seems, can damage your health. Research by the National Rheumatism and Arthritis Council showed that workers who feel undervalued or out of control at work, are significantly more likely to suffer from back problems. Depression, a spokesman claimed, is actually far more likely to cause backache than heavy lifting. Professor Warburton of Reading University believes that one of the greatest health threats comes from negative feelings such as depression or guilt, which create stress hormones, producing cholesterol. 'It's quite likely that by worrying about whether or not you should be eating a chocolate bar you are doing yourself more harm than just getting on and eating it,' says the professor!

## Lack of bright light

Scientists have known for some time about Seasonal Affective Disorder (SAD): a form of depression caused by lack of light in winter, and thought to explain the relatively high suicide rates in countries such as Sweden, where for parts of the year days are very short. However, recent research has shown that those working night shifts in factories can suffer from the same problem, leading to stress and depression. The problem can be overcome by illuminating workplaces with lights three times brighter than usual, making workers feel happier and more alert.

## A low-fat diet

A low-fat diet may be good for your waistline, but the latest research suggests that it is less beneficial psychologically. A team of volunteers at Sheffield University, asked to follow a diet consisting of just twenty-five per cent fat (the level recommended by the World Health Organisation) reported a marked increase in feelings of hostility and depression. And an earlier piece of research revealed, startlingly, that people on low-fat diets are more likely to meet a violent death!

## Drinking coffee

Many of us are already aware that drinking coffee raises your blood pressure and can cause anxiety, but according to the latest research it can also make you bad-tempered. Mice who were given regular doses of caffeine by researchers, were found to be unusually aggressive!

## The wrong genes

Despite all the changes we make to our behaviour, diet, and environment, there is growing evidence that at the end of the day, whether we are cheerful or miserable is largely a question of our genes. 'Of course what happens to you in your life will make a difference to how happy you are,' say scientists, 'but there are two or three vital genes which probably decide how cheerful you are in comparison to others in a similar situation.'
So whatever else you do, make sure you choose your genes carefully!

**5** **a)** Work in pairs with someone who has been reading the other text. Tell your partner about the topics mentioned in your text, including:

- the main points being made.
- examples and evidence used to support them.

**b)** Discuss your reactions. Which findings did you think were:

- obvious if you think about it.
- surprising but interesting.
- unconvincing.

**c)** Has the article made you feel that you should change any of your own habits or attitudes? Think about:

- what you eat and drink.
- how much exercise you get.
- your work and hobbies.

What about other people you know?

# Vocabulary

## Word building with abstract nouns, verbs and adjectives

**1** Use your mini-dictionary to complete the table, marking the word stress as in the example. In the box marked *, there is more than one possible answer.

| | noun | verb | adjective | person |
|---|---|---|---|---|
| | psychólogy | – | *psychológical* | *psychólogist* |
| a | anxiety | – | | – |
| b | | – | aware | – |
| c | depression | | * | – |
| d | | – | | scientist |
| e | | to suffer | | |
| f | support | | | |
| g | | | involved | – |

> ## Pronunciation
>
> 1 [image] [2.1] Did you find that different syllables were stressed in any of the word families in the table? Listen and check your answers.
>
> 2 In many of the suffixes (and other non-stressed syllables) there are /ə/ sounds. Mark where you think they are, like this:
>
> /ə/ /ə/ /ə/
> psychology psychological
>
> Listen again to check your answers, and practise the pronunciation of the words.

**2** There are a number of adjectives to describe feelings which have an *-ing* and an *-ed* form, for example *depressing* and *depressed*. What is the difference in meaning? Can you think of any more pairs of adjectives like this?

**3** A number of nouns and verbs in English are exactly the same (for example *support*). Find at least five more examples like this in the text. Can you think of any more?

Personal vocabulary

## Task: devise a list of what makes you happy, angry, etc.

What makes you laugh?

What makes you happy?

What helps you to relax?

What really annoys you?

### Useful language

**Describing different feelings**

"... really annoys / frightens / embarrasses / depresses me ..."

"One thing that really annoys / frightens, etc. me is ..."

"I hate it / it really annoys me when ..."

"I find ... embarrassing / relaxing."

"... makes me feel really annoyed / depressed / happy."

**Phrases for describing negative feelings**

"I can't cope with ..."

"I find ... really hard to cope / deal with."

"I have a problem with ..."

**Ways of generalising**

"People who ... (really annoy me)."

"I like / don't like the thought / the feeling / the way / the idea that ..."

What makes you embarrassed?

What makes you depressed?

What makes you nervous?

## Preparation for task

1 You are going to hear a group of people discussing these questions on the left. Make sure you understand exactly what the questions mean. Check in your mini-dictionary if necessary.

2 **a)** 📼 [2.2] Listen and decide which question they are discussing in each section.

**b)** What answers do they give in each case? Do you have the same feelings about the things they mention or not?

## Task

1 **a)** Work in groups. Each group should choose a different question.

**b)** You are going to write a list of about fifteen things that annoy you / make you happy, etc. Spend a few minutes making an individual list first. Ask your teacher about any words or phrases you need, and write them in your *Personal vocabulary* box. Look at the phrases in the *Useful language* box to help you express your ideas.

2 Compare your individual lists, explaining exactly what and why these things make you feel the way they do. Make a group list including the best ideas / the ones you all agree about. Spend a few minutes making sure that you can explain your ideas to the rest of the class.

3 Form new groups with people who discussed different topics. Tell the other students your ideas. Do they agree with you? Do they have any other suggestions?

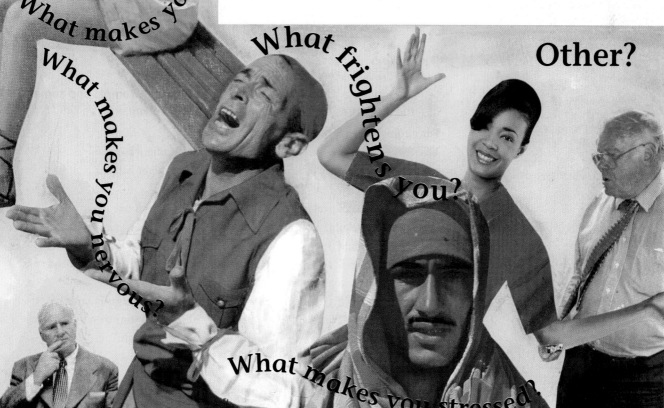

What frightens you?

Other?

What makes you stressed?

# Part B **Language**

Expressing abstract ideas
The use of prefixes and suffixes
Wordspot: *over*
Real life: responding
sympathetically

## Language focus 1

### Expressing abstract ideas

Read the quotes about the topics on pages 22-23 and answer the questions in *Analysis*.

**a** 'Waking up on a Sunday morning and thinking that I have nothing to do, nowhere to go, nowhere that I need to be ... the feeling of being able to do what I like all day ... that makes me feel happy ...'

**b** 'People not sharing sidewalk or pavement space ... sort of pushing me out of the way – that really annoys me.'

**c** 'There are two things that really annoy me ... meanness, you know, people who never give anything away, and hypocrisy – the way that some people pretend to be so nice, but really they're just being dishonest ...'

**d** 'Being followed by a police car makes me really nervous ... even when I know I haven't done anything wrong ... it's terrible!'

**e** 'One really embarrassing thing is when someone knows your name, and it's past the point of being able to ask them their name, you're just supposed to know – that's really awful.'

**f** 'I get very stressed by traffic jams, definitely, and the thought that I'm going to be late, I can't cope with that.'

**g** 'Swimming in the sea on a lovely sunny day, somewhere really peaceful, with beautiful scenery to look at ... that's my idea of happiness ...'

## Analysis

**Nouns**
Many nouns describe abstract ideas, for example *happiness*. Find two more abstract nouns like this in the quotes. Can you think of any more examples of your own?

**Gerunds (-ing forms)**
Gerunds are also often used to describe general / abstract ideas. Very often they come at the beginning of the sentence. Underline the examples in the quotes. Can you find an example of:
a  a negative gerund .........?          d  a passive gerund .........?
b  gerund + object .........?             e  preposition + gerund .........?
c  subject + gerund .........?

**Phrases**
There are a number of other phrases with nouns that are used to describe general / abstract ideas:
feelings:      *the feeling of* being able to do what I like all day
behaviour:    *the way that* some people pretend to be so nice
thoughts:     *the thought that* I'm going to be late
Here are some more common phrases. What abstract ideas do they express? Think of an example sentence for each.
*the knowledge that    the belief that    the idea that*
*a sense of    a lack of*

***Now read Language summary A and B on page 148.***

## Practice

**1** **a)** Complete the dictionary definitions. Use the prompts and some of the structures and phrases in *Analysis* to help you.

**For example:**
~~▓▓▓▓▓▓▓▓▓▓~~ a sense/ fear or worry about what might happen.
**nervousness**  a sense of fear or worry about what might happen.

1  ~~▓▓▓▓▓▓▓▓~~ feel / bad because you feel you have done something wrong
2  ~~▓▓▓▓▓▓▓▓~~ feeling / unfriendliness towards people or ideas
3  ~~▓▓▓▓▓▓▓▓~~ sense / shyness or shame, often because you or someone else has done something silly
4  ~~▓▓▓▓▓▓▓▓~~ be / tense and worried because of problems in your life
5  ~~▓▓▓▓▓▓▓▓~~ have / a low opinion of yourself, and your own importance
6  ~~▓▓▓▓▓▓▓▓~~ way / feel when you are calm and peaceful
7  ~~▓▓▓▓▓▓▓▓~~ feel / quite angry but not very angry

**b)** What feeling is being described in each case? If necessary, you can use the box on page 142 to help you.

**2 a)** Work in pairs. Student A writes definitions for the words in box A, and Student B for the words in box B. Write the definitions in your own words on a piece of paper, using the structures in *Analysis* and your mini-dictionary if necessary.

| A | confusion pride contentment curiosity jealousy |
|---|---|

| B | delight envy disappointment fury frustration |
|---|---|

**b)** Read out your definitions to your partner. Your partner looks at your box and says which word you are defining.

**c)** Work in groups. Think of some common situations in which people often experience the feelings in **a**.

# Language focus 2

## The use of prefixes and suffixes

## Analysis

### Prefixes

a Prefixes (and one or two suffixes) change the meaning of a word. Look at the words below, taken from the text on pages 19-20. What meaning do they add to the word?
*unmarried self-indulgence undervalued*

b Think of at least two more prefixes that mean 'the opposite of'.

c Can you think of any other prefixes which change the meaning of a word in other ways?

### Suffixes

Suffixes (at the end of words) generally show the grammatical form of a word: whether the word is a noun, adjective, verb, etc.

a Look at the words in boxes A and B above and underline some common suffixes for nouns. Think of two more examples of each suffix.

b Look back at Exercise 1 on page 21. Can you see any more common suffixes for either nouns or adjectives? Write down two more examples of each.

***Now read Language summary C, D and E on pages 148–149.***

# Practice

**1 a)** Read the phrases, and check the meaning of the prefixes in **bold** if necessary. Then write down:

1 a word either in English or your own language that people often **mis**spell.
2 one profession in which you think that people are **over**paid, and one in which you think they are **under**paid.
3 three public places which are usually **non**-smoking in your country.
4 the name of one newspaper in your country which is considered to be **pro**-government and one which is **anti**-government.
5 two famous **multi**national corporations.
6 the names of two **ex**-presidents of the USA.
7 an example of the kind of behaviour that you would expect from someone who is very **self**-centred.
8 two professions which require **post**-graduate qualifications.
9 the names of some people or places that look after **pre**-school children.
10 the name of a book that you would like to **re**-read.
11 one bad habit which fortunately you have now **out**grown.

**b)** Close your books and compare answers in groups. Use the phrases with prefixes above to explain what you wrote.

> I wrote 'shopping' because it's a word I often misspell in English.

**2** Look at the words in the box. How many prefixes can you add to them?

For example:
**pre**cooked **under**cooked **over**cooked

| cooked used government confident communist |
|---|

**3 a)** The box shows a number of personal characteristics. If necessary, check the meaning of the words in your mini-dictionary or with your teacher.

| a sense of fairness self-confidence talent determination loyalty ambition good communication skills self-discipline creativity high moral standards tact tolerance a sense of humour |
|---|

**b)** What is the adjective, if any, in each case?
**c)** With your partner, think of at least three other personal qualities to add to the list above.

## Follow-up task

**1**  Work in groups. Choose three of the people in the list and think of six qualities that they need. You can use the qualities in Exercise 3 on page 25 or ideas of your own. Ask your teacher about any words or phrases you need.

- a good boss
- a successful teacher
- a good parent
- a religious leader
- a successful rock star or actor
- a great leader
- a good friend
- a top sports star
- a good partner

**2**  Present your ideas to the rest of the class and find out whether they agree with you.

**3**  Which of the people do you think the person below is writing about? Choose a person from the list in Exercise 1 and write a similar description.

> For me, the most important qualities in a ▬▬▬▬ are tolerance and understanding – I hate the thought of being criticised and judged all the time. It's also important to have someone who's supportive, who you can lean on when you have a problem, but someone discreet, who doesn't go around telling everyone your secrets. I think it's also important that your ▬▬▬▬ shares some of the experiences that you've had, and that they have a similar sense of humour, so that you understand each other better.

# Wordspot

*over*

**1**  Some meanings of *over* are shown in the diagram. Check you understand the examples.

(a) *above*
...*flying over Milan.*

(b) *more than (with numbers / ages, etc.)*
*over 200 years old*

(g) *across / covering*
*a bridge over the river*

(f) *prefix = too much*
*overweight*
*over-confident*

**OVER**

(c) *= finished*
*The party's over.*

(d) *for a period of time*
*over the last few weeks*
*over the next month*

(e) *other phrases and phrasal verbs*
*over here / there*
*get over a shock*

**2**  Here are some more common phrases with *over*. Put them in the correct place on the diagram.

> all over the world    over £1,000,000    over the last decade
> to go over the speed limit    to go over (an exercise)
> over a week / month, etc. ago    oversleep
> over and over again    an overdose    to pull over
> to lean over someone    it's all over

**3**  In each of these sentences, replace the phrases in **bold** with a phrase with *over*.

a  Cola is a popular soft drink **in every country**.
b  Sorry I'm late, I **slept longer than I wanted to**!
c  The referee is looking at his watch ... and ... **it's finished**! Brazil have won!
d  When I woke up, I found myself lying on a bed with a doctor **bending towards** me.
e  It's a shame we've lost touch with Mark – he hasn't written for **more than a year**.
f  He was admitted to hospital after **taking too much of a drug at one time**.
g  He wears his hair very long, **covering his shoulders**.
h  I don't like the sound of the engine: we'd better **stop at the side of the road** and have a look.
i  One way of learning a telephone number is to say it to yourself **a large number of times**.
j  The new terminal will cost **more than £25 million**.
k  There are some points I still don't understand in this exercise: can we **check** it again?

# Real life

Responding sympathetically

a Never mind, these things happen!

b Don't take any notice (of him / her / them)!

c Don't worry, it doesn't matter at all!

d It / he / she sounds really awful / difficult / worrying, etc.

e You must be really worried / upset / disappointed, etc.

f Try not to worry about it too much!

g What a shame!

h Come on, pull yourself together!

i Just try and ignore it!

j There's no point in getting upset about it!

k Calm down!

l How awful/ annoying.

**1** Read the situations in the box below. For each situation decide which of the responses above would be:

- totally inappropriate.
- a bit insensitive.
- just right in that situation.

1 A visitor to your home is obviously feeling embarrassed because she's dropped a drink onto your carpet.

2 A child you know tells you that some of his classmates are being unkind to him at school.

3 A friend of yours is feeling upset and angry because his new boss is treating him badly.

4 Your partner is getting very irritated because he's phoned a government office about eight times and still not got a proper answer to his query.

5 A friend phones you very upset because she has just had a terrible row and split up with her boyfriend.

6 A friend is obviously getting a bit upset because everyone is teasing him about his new hairstyle.

7 A friend is feeling worried because her mother is about to go into hospital for a serious operation.

## Pronunciation

1 [2.3] Intonation is also very important if you want to sound sympathetic. Listen to the phrases above. In two cases the speaker does not sound very sympathetic. Which ones? How could you say these phrases more sympathetically?

2 Practise saying all the phrases as sympathetically as possible.

**2** [2.4] You will hear a conversation about one of the situations in Exercise 1. Listen and answer the questions.

a Which situation is being discussed?

b How does the man describe the other person and his / her behaviour?

c Is his friend supportive?

d What comfort / advice does his friend give?

e Which phrases does she use?

**3 a)** Choose one or more of the other situations in Exercise 1 and write a similar conversation, using some of the phrases from the speech balloons. Use intonation in your conversation to show whether the listener is really sympathetic or not. Ask your teacher for any other words and phrases you need.

**b)** Practise your conversation with your partner.

**4** In pairs, act out your conversation for the rest of the class. They must listen and say which situation(s) you are acting out, and whether or not the listener is really sympathetic.

# Do you remember?

## 1

**In pairs, discuss why people:**

- suffer from high blood pressure.
- follow a low-fat diet.
- suffer from stress.
- feel out of control.
- feel under-valued.
- have low self-esteem.

## 2

**Find the odd one out in the groups of words. Explain why.**

a) annoyed   nervous   furious
b) delighted   disappointed   contented
c) stressed   relaxed   frustrated
d) curious   envious   jealous

## 3

**What are the noun forms of the adjectives below? Put them in the correct column, and mark the stress as in the example. Practise saying them with a partner.**

> aware   ~~depressed~~   creative
> curious   disappointed   determined
> embarrassed   envious   frustrated
> furious   jealous   nervous

-ion   -ation   -ment   -ness   -ity   -y

- depression

## 4

**a) Work in pairs or groups to discuss the following. Which is worse, in your opinion:**

- being overworked or not having enough to do?
- feeling too hot or too cold?
- having to get up really early for work every day, or having to work late every evening?

**b) Which of the following regularly depresses you:**

- the thought that you haven't got any money?
- the thought of winter coming?
- the thought of going to school or work on Monday morning?
- the thought of getting old?

**c) Which of the following would you most like to have:**

- the ability to remember large amounts of information?
- the ability to sing or dance really well?
- the ability to read quickly?
- the ability to draw really well?
- the ability to make other people laugh?

## 5

**a) Here are some common words with prefixes. Mark them as follows:**

(✓✓)   if you already know the meaning.
(✓)   if you can guess.
?   if you need to check.

> overtired   outlive   multi-cultural
> multi-coloured   re-read
> non-fiction   reappear   rebuild
> non-violent   anti-clockwise
> non-alcoholic   outgrow   antibiotic
> anti-government   outnumber
> self-discipline   overpriced
> multimedia   self-confidence
> overworked   self-esteem

**b) Compare your answers with a partner. Check the meaning of any words you have marked *?* in your mini-dictionary or with your teacher.**

**c) In pairs, spend three minutes memorising the words. Close your books. You have two minutes to remember as many of the words as you can. Which pair remembered the most words?**

## 6

**Put the word *over* in an appropriate place in the sentences. What does it mean in each case?**

a) This bridge is where the railway crosses *over* the road.
b) Her grandmother is ninety.
c) My brother is the one there in the black leather jacket.
d) The last few months I've got to know Alex a lot better, and I must say, I really like him.
e) I think Paul failed the exam because he was confident, and didn't bother to do any revision.
f) What a shame the summer is now.

28

# module 3
## Adventures and mishaps

### Part A Task

Speaking: *Are you a risk-taker?*
Vocabulary: verb and adverb combinations for movement
Reading and speaking: *The Gentle Touch*
Preparation for task: an unfortunate incident
Task: tell a story from two different points of view

### Speaking

1 Work through the quiz discussing the questions with a partner, like this:

> I'd probably ...

> I wouldn't do any of those – I'd ...

> I definitely wouldn't ...

Make a note of each other's answers.

## Are you a risk-taker?

**1 An entrepreneurial friend of yours offers you an exciting job in a new venture of his, but it will mean giving up your secure, but rather boring job in the civil service. Do you:**
a Turn the offer down straightaway – most of his schemes are a bit wild.
b Spend several days thinking about the pros and cons – you could make a lot of money, but then again, you could end up with nothing.
c Say yes without much hesitation – what have you got to lose?

**2 It's Saturday night. You and a friend are walking along the street with nowhere special to go. Some interesting, but rather unusual people who you met briefly at a party last weekend drive up in their car. They invite you to another party about fifty kilometres away. Do you:**
a Refuse politely and walk off.
b Take the address of the party, and find out if your friend thinks you should go.
c Jump into their car straightaway, dragging along your unwilling friend.

**3 Some friends of yours have got together to buy you a special birthday present. A 200 metre bungee jump! How do you respond?**
a Angrily – why have they wasted money on something they know you won't do?
b You agree to do it, but spend the weeks before the jump feeling terrified.
c Enthusiastically – it sounds like a great challenge!

**4 You want to go away for a holiday, but your budget is limited. Which of the following options most appeals to you?**
a Booking into a nice hotel in a neighbouring region for a few days and hiring a car to drive around in.
b Spending a week or two in a neighbouring country, staying in cheap rooms and travelling around on local trains and buses.
c Spending a few weeks further away, camping and hitch-hiking to keep costs down.

**5 Mark the situations *a b* or *c* according to how you view the activities:**
a = foolish / dangerous / irresponsible
b = not something I would usually do myself, but okay for other people
c = normal / good fun

- motorcar racing ____
- driving at very high speeds ____
- mountaineering ____
- going on dates with strangers ____
- taking illegal drugs ____
- gambling ____
- boxing ____
- walking around alone late at night ____
- smoking ____
- sunbathing ____

2 Check the results of the quiz on page 142. Do you agree with them? Tell the rest of the class anything surprising you discovered about your partner.

# Vocabulary

## Verb and adverb combinations for movement

**1** The verbs in the box all come from the quiz. Match each verb to one of the pictures below. What is the meaning of the second word in each combination?

drive up (to ...)    walk off    walk along    drive around    go away

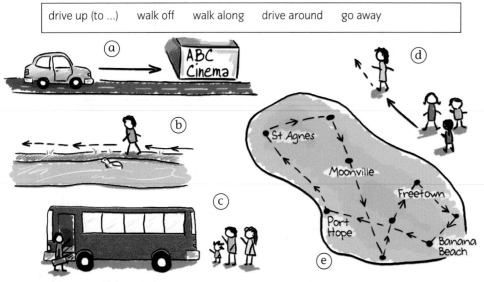

**2** **a)** Can you work out what the verbs in box B mean? The pictures above may help.

| A | B |
|---|---|
| being on holiday | rushing around |
| being late for your next appointment | running away |
| sightseeing | rushing off |
| the end of the working day | driving around |
| children playing in the park | driving along |
| being lost and needing directions | running around |
| being very frightened | walking home |
| missing your last bus home | wandering around |
| travelling on a motorway | going home |
| being far too busy | walking up to someone |

**b)** Work with a partner. Which verbs in box B do you associate with the situations in box A?

**3** Complete the diagrams with appropriate word combinations.

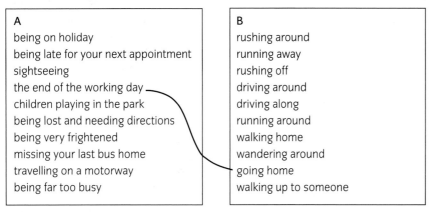

# Reading and speaking

**1** Look at the picture opposite. What can you see? Think of three possible interpretations of the situation.

**For example:**

It could be a demonstration.

**2** **a)** Skim the text. Which was the correct interpretation?

**b)** Answer these questions.

1 Which city was the writer in?
2 What attracted his attention?
3 What had the boy done?
4 How did the police officers behave?
5 What will happen to the boy?

**3** In the text, which words or phrases tell you that:

a the police officers were speaking kindly to the boy?
b the boy was in a confused state?
c the boy had fallen and hurt himself?
d the police officers looked capable and efficient?
e there is very little crime in Denmark?
f the author was treated harshly by the American police?
g the writer had a positive opinion about the way the police officers dealt with the situation?

**4** Discuss the following questions in groups.

- Do you agree with the approach of the Danish police officers?
- Do you believe a lenient or a tough approach to crime is more effective?
- Are there any crimes in your country that you think are treated either too harshly, or too leniently?

# The gentle touch

*The author is walking across a square in Copenhagen, the capital of Denmark, when he sees a small crowd by the town hall. He stops to have a look.*

Two police officers, a man and a woman, 5 both young and blond and as gorgeous as everyone else in the city, were talking softly and with sympathy to a boy of about seventeen who had clearly taken the sort of drugs that turn one's brain into an express 10 elevator to Pluto. Disorientated by this sudden zip through the cosmos, he had apparently stumbled and cracked his head; a trickle of blood ran from above his hairline to his cheek. The police officers were 15 wearing the smartest commando-style uniforms I have ever seen. They looked as if between them they could handle any emergency, from outbreaks of Lassa fever to disarming a nuclear submarine. 20

And the thing is, this was probably the biggest thing they would have to deal with all evening. The Danes are almost absurdly law-abiding. The most virulent crime in the country is bicycle theft. In 1982, a year for 25 which I just happen to have the facts, there were six murders in Copenhagen, compared with 205 in Amsterdam, a city of similar size, and 1,688 in New York. The city is so safe that Queen Margarethe used to walk 30 from Amalienborg Palace to the shops every morning to buy flowers and vegetables just like a normal citizen. I once asked a Dane who guarded her in such circumstances, and he looked at me with surprise and replied, 35 'Why, we all do,' which I thought was rather sweet.

The police officers helped the boy to his feet and led him to the patrol car. I found myself following them almost involuntarily. 40 I don't know why I was so fascinated, except that I had never seen such gentle police. I said in English to the female officer, 'Excuse me, what will you do with the boy?' 'We'll take him home,' she said simply, 'I 45 think he needs his bed.'

I was impressed. I couldn't help thinking of the time I was stopped by police in America, made to stand with my arms and legs spread against a wall and frisked, then 50 taken to a police station and booked because of an unpaid parking ticket. I was about seventeen myself at the time. God knows what they would have done with me if they had found me drugged on a city 55 bench. I suppose I'd be getting out of jail about now. 'Will he be in trouble for this?' I asked.

'With his father, I think so, yes. But not with us. We are all young and crazy 60 sometimes, you know? Good-night. Enjoy your stay in Copenhagen.'

'Good-night,' I said, and with the deepest admiration watched them go.

Adapted from *Neither Here Nor There* by Bill Bryson.

**Personal vocabulary**

# Task: tell a story from two different points of view
## Preparation for task

1 The pictures show an unfortunate incident that happened to Bill, a young Englishman, while visiting a friend in Hungary. The words and phrases in the box all relate to the story.

**a)** If necessary, check the meaning of the words in the box in your mini-dictionary or with your teacher.

**b)** Which words are illustrated in the pictures?

| | | |
|---|---|---|
| to be aggressive | to be arrested | to break into somewhere |
| to be drunk | to fall over | heavy snow |
| to hold onto something | thick ice | a police cell |
| to rob someone | to be slippery | to shout at someonea |
| steep hill | to sway all over the place | to swear at someone |
| to be terrified | to be in your underwear | |

## Useful language

**a For telling the story**

"He / She was just ... when ..."

"All of a sudden / Suddenly ..."

"She saw / heard them ... -ing"

"So then he / she ..."

"So anyway he / she ..."

**b For comparing the two accounts**

"According to (Bill / the old lady) ..."

"He / She claims that ..."

"He / She insists that ..."

"He says ... whereas she says ..."

"He / She is absolutely certain that ..."

"(Bill / The old lady) mentioned / didn't mention ..."

Several years ago, Bill was staying in Budapest with Feri, a Hungarian friend he'd met a few years earlier. One winter night as they were walking home from a party through a smart area of the city ...

**2** In groups, discuss briefly what you think happened to Bill. Is there anything that you do not understand from the pictures? Make a list of questions.

**3** Listen to two different accounts of what happened. Listen as many times as necessary in order to be sure of the details.

📼 [3.1] Group A will hear Bill's side of the story, as described to a British consulate official the next morning.

📼 [3.2] Group B will hear the statement that the old lady gave to the police.

## Task

**1** Work with other students from the same group. Check what you understood from the cassette and practise re-telling the story you heard. Look at the phrases in **a** in the *Useful language* box. Ask your teacher about any further words and phrases you need, and write them in your *Personal vocabulary* box.

**2** **a)** Work in pairs, one person from Group A, and one from Group B.

- Person A is the consulate official explaining to the police Bill's account of what happened.
- Person B is a police representative explaining what the old lady reported to the police.

**b)** Listen to each others' accounts and find:
- five contradictions between the two sides of the story.
- any information that one person mentioned, but the other didn't.

**3** With the rest of the class, make a list of the differences and contradictions that you found. Look at the phrases in **b** in the *Useful language* box to help you.

**4** Whose side of the story do you believe? Were the police right to arrest Bill and Frank? What action should they take now?

# Part B **Language**

Verb forms in narrative
Continuous aspect in other tenses
**Writing skills:** avoiding repetition
**Real life:** responding to unexpected problems

## Language focus 1

Verb forms in narrative

**1** The sentences below come from the story of Bill's arrest on page 33. Mark them **(B)** if you think Bill said them, and **(OL)** if you think the old lady said them.

**2** 🔲 [3.3] Which verb form is best in each case? Listen and check your answers.

**a** "We *had just left / had just been leaving* a party, when the incident *happened / was happening*. 🔲"

**b** "It *had snowed / had been snowing* for several hours – the streets were very slippery and we *fell / were falling* all over the place. 🔲"

**c** "I *went / was going* to the window – in the street, there were two young men *sway / swaying* and *fall / falling* everywhere. 🔲"

**d** "They *had obviously drunk / had obviously been drinking* alcohol. 🔲"

**e** "I could hear them *shout / shouting* and *swear / swearing*. 🔲"

**f** "We *laughed / were laughing* and *called / were calling* for help. 🔲"

**g** "Eventually we *decided / were deciding* to hold onto the car doors for support. 🔲"

**h** "I saw them *bang / banging* on all the car windows: they *obviously tried / were obviously trying* to break into them. 🔲"

**i** "Suddenly, the police *arrived / were arriving* and *arrested / were arresting* us. 🔲"

## Analysis

**Narrative tenses**

**a** Look at the four past verb forms in sentence **a** and complete the table:

| Past Simple | Past Continuous |
|---|---|
| *verb + -ed*<br>*happened* | |
| **Past Perfect Simple** | **Past Perfect Continuous** |

**b** Which forms refer to events **before** the main events of the story? Find two more examples above.

**Continuous aspect**
Continuous verbs:
• emphasise duration / repetition of the action

• describe an action in progress at a particular moment

  Look at Bill's sentences. Can you explain why the continuous form is used / not used?

**The present participle in narrative**
In sentence **c** above, the present participle (-*ing* form) is used without an auxiliary:
  *swaying* and *falling* everywhere.
The meaning is similar to that of continuous verbs. See above.
After the verbs *see* and *hear* two forms are possible. What is the difference?
  *I heard them shout and swear.*
  *I heard them shouting and swearing.*

***Now read Language summary A, B, D and E on pages 149-150.***

# Practice

**1** **a)** Look at the pictures and the title of the story and guess what happened. Read the text quickly to see if you guessed correctly. Do not complete the gaps yet.

## AN UNFORGETTABLE JOURNEY

One hot summer's day, Mr and Mrs X, from San Francisco, **(1)** _____ *(travel)* home from Arizona where they **(2)** _____ *(visit)* Mrs X's elderly grandmother.  During the visit, Mrs X **(3)** _____ *(persuade)* her husband to let the old lady come and live with them and so they **(4)** _____ *(bring)* her home with them to San Francisco.

They **(5)** _____ *(drive)* along through the desert, quite happily, the old woman **(6)** _____ *(sit)* on the back seat, the couple **(7)** _____ *(chat)* in the front. After a while, they **(8)** _____ *(realise)* that the old woman **(9)** _____ *(not speak)* for some time. The wife **(10)** _____ *(turn)* round to ask her if she was okay, as, earlier on, she **(11)** _____ *(complain)* about the terrible heat. However, the grandmother **(12)** _____ *(not reply)*, instead they heard her **(13)** _____ *(splutter)* and **(14)** _____ *(groan)*, then a strange silence.

Alarmed, they stopped the car and rushed round to the back seat, only to find that unfortunately, the old woman **(15)** _____ *(die)*. Horrified, they decided they should lie her body flat, but **(16)** _____ *(be)* rather a large woman, she would not fit on the back seat, so, in the end, they **(17)** _____ *(tie)* her onto the roof-rack instead.

After they **(18)** _____ *(drive)* across the desert for some time, they came across a petrol station and **(19)** _____ *(decide)* to stop and phone the rest of the family with the dreadful news. However, as they **(20)** _____ *(come)* out of the petrol station, to their horror, they saw  their car **(21)** _____ *(disappear)* into the distance, the old woman's body still **(22)** _____ *(lie)* on the roof. While they **(23)** _____ *(phone)*, someone **(24)** _____ *(steal)* their car!

**b)** Complete the gaps using the correct form of the verbs in brackets. More than one form is possible in some cases.

**2** **a)** Present participles often improve the style of a narrative and reduce the number of words needed. Find <u>six</u> places in the following story where a present participle can be substituted for a full verb. The story will be eleven words shorter and you will need to change the punctuation.

> Some years ago, Denis Thatcher, husband of the then Prime Minister, Margaret Thatcher, was on a train, ~~which was~~ travelling back to London. The train stopped, and Mr Thatcher looked up from his papers to see a group of inmates from a psychiatric institution who were getting into his carriage – their supervisor was following them. They all sat down and the supervisor began to count them. 'One, two, three, four, five,' she counted, but she stopped when she got to Mr Thatcher. 'Who are you?' she asked - she was frowning. 'I'm the Prime Minister's husband, actually,' he replied – he was looking surprised. 'Oh, right,' she continued, she was smiling kindly now, 'six, seven, eight, nine ...'

**b)** 🔲 [3.4] Listen and check your answers.

## Pronunciation

**1** 🔲 [3.5] Read aloud the new version of the story, copying the pronunciation on the cassette. Practise phrase by phrase, stressing the most important words:

*Some years* ago, // *Denis Thatcher,* // *husband* of the then *Prime* Minister, // *Margaret Thatcher,* // was on a *train* travelling back to *London.*

Which words in the sentence above have a weak pronunciation?

**2** Read aloud the rest of the story, paying attention to stressed and weak forms.

*Follow-up task*

**1**   Work in groups. Choose one of the options below. *Either:* think of an adventure or mishap that you or one of your friends have had while travelling. It could be an interesting or amusing encounter with authorities like the ones on pages 31-33 or any other interesting incident. Tell the story to the other students in your group.

*Or:* choose one of the stories you have read in this module (the text on page 31 or one of the stories in Practice 1 and 2), and re-tell it from the point of view of one of the other characters, for example one of the police officers. Think what changes of emphasis the story might have from this person's point of view. The other students should listen and decide:
*   which story you are re-telling.
*   which character's point of view you are telling the story from.

**2**   Before telling your story, spend a few minutes planning what you will say. Use what you have learned about verb forms in narratives when you tell your story.

# Language focus 2

Continuous aspect in other tenses

## Analysis

**1**   What are the forms missing from the table? Look back at the table on page 34. Can you see a pattern in the way the continuous is formed?

| Present Perfect Simple | Present Perfect Continuous |
| --- | --- |
| *I've tried* | |
| Future Simple | Future Continuous |
| *I'll wait* | |

**2**   Look back at explanations of the continuous forms in *Analysis*, Language focus 1, then try Practice 1.

***Now read Language summary C on page 150.***

## Practice

**1**   **a)**   Circle the best verb form in each case. Why is it the best?

① So how are you anyway? Done anything exciting since I saw you?

No, nothing at all. *It's rained / It's been raining* all weekend. *I haven't been / I haven't been going* out once!

② I'll phone you tonight to discuss the details, say about eight o'clock?

Could you make it a bit later? *We'll have / We'll be having* dinner at that time.

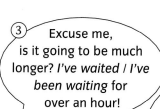

③ Excuse me, is it going to be much longer? *I've waited / I've been waiting* for over an hour!

I'm sorry, the computer's *broken down / been breaking down* and *we've lost / we've been losing* all our records. Dr Greenway will see you as soon as he can.

④ Put the camera down please, *you'll break it / you'll be breaking it*.

No, I won't!

**b)**   🎧 [ 3.6] Listen and check your answers.

**2** **a)** Work in pairs. Student A looks at card A on page 142, and Student B looks at card B on page 146. On a piece of paper, write true answers to the questions. Write notes, not complete sentences.

**For example:** *1 jeans & green t-shirt*

**b)** Swap papers with your partner. Ask questions to find out why your partner wrote those answers.

> Why did you write 'jeans and green t-shirt'?

> Because I was wearing jeans and a green t-shirt yesterday.

**c)** Write complete sentences for each question in cards A and B, paying attention to the verb forms.

# Writing skills

## Avoiding repetition

**1** Read Marisol's story. If necessary, check the meaning of the words in the box in your mini-dictionary. In pairs, discuss briefly what happened.

| a hairpin bend    to freewheel    the crater of a volcano |
| --- |

**2** The grammar Marisol uses is correct, and many of the expressions she uses are very good, but she keeps repeating the same words which makes the story sound unnatural. Her teacher has corrected the first paragraph, showing her how to avoid this:

a   by using pronouns to replace nouns.
b   by using auxiliary verbs to replace full verbs.
c   by using alternative words with the same or a similar meaning.
d   by omitting the repeated words, if possible.

Read the first paragraph and find examples of each.

**3** Look at the second paragraph of Marisol's story. Her teacher has underlined the unnecessary repetitions, but has not corrected them. Correct them using the methods in Exercise 2.

**4** The third paragraph has not been corrected. Find examples of unnecessary repetition and correct them. When you have finished, read through the whole story checking that it sounds natural.

**5** Write a story of your own about a frightening experience that you or one of your friends has had. If you cannot think of a true story, invent one.

The most frightening experience of my life

One of the most frightening experiences of my life happened while I was spending Christmas in Tenerife, in the Canary Islands. My brother José was working ~~in Tenerife~~ *there* and unfortunately ~~my brother José~~ *he* couldn't get any time to come home, so I ~~went to spend~~ *spent* the holiday with ~~my brother José~~ *him*. On the last day of my ~~holiday~~ *visit* we decided to go up Mt Teide - ~~Mt Teide is~~ a volcano in the centre of ~~Tenerife~~ *the island* and officially ~~Mt Teide~~ is the second largest mountain in Europe. We hired a little car for the day - I couldn't drive at the time, but my brother could ~~drive~~.

José and I set off in brilliant sunshine, before long it got much colder and by the time we reached the crater of Mt Teide it was snowing. What is more, all the restaurants, hotels and petrol stations <u>at the top of</u> Mt Teide were shut. It was then that <u>José and I</u> realised that we had almost run out of petrol. <u>Running out of petrol</u> was particularly desperate because I had to catch the plane home that evening, and if <u>I didn't catch the plane</u>, I would have to pay for a new ticket. So José decided to do something incredibly dangerous - <u>José decided</u> to switch off the engine of the car and freewheel down the other side of Mt Teide. <u>José freewheeled down the side of</u> Mt Teide for several kilometres, along hairpin bends on dangerous icy roads. I was absolutely petrified, but for some reason I didn't tell <u>José</u> to stop.

Then my worst nightmare happened: the car slipped on the slippery road, and the two front wheels went over the edge. We were very lucky that the rest of the car didn't go over the edge. José and I sat in the car for about half an hour, not daring to move and freezing cold. No other cars even passed by, until suddenly a car came round the corner and out jumped three enormous men. Without saying a word, the three men surrounded the car and literally lifted it back on the road. When my brother and I got out to thank them, the three men just repeated 'Norway' several times - my brother and I assumed that Norway was where the three men came from - then the three men got back into their car and drove off. We got back into our car and continued down the side of Mt Teide. I have never felt so relieved in my life as I felt when we reached the town - and the petrol station - at the bottom!

# Real life

## Responding to unexpected problems

**1** Look at Person A's part in the five conversations below. Where does the conversation take place? How do you imagine that Person B responded?

> *a* Excuse me, can you tell me which stop to get off at for the National Museum of Film?

> *b* Er ... we'd both like the chicken in mushroom sauce, please.

> *c* I'd like to book two tickets for the performance on Wednesday evening, please. Can you tell me what tickets there are available?

> *d* Can I change these dollars into Turkish lira, please?

**2** [3.7] In each conversation, Person B replies with an unexpected problem. Listen and imagine that you are Person A. Try to respond to the difficulty immediately. How successful were you? What was the problem in each case?

**3** [3.8] Listen to the whole conversation. How did A respond in each case? What happened?

## Pronunciation

**1** [3.9] These phrases can all be used to respond in unexpected situations. Listen and mark them as follows:

| | |
|---|---|
| ✓✓✓ | to show polite acceptance. |
| ✓✓ | to be polite, but to show slight annoyance. |
| ✓ | to show the person is annoyed / does not accept the situation. |

a What a pity ...  ☐
b Oh dear.  ☐
c You must be joking!  ☐
d What a nuisance!  ☐
e Right, I see ...  ☐
f This is ridiculous!  ☐
g Oh, for goodness sake!  ☐
h Oh dear, that's a shame ...  ☐
i Oh, right ...  ☐
j Oh, no!  ☐

**2** You can tell how the person feels from the words they choose, but also from their intonation. Listen again and copy the intonation on the cassette.

**3** Practise the conversations in Exercise 3 with a partner. You do not need to use the exact words on the cassette, but include some phrases above.

**4** [3.10] Listen to some more unexpected problems in everyday situations. Your teacher will stop the cassette after each one. Write down a possible response and compare it with other students. Then act out the conversations in pairs.

> *e* Can I have a packet of Mellow cigarettes, please?

# Do you remember?

 **1**

**Work in pairs. Think of as many reasons as you can why the following might happen:**

a) You rush around your house at top speed, tidying up.

b) You drive around a strange town for three-quarters of an hour.

c) You walk home along the middle of the road.

d) A stranger comes up to you in the street, says something to you and you immediately walk off.

e) You jump into your car and drive off at 120 kmph.

f) You wander around the streets aimlessly, looking in shop windows.

g) You run home from the bus stop.

h) You shout 'go away!' to someone.

**Compare answers with the rest of the class.**

 **2**

**Which verbs are better in the continuous form? Change the sentences where appropriate.**

a) It <u>had rained</u> all night and everywhere was soaking wet.

b) I <u>phoned</u> her to see if she <u>wanted</u> to come to the cinema with us, but she's busy.

c) They <u>had gone</u> out together for years before he asked her to marry him.

d) Two hours before the speech, he still <u>hadn't decided</u> what he would say.

e) She <u>vacuumed</u> upstairs, so she didn't hear the phone.

 **3**

**Join the sentences together, using a present participle (-*ing* form).**

a) I stood outside the cinema for about half an hour. I was waiting for you.

*I stood outside the cinema for about half an hour waiting for you.*

b) The old man stood on his doorstep. He was smoking his pipe and chatting to his neighbours.

c) That's Marina over there. She's wearing a big black hat.

d) She sat for ages. She was staring into space. She was thinking.

e) Richard stood in the corner of the room. He watched the others dancing. He didn't dare to ask anyone to dance with him.

 **4**

**Work with a partner. Look at the pairs of sentences, and discuss the difference in meaning between them.**

a) Kristina's gone to the gym. Kristina's been going to the gym.

b) He changed his mind. He was changing his mind.

c) She had phoned my boyfriend secretly. She had been phoning my boyfriend secretly.

d) I've remembered what happened last night: it's so embarrassing! I've been remembering what happened last night: it's so embarrassing!

e) I'll read the report at the weekend. I'll be reading the report at the weekend.

 **5**

**Match the verbs in A with an appropriate ending from B.**

| A | B |
|---|---|
| take | an offer |
| slip | a date |
| waste | a risk |
| turn down | someone's house |
| | |
| run out | money |
| go on | a hotel |
| break into | on the ice |
| book into | of petrol |

# Developing the mind

## Part A **Task**

Listening and reading:
types of intelligence
Vocabulary: qualities of mind
Preparation for task: quiz –
*What kind of mind have you got?*
Task: analyse the results of a quiz

## Listening and reading

**1** Have you ever done a test like this? What does it test?

1. What is the next number in this series?

   6520, 7522, 8524, ……. .

2. If some criminals are millionaires, and all tycoons are millionaires, then some criminals are definitely tycoons.
   We can say with certainty that this statement is:

   **True   False   Neither**

**2** 🖳 [4.1] You are going to hear extracts from a radio programme about intelligence tests (Intelligence Quotient or IQ). Read the notes, then listen and add to the information.

a The first IQ tests: where / when?

b First widely used: when / why?

c Average IQ:

d Genius level:

e How different groups perform:
• women
• people from East Asia
• people over twenty-three

f Advice for people doing IQ tests:

**3** **a)** There has been criticism of IQ tests, partly because they only seem to test logical thinking and ignore things like emotional intelligence. What do you think this is? Discuss with a partner.

**b)** Read the text quickly to see if you were right. What is the connection between each of the pictures and emotional intelligence?

## EMOTIONAL INTELLIGENCE

### 1

It turns out that a scientist can see the future by watching four-year-olds with a sweet. The researcher invites the children into a plain room. You can have this sweet right now, he says. But if you wait while I go out for a few minutes, you can have two sweets when I get back. And then he leaves.

### 2

Some children grab the treat the moment he's out the door. Some last a few minutes before they give in. But others are determined to wait. They cover their eyes, they put their heads down, they sing to themselves, they try to play games or even fall asleep. When the researcher returns, he gives these children their sweets. And then, science waits for them to grow up.

### 3

By the time the children reach high school, something remarkable has happened. A survey of the children's parents and teachers found that those who as four-year-olds were strong-minded enough to hold out for the second sweet generally grew up to be better adjusted, more popular, adventurous, confident and dependable teenagers. The children who gave in to temptation early on were more likely to be lonely, easily frustrated and stubborn.

### 4

When we think of brilliance, we see Einstein — deep-eyed, woolly-haired, a thinking machine. High achievers, we imagine, were born for greatness. But then you have to wonder why, over time, natural talent seems to flower in some, yet disappear in others. This is where the sweets come in. The ability to defer gratification is a master skill, a triumph of the reasoning brain over the impulsive one. It is a sign, in short, of emotional intelligence. And it doesn't show up on an IQ test.

### 5

In his book *Emotional Intelligence*, Daniel Goleman argues that brain power as measured by IQ actually matters less than qualities of mind like understanding one's own feelings, empathy — being sensitive to other people's feelings — and the ability to manage your own emotions. EQ is not the opposite of IQ. What researchers are trying to understand is how they complement each other. Among the ingredients for success, researchers now generally agree that IQ counts for about twenty per cent: the rest depends on everything from luck, to social class ... and emotional intelligence. In the business world, according to personnel executives, IQ gets you a job, but EQ gets you promotion.

**4** Read the text again and choose the best summary of each paragraph.

### Paragraph 1

a   The experiment started with each child eating a sweet.

b   In the experiment, the children were not allowed to eat their sweets straightaway.

c   In the experiment, the children were promised an extra sweet if they were patient.

### Paragraph 2

a   Most of the children decided to eat their sweet straightaway.

b   The researchers were most interested in the children who found ways of passing the time in order to get an extra sweet.

c   Once the researchers had left, many of the children forgot about the sweets.

### Paragraph 3

a   Success in IQ tests usually means that people are successful in life.

b   You have to be as brilliant as Einstein to be a success in life.

c   The scientists found that the children who were more patient were happier as teenagers.

### Paragraphs 4 / 5

a   IQ is still considered the most important factor for success at work.

b   According to Daniel Goleman, emotional intelligence is more important than IQ for success in the long-term.

c   People with a high IQ tend not to be very emotionally intelligent.

**5** Do you agree that emotional intelligence is more important than IQ for success in life? Make a list of specific occasions when one or the other is important (for example passing exams, looking after children).

# Vocabulary

## Qualities of mind

**1** **a)** Check the meaning and pronunciation of these adjectives from the text in your mini-dictionary.

| determined   strong-minded   well-adjusted   adventurous   confident
dependable   lonely   stubborn   brilliant   popular   awkward   impulsive |
|---|

**b)** Complete the sentences with one of the adjectives.

1 A .................. person is exceptionally intelligent or skilful.

2 A .................. person is very unwilling to change his mind.

3 An ................ person is shy and easily embarrassed in a social situation.

4 An ................ person is willing to take risks and try new things.

5 A .................. person knows what he wants to do and won't let anything stop him doing it.

6 A .................. person can resist temptation.

7 A .................. person is a person most people like.

8 A .................. person is unhappy because he has no one to talk to.

9 An ................ person does things suddenly, without thinking first.

10 A .................. person is calm and good at controlling her emotions.

11 A .................. person is someone you can rely on.

12 A .................. person is very sure of herself.

**2** Discuss the following questions with a partner. Which adjectives are:

*   usually positive (+)?   *   usually negative (−)?   *   both / it depends (+ −)?

Give examples to explain why.

**41**

**Personal vocabulary**

# Task: analyse the results of a quiz

## What kind of mind have you got?

1   How many sides does each figure have?

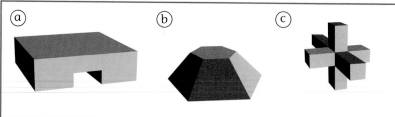

ⓐ          ⓑ          ⓒ

2   Look at the items in the picture on page 142 for **one** minute, then turn back to this page and write as many items as you can remember in the space below.

——— ——— ——— ———
——— ——— ——— ———
——— ——— ——— ———

3   You've taken a group of four-year-olds to the park, and one of them starts crying because the others won't play with her. What do you do?

_____

_____

4   Write down as many possible uses for a newspaper as you can in **two** minutes. (If you don't know how to express the ideas in English, you can make notes in your own language to ask your teacher about later.)

## Useful language

**a Comparing answers**

"What did you get for ...?"

"How do you work that out?"

"Do we all agree on that one?"

"Couldn't the answer be ...?"

"I'm not so sure about that ..."

**b Presenting your conclusions**

"All / Some of us thought that ..."

"We are all absolutely sure that ..."

"We couldn't agree about ..."

"We're not sure whether ..."

"We thought this question was fairly obvious / the hardest ..."

## Preparation for task

1   **a)** People can be intelligent in many different ways. Here are some of them. Thinking about yourself, put them in order, with your strongest point as 1 and your weakest as 6.
- artistic / visual intelligence
- logical thinking
- creativity
- good memory
- sensitivity to other people / emotional intelligence
- practical problem-solving skills

**b)** Compare notes in groups. What are the main differences between you?

2   The quiz tests different types of intelligence. Work through it individually. You have a maximum of fourteen minutes. If you find one question difficult, go on to the next.

5 You are the manager of a small hotel. You have eight rooms, and eight sets of guests. Put the guests in the right rooms so that everyone is happy, using the information below.

- Mr and Mrs A would like a room next to their children so they can keep an eye on them.
- The children would like a room overlooking the swimming pool.
- Miss C wants a room overlooking the sea.
- Mr and Mrs D would prefer a quiet room at the back of the hotel.
- Mr E always stays in room 2.
- Mr F, Mr and Mrs G, and Miss H would like adjoining rooms if possible.

sea

| Room 1 | Room 2 | Room 3 | Room 4 | swimming pool |
| Room 5 | Room 6 | Room 7 | Room 8 | |

6 You and your partner have got into an argument. You are both upset and, in the heat of the argument, start making personal attacks you don't really mean. What's the best thing to do?

_____

_____

## Task

1 a) Work in groups. Compare and explain your answers. Ask your teacher for any words or phrases you need and write them in your *Personal vocabulary* box. Look at the *Useful language* box (Comparing answers) to help you.

b) When you have answered each question, complete columns A and B.

| A Kind of intelligence being tested | B Best answer |
| --- | --- |
| | |

2 Compare conclusions briefly with the rest of the class. Look at the *Useful language* box, (Presenting your conclusions) to help you.

3 [4.2] Listen to the correct answers.

a) If your answers are the same as the answers on the cassette, tick (✓) them. Change any answers you got wrong.

b) Make a note of any extra information given. Were you surprised by any of the answers?

# Part B **Language**

Passives and alternatives
to the passive
Basic word order patterns
in English
**Real life:** explaining how
things work
**Writing skills:** writing a note
explaining how to use something
**Wordspot:** *mind*

## Language focus 1

Passives and alternatives to
the passive

**1** Read the article about mice
and brain cells. Choose the
best headline for the article.
Why is it the best?

a   Sweets can make you stupid
b   Why mice love popcorn
c   Luxuries improve your
    intelligence
d   Why children who eat sweets
    do worse at school

Your brain power can be improved by life's little luxuries according to research by Professor Fred Gage of The Salk Institute in La Jolla, California which was published recently. It has been discovered that mice who are fed on popcorn and sweets have up to fifteen per cent more brain cells than mice who are kept in normal laboratory conditions. Being kept in cages full of brightly-coloured toys has a similar effect. It is claimed that the same may be true for humans, which possibly explains why children from poorer homes tend to do less well at school and in life generally.

**2** What do you think of the ideas in the article? Do you believe that luxuries can improve your brain power?

**3** 🖭 [4.3] The two people in the picture are talking about the article. Listen and complete the conversation.

MAN:    Have you read this article
        about mice and popcorn?
WOMAN:  No, why?
MAN:    Apparently (a)_____
        your brain power by eating
        sweets!
WOMAN:  Oh, yeah?
MAN:    Yeah, really! (b)_____
        that if (c)_____
        popcorn and sweets to mice
        and (d)_____
        in cages with toys and things,
        they have bigger brains than
        the ones (e)_____
        in ordinary cages ...
WOMAN:  Really?
MAN:    Yeah, and (f)_____
        it might be true for humans
        too!
WOMAN:  Amazing ... perhaps you
        should eat more sweets then!

## Analysis

**The passive**

**1** What is the subject of each of the sentences below?
 a  *They feed the mice on popcorn and sweets.*
 b  *The mice are fed on popcorn and sweets.*
 c  *Your brain power can be improved by life's little luxuries.*

**2** Who feeds the mice in sentence **b**? Why is the passive used?

**3** What improves your brain power in sentence **c**? Why is the passive used?

**4** Read the article again and underline any other examples of the passive. How do we form the different tenses in the passive?

**Alternatives to the passive**
Compare the newspaper article with the conversation. How do the passive forms change in the conversation? Why? What do *you* and *they* mean?

***Now read Language summary A, B and C on pages 150-151.***

# Practice

Read the extract from a brochure giving information about English language exams. The verbs in brackets are all in the active form. Decide which to change to passive forms, and which tenses they should be.

## CERTIFICATE IN ENGLISH FOR BUSINESS COMMUNICATION

- The Certificate in English for Business Communication (1)_____ (*has offered*) since June 1995.

- A new, revised version of the examination (2)_____ (*introduce*) in June 1998.

- The examination can (3)_____ (*take*) in over 200 centres in 40 countries throughout the world.

- In order (4)_____ (*accept*) as an Examination Centre, Institutions must (5)_____ (*complete*) a Centre Registration form.

- The four papers (6)_____ (*test*) the students' communication skills in listening, speaking, reading and writing.

- It is not necessary for the papers (7)_____ (*take*) in any particular order.

- Each paper (8)_____ (*lasts*) approximately ninety minutes.

- Monolingual dictionaries can (9)_____ (*use*) for the Reading and Writing papers.

- Results (10)_____ (*will send out*) to candidates approximately eight weeks after the last examination.

- A number of changes to the examination (11)_____ (*introduce*) in the near future. A full list of changes (12)_____ (*will supply*) on request.

· · · · · · · · · · · · · · · · · · · · · · · · · · · · · · · · · · · ·

## Follow-up task

1 Discuss the following questions in groups.
- How many ways of learning a language can you add to the list?
- How many of them have you experienced yourself?

*Being sent to a bi-lingual school when you're a child*

*Getting a job in a country where the language is spoken*

**2a** Look at the advertisements for different ways to learn English. What is the method in each case?

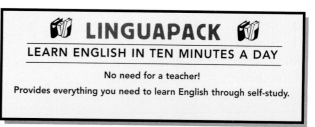

**b** To find out more about each method, read the information at the back of the book.

**Student A:** look at the information on page 142 about Linguapack.
**Student B:** look at the information on page 145 about The English Centre.
**Student C:** look at the information on page 146 about OnLine English.

**c** If necessary, check the meaning and pronunciation of any words in your mini-dictionary. Then spend a few minutes thinking how you can best summarise the information for the other students. Use your own words. Think about when to use the passive.

**3** Listen to the other students, and make a note of any extra information about each method.

**4** Discuss the following questions.
- What are the advantages and disadvantages of each method?
- What kind of people might benefit from each? What kind of people would not enjoy them?
- Which do you think is the best way to learn a foreign language? Why?

· · · · · · · · · · · · · · · · · · · · · · · · · · · · · · · · · · · ·

# Language focus 2

## Basic word order patterns in English

**1** Madeleine is talking to a friend about how she learned English. You will see a word printed in **bold** at the end of each line and two possible spaces in the sentence. Write each word in the best place in the sentence. The first example is done for you.

| | |
|---|---|
| (a) _____ I hated (b) _languages_ at school. | 1 **LANGUAGES** |
| I just wasn't interested in learning, so (a) _____ I (b) _____ did my homework | 2 **NEVER** |
| and (a) _____ I was (b) _____ bottom of the class when it came to exams! | 3 **ALWAYS** |
| Maybe it wasn't her fault, but I really didn't get on with my teacher. | |
| She seemed to think I was a (a) _____ young (b) _____ girl just because I didn't | 4 **STUPID** |
| know a past participle from an auxiliary verb (I still don't, actually). And | |
| even if I did learn English, there were no English-speaking people in my town, | |
| so (a) _____ who would I ever speak English (b) _____? | 5 **TO** |
| Things started to change when I got my first job, though. I spent my | |
| (a) _____ two (b) _____ years in the Sales Department, and I had to speak | 6 **FIRST** |
| English on the phone almost every day, which wasn't easy. I didn't really | |
| have (a) _____ time (b) _____ to go to classes, so at first I tried to study on | 7 **ENOUGH** |
| my own. | |
| I also persuaded an English-speaking friend to give | |
| (a) _____ some private lessons (b) _____ and I started to make progress. | 8 **ME** |
| I don't know when (a) _____ it (b) _____ exactly that I realised my English was | 9 **WAS** |
| (a) _____ good (b) _____ to do First Certificate, but I did ... and I passed! | 10 **ENOUGH** |
| So, I don't hate English any more. In fact it's made (a) _____ a (b) _____ | 11 **QUITE** |
| big difference to my life! | |

**2** 🔲 [4.4] Listen and check your answers.

## Analysis

**1** Find examples above of the following:
a an adjective   b an adverb   c a preposition
d a subject   e an object   f a direct object
g an indirect object   h an auxiliary verb

**2** a What's the usual order of subject, object and verb in an English sentence?

b If you have two objects (an indirect and a direct object), which comes first?

c Do adverbs like *always* or *never* go before or after the verb?

d Which come first, opinion or description adjectives?

e Does *enough* go before or after an adjective? What about a noun?

f Can you put a preposition at the end of a question?

g Do you use a question form after phrases like *I don't know when*?

***Now read Language summary D on page 151.***

## Practice

Here are some sentences you might hear in a language classroom, but the words are jumbled up. Put the words into the best order, as in the example.

1 the subject / we / of the sentence / usually / put / before the object
*We usually put the subject of the sentence before the object.*

2 start / easy / we'll / with / question / a / nice

3 look it up / don't know / if you / you can / always / in a dictionary / a word

4 enough / everyone / chairs / are there / to sit down / for / ?

5 anyone / means / this word / know / does / what / ?

6 have you / time / had / enough / or / a few / minutes / do / you need / more / ?

7 each group / I'm going / to / different / a / reading passage / give

8 any homework / last week / did / I / give / you / ?

9 the / of the book / this term / first / modules / we're going to / four / cover

10 very well / you've all / done / quite / exercise / a / difficult

# Real life

## Explaining how things work

**1** Have you ever used a video camera or have you been videoed? Why? What happened? Label the parts of a video camera with the words in the box.

| handle   lens cap   viewfinder   record button |

**2** [4.5] Listen to Kate explaining how to use a video camera. Number the pictures below in the order they occur in the conversation. The first example is done for you.

**3 a)** Look at these phrases. Are they used for explaining how to use something or for asking about how to use something?

| | |
|---|---|
| First of all ... | Can you see a switch that says ... |
| Look out! | If you want to ... then you ... |
| What if I want to ...? | You should be able to see a ... |
| The next thing is to ... | This one / thing here? |
| Hang on a minute ... | Have you got that? |
| What you need to do is ... | |

**b)** Listen again and tick (✓) any of the phrases from the box that you hear. Practise saying them.

## Pronunciation

**1** In fast speech, consonants at the end of words often link onto vowels at the beginning of the next word.

**For example:**

First_of_all take_it_out_of the case...

Can you find examples of the same thing in the phrases below?

a  take off the cap
b  pull it out at right angles
c  rest it against your shoulder
d  press it at the top
e  switch it on
f  hold it by the handle
g  turn it round

**2** [4.6] Listen and check your answers. Practise saying the phrases.

**4 a)** Work in pairs. Imagine you have to explain how to operate one of these objects to someone who has never used it before. Ask your teacher about any words or phrases you need.

- a photocopier
- a coffee maker
- a video recorder
- a washing machine
- another machine that you are familiar with

**b)** Act out your conversation for the rest of the class. Do **not** say what the object is. The other students have to guess!

# Writing skills

## Writing a note explaining how to use something

**1** You are using a friend's computer and want to send an e-mail to Richard Bell, a friend in America, congratulating him on the birth of his new baby. You know his e-mail address, which is richardbell@.... Unfortunately you don't know how to send the message. Follow the instructions.

a  Mark the places you should click with an X.
b  Put an arrow to show where the address goes.
c  Write an appropriate message to your friend Richard Bell.

**2** Read through the instructions again, and underline any useful phrases for giving different types of instructions (both for using computers and generally).

For example:  *you'll see  you do this by ...-ing ...*

**3** Choose one of the machines in Exercise 4a on page 47 and write a note to a friend or colleague explaining how to use it. Ask your teacher for any words and phrases you need.

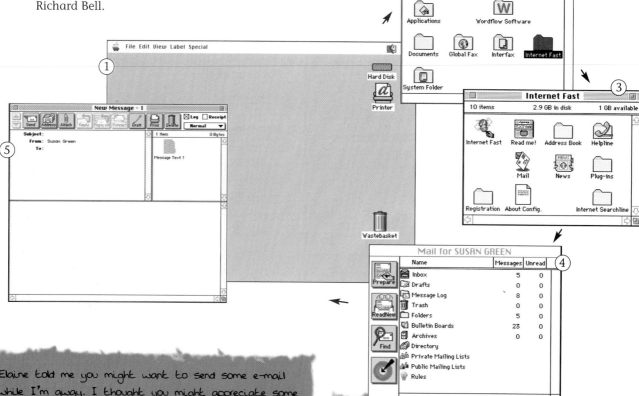

Elaine told me you might want to send some e-mail while I'm away. I thought you might appreciate some help in case you haven't used it before. (I'm assuming the computer is on, by the way!)

1. In the top right hand corner of the screen, you'll see an icon marked Hard Disk. Click on this (you do this by moving the mouse so the arrow goes to the icon). Then press the front bit of the mouse quickly.

2. The screen display will change, and the Hard Disk window should appear: look for the Internet Fast icon and click on it.

3. The screen display will change again. Now look for the Mail icon and click on that.

4. You'll see a window called Mail which shows all the mail you've sent and received. On the left of the screen, there's a bar with various icons: click on the one which says Prepare.

5. A new window will come up, which says New Message. Where you see 'To' type in the address of the person you want to send your e-mail to. (You must type in the address exactly: don't change any small letters into capitals and make sure you put the dots (.) in the right place, or the message won't go!

6. Then click on the box labelled Subject: you can put a title to your message if you want to give it one.

7. Below the four boxes is the actual space for you to write your message: just type it in, and when you've finished, go back to the icons at the top and click on Send. You'll hear a few strange noises and in seconds your e-mail will be on its way!

Hope this makes sense. If you have any problems, you could always phone!

# Wordspot

*mind*

**1** Replace the words underlined with a phrase using *mind* from the diagrams. (You may need to change verb forms.)

**For example:**

I'm really sorry about not phoning you yesterday. I had a lot to do and ~~I forgot all about it!~~ *it slipped my mind*

a   Look, there's nothing wrong with you – <u>you're just imagining it!</u>

b   Hurry up and <u>decide!</u> The shop's shutting in about half a minute.

c   Where have you been until this time of night? Your mother's been <u>really, really worried!</u>

d   Well, I'm afraid I'm the sort of person who <u>says what I think</u>, and I think you're making a big mistake!

e   Actually I think I've <u>changed my decision</u>. I will come with you, after all!

f   <u>Be careful of</u> the step just before the bathroom door. A lot of people don't notice it!

g   <u>Could you possibly lend</u> me some money. I don't seem to have brought any cash with me.

h   <u>I hope you won't be annoyed</u>, but I borrowed your black top to go out in.

i   <u>It's got nothing to do with you</u> – it's private!

**2  a)** The sentences in Exercise 1 all come from conversations. Read them again and decide:

- Who are the speakers?
- What is the situation / topic of conversation?
- What might they say before / after this?
- What mood are they in (annoyed, impatient, etc.)?

**b)** Work in pairs. Expand four of the lines into conversations, like this.

MAN:   Hi! How are you today?

WOMAN: Okay.

MAN:   I'm really sorry about not phoning you yesterday! I had a lot to do, and it slipped my mind!

WOMAN: Yeah, you always have a lot to do, don't you?

MAN:   Look, I said I'm sorry. What's the big problem?

WOMAN: I've just had enough, do you understand? I've had enough of waiting around for you to phone me. I don't want to ...

**c)** Act out some of your conversations for the rest of the class.

**3** Look at the other phrases with *mind* in the diagrams. Write sentences (or more conversations) using some of them.

**4** Copy the diagrams in Exercise 1 to make a poster for your classroom wall. There are many idiomatic phrases with *mind*. Are there any more that you can add?

# Consolidation
## modules 1–4

### A Vocabulary: word hunt

**1 Work in pairs or groups. Complete the gaps in the word hunt. If necessary, look back at the appropriate page in your book. (The page numbers are given in brackets.)**

**a** (Module 1, page 6) Find words to describe someone's lifestyle which mean the opposite of:
secure and conventional _____
exciting _____
admirable _____

**b** (Module 1, page 13) Find two more phrases meaning *arrange for someone to do something* using this construction:
*get your hair cut* _____ _____

**c** (Module 2, page 18) Find the words for:
two negative emotions _____ _____
two health problems _____ _____

**d** (Module 2, page 25) Find words that mean:
not paid enough _____
selfish _____
spell wrongly _____

**e** (Module 2, page 26) Find three words where *over* means *too much*:
_____ _____ _____

**f** (Module 3, page 32) Find:
two words relating to crime
_____ _____
two words relating to aggressive behaviour
_____ _____
two words that might relate to accidents
_____ _____

**g** (Module 4, page 41) Find:
two characteristics of a person who is successful socially _____ _____
two characteristics of a person with a strong character _____ _____

**h** (Module 4, page 49) Find a phrase with *mind* that means:
to decide _____
to be crazy _____
to forget _____
to be careful of your head _____

**2 Discuss the following questions with other students.**

a How well have you remembered the new vocabulary from Modules 1–4:
• very well?  • quite well?  • not very well?
b Which areas do you need to look back at again?
c Is there anything you can do in the future to ensure that you remember the vocabulary as effectively as possible?

### B Verb forms: active and passive

**1 Complete these true stories with the verbs in brackets. You can use both active and passive forms. In some cases more than one answer is possible.**

> ## It must be true, I read it in the tabloids
>
> **a** Magistrate Isabelle Le Tessier (1) _____ (*sentence*) her old school teacher for speeding in Rouen, France, last week. He (2) _____ (*force*) to write 'I must not break the speed limit' 25,000 times.
>
> **b** Cuban Raul Blanco, who (3) _____ (*lose*) three fingers in an accident several years ago, (4) _____ (*refuse*) US citizenship because he cannot provide a full set of fingerprints.
>
> **c** Lars Homberg and Anka Edlund of Karlstad, Sweden, (5) _____ (*decide*) to get married after spending nineteen hours stuck in a lift together earlier this month. They (6) _____ (*never meet*) before their ordeal.
>
> **d** André Gurnham of Lyons, France, (7) _____ (*try*) to find romance. Recently, he placed an advertisement in the local paper saying, 'Ladies, write in if you are bored with the man in your life!' Checking through the replies, he was dismayed to discover that both his wife and his mistress (8) _____ (*answer*).
>
> **e** The state of Andhra Pradesh in India (9) _____ (*pass*) a new law saying that anyone who (10) _____ (*catch*) cheating in school exams (11) _____ (*send*) to jail for ten years.

**f** A sales assistant (12) _____ (*lie*) dead in the window of a Johannesburg furniture store for a week before being noticed. He (13) _____ (*arrange*) the waterbed display when he collapsed, and passersby assumed he (14) _____ (*demonstrate*) how comfortable the beds were. Indeed he (15) _____ (*look*) so comfortable that waterbed sales quadrupled in the seven days that he (16) _____ (*lie*) there.

**g** Failed pilot, Larry Walter, attached forty-two helium balloons to a kitchen chair, and spent fourteen hours (17) _____ (*float*) three miles above Los Angeles earlier this week. Mr Walters, who (18) _____ (*turn down*) by the US air force because of bad eyesight, was determined to fly. When wind unexpectedly (19) _____ (*sweep*) him over the city's airport, two planes almost hit him and a pilot told air traffic control, 'You're not going to believe this, but we (20) _____ (*just pass*) a man (21) _____ (*fly*) in a chair!'

**2** 🖭 **Listen and compare your answers to those on the cassette. Which story do you like best? Why?**

## C Speaking: talking about general ideas

**1 Discuss the following in groups.**

a The characteristics in the list all contribute to the first impression people make. Which are most important when you meet a new colleague or neighbour?

b Are the same things important when you meet an eligible member of the opposite sex?

---

### *First impressions*

- your voice and the way you speak
- the way you dress, and how smart / stylish you are
- being able to chat easily about lots of different things
- how much you smile
- the ability to make other people laugh
- appearing self-confident
- giving the impression of being intelligent / educated
- how good-looking you are
- being friendly and open
- being cool and mysterious
- sincerity and lack of pretentiousness

---

**2 Is there anything else that you always notice when you meet new people? Is there anything in particular that would put you off someone?**

## D Speaking: real life

**1 Work in pairs. What would you say in the following situations? If you cannot think of any suitable phrases, look back at the appropriate page in your book for help. (The page numbers are given in brackets.)**

a You are walking down the street with a friend. A man starts shouting insults at your friend for no reason. Your friend is getting very tense and angry. (Module 2, page 27)

b You are chatting to an acquaintance. She is keen to continue the conversation, but you have a lot to do, so you want to end the conversation politely. (Module 1, page 16)

c You have just started a new job, and don't know how to work the photocopier. The only person around is a colleague you've never spoken to before, who looks deeply engrossed in some reading. (Module 1, page 16)

d Your central heating / air conditioning is broken. You phone up to get it fixed, but no one can come for another three days, and even then they can't give you a particular time, so you'll have to stay in all day and wait for them. (Module 3, page 38)

e You are explaining to a friend how to use one of the following:
- your camera  • your personal stereo
- your mobile phone  • your electronic dictionary
- another small appliance that you have with you
Your friend does not understand, and you have to explain several times. (Module 4, page 47)

**2 Choose one conversation to act out in front of the other students.**

# Unusual achievements

## Part A Task

---

**Reading and vocabulary:**
different kinds of achievement
**Vocabulary:** verb-noun word combinations
**Preparation for task:** the most important human achievement
**Task:** what is the greatest achievement of the last 150 years?

---

## Reading and vocabulary

### Different kinds of achievement

**1** The people in the pictures have achieved something unusual. Can you guess what?

**2** Match the pictures with the texts. Were your predictions correct? Summarise what each person has achieved in a sentence.

(a) On 15–16 July 1994, Ricardinho Neves (Brazil) juggled a regulation soccer ball non-stop for 19 hours 15 minutes 31 seconds with feet, legs and head, without the ball ever touching the ground at the Los Angeles Convention Center, California, USA. The record time for ball control by a woman is 7 hours 5 minutes 25 seconds by Claudia Martini (Brazil) at Caxias do Sul, Brazil, on 12 July 1996.

From *The Week*

(b) A grandmother who took ninety-seven days to fly around the world in a helicopter has raised £500,000 for Save the Children. On the way, Jennifer Murray, 57, broke three world records and saw the Monaco Grand Prix, the Valley of the Kings and the Hong Kong handover. She spent her birthday with tribesmen in Borneo and was surrounded by armed militia at a remote airfield in the Philippines. Back in England she said, 'It is going to be very difficult to settle down into the old routines again.'

From *The Week*

(c) Nicola Foulston, 29-year-old managing director of Brands Hatch, the venue for British Formula 1 racing, inherited the racing track when her father was killed in a car crash. This week she won the Veuve-Clicquot Businesswoman of the Year Award. Since taking over, she has turned around a struggling company, which now has a market value of £36 million, and she is thinking of buying other sporting venues. One casualty of her success has been her personal life, as marriage to a flying instructor ended in divorce after only a year. She told *The Sunday Times* that she will never marry again and would, 'never have children while I had this career.'

From *The Week*

(d)

Harrison Ford has been voted the greatest film star of all time. Readers of the film magazine *Empire* cited his 'laconic attitude' and 'sloppy charm' as the reason for his popularity, placing him above such Hollywood legends as Steve McQueen, John Wayne and Cary Grant. Ford's definition of a good actor for example, is 'someone who shows up on time and doesn't knock over the furniture'. He is an actor, says the critic Christopher Hemblade, 'who seems to have a certain integrity and honesty and usefulness.'

From *The Week*

(e)

A student who went blind while waiting to go to university has gained a first class degree in Latin and Greek from Oxford. Ben Merrick's sight began to fail after he left school, due to a rare hereditary disease, but he ignored doctors who advised him to abandon his plans to study Greek and Latin. Mr Merrick thanked the Oxford Recording Centre for the Blind, who put hundreds of passages on tape. 'When someone has gone to the trouble of putting whole books on tape, you feel morally obliged to listen to them all,' he said.

From *The Week*

**3 a)** If necessary, check the meaning and pronunciation of the words in **bold** in your mini-dictionary or with your teacher. Then decide which things you think each person in Exercise 2 has done. Compare and explain your answers in pairs.

has **raised** a large sum of **money** for charity ..........

has **overcome** a lot of **difficulties** ..........

has **made** a lot of **sacrifices** in order to achieve what he / she wanted ..........

has **taken** huge **risks** ..........

has had **to cope with** unexpected problems ..........

has done something rather **pointless** ..........

seems very **modest about** his / her achievements ..........

seems to have no **sense of** danger ..........

has succeeded **against the odds** ..........

has shown a lot of **dedication** and **stamina** ..........

has **achieved something** really **worthwhile** ..........

has **got** their **priorities wrong** ..........

**b)** Whose achievement do you think is the most / least worthwhile? Explain why.

# Vocabulary

## Verb-noun word combinations

**1 a)** In the boxes below are some verbs and nouns which are often found together. Without looking back at Exercise 3, match them up.

> A   achieve   break   make   overcome   raise   show   take   take over   cope with   win

> B   an award   problems   a company   difficulties   a world record   something worthwhile   a sacrifice   stamina   money for charity   a risk

**b)** In pairs, think of examples of how the word combinations can be used.

**For example:**

*Kim Basinger has just <u>won an award</u> for her new film.*

**2** Look at other combinations with some of the verbs. Cross out any combinations which are not possible. Can you explain why?

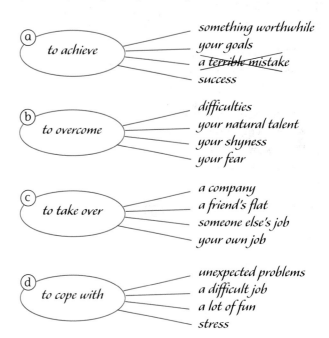

a) to achieve — something worthwhile / your goals / a terrible mistake / success

b) to overcome — difficulties / your natural talent / your shyness / your fear

c) to take over — a company / a friend's flat / someone else's job / your own job

d) to cope with — unexpected problems / a difficult job / a lot of fun / stress

**3** It is very important to notice and remember words that go together in English. Discuss with other students which of the following are most useful for remembering word combinations:

- underlining them in things that you read.
- writing them in your vocabulary book.
- repeating them to yourself.
- making sentences of your own with them.
- making notices for the wall or posters to remind you of them.
- other ideas.

## Personal vocabulary

# Task: what is the greatest achievement of the last 150 years?
## Preparation for task

**1** Close your books and work in groups. Without reading the ideas below, make your own list of some of the most important human achievements of the last 150 years. (Think about politics, society, technology and medicine.)

**2** Look at the list below. How many of these things did you put on your list? Did you have anything that is not mentioned below?

- the invention of the telephone
- the discovery of penicillin
- the invention of the car
- the liberation of women
- the invention of television and film
- the exploration of space
- the invention of the aeroplane
- the development of rock-and-roll music
- the invention of the microchip
- the spread of democracy throughout the world

**3** [5.1] Listen to someone talking about one of these achievements and its importance.

a   Which of the achievements on the list is he talking about?
b   Give four reasons why he believes it has been so important.
c   How was life different before this?
d   Do you agree with the arguments he gives, or not?

## Useful language

"The invention / discovery / exploration, etc. of
   ... has led to ..."

   ... has meant that ..."

   ... has provided ..."

   ... is of great importance because ..."

   ... has completely changed our lives because ..."

"As a result of this, people have been able to ..."

"Without (the car, etc.) we wouldn't be able to ... / we wouldn't have ... / we wouldn't know about ..."

"Previously, we couldn't ... / didn't have ..., etc. whereas now ..."

"Because of this, one day we may be able to ..."

## Task

1 Work either in pairs or individually. You are going to prepare a short talk similar to the one on the cassette. Choose one of the topics on the list or another idea of your own.

2 Spend about twenty minutes preparing your talk. It should last about two minutes. Think about:

a the consequences of this achievement.
b how life would be different without it / what life was like before it happened.
c what difference (if any) it makes to your life personally.
d what future possibilities it offers.

Look at the special fact file on page 143 for information and statistics to support your case, but think of your own ideas first. Ask your teacher for any words or phrases you need, and write them in your *Personal vocabulary* box. Look at the phrases in the *Useful language* box to help you. Spend a few minutes practising what you will say.

3 Work in groups with students who prepared talks on different topics. Take it in turns to give your talks. Listen to the other students. At the end, ask any questions or make any points of your own about what they said. After everyone has spoken, vote which you think is the most important achievement (you cannot vote for yourself!).

4 Compare results with the other groups. Do you agree with your group's decision? Why? / Why not? What do you think will be the most important achievements of the next hundred years?

# Part B **Language**

Perfect aspect in the past, present and future
More about the Present Perfect Simple and Continuous
**Writing skills:** describing a film or book you have enjoyed
**Wordspot:** *up*

## Language focus 1

Perfect aspect in the past, present and future

Read the texts and tick (✓) the best ending to the sentences below.

①

Mederda de Jesus Leon de Uzcatefui – alias 'La Maestra Chucha' – must be the most experienced teacher in the world. She still teaches at her own school in Caracas, Venezuela, where she began teaching in 1911, when at the age of twelve, she and her two sisters set up a school named *Modelo de Aplicacion*.

La Maestra Chucha
a  has been a teacher for more than eighty-five years.
b  was a teacher for more than eighty-five years.
c  had been a teacher for more than eighty-five years.

②

Git Kaur Rhandawa, from Hayes in West London, had more reason than most people to be nervous when she took her driving test on 19 June 1987. It was her forty-eighth attempt at the test. Imagine her joy when the examiner said, 'Congratulations Mrs Rhandawa ...'

Git Kaur Rhandawa felt really happy because
a  she's finally passed her driving test.
b  she was finally passing her driving test.
c  she'd finally passed her driving test.

③

John Hughes, thirty years old, is believed to be the world's biggest film addict. After seeing his first film at the age of six in 1975 (his parents took him to see *Pinocchio* as a Christmas treat), he has seen over 6,000 feature films. He currently goes to the cinema at least six times a week, and watches an average of ten videos a week – an average of about 800 films a year. He

records every title he has seen in his diary (with a star rating), and given his current rate of viewing he hopes to achieve his ambition of seeing 10,000 films before his thirty-fifth birthday. When asked for his favourite among the films he has already seen, Mr Hughes – who is unmarried – has no hesitation, '*Pinocchio*,' he says.

By the time he is thirty-five, John Hughes hopes he
a  has seen 10,000 films.
b  will have seen 10,000 films.
c  will see 10,000 films.

**56**

# Analysis

**1** Look at the sentences you chose, and answer the questions.

a <u>She's been a teacher for over eighty years.</u> Which tense is this? When did she become a teacher? Is she still a teacher now?

b <u>She felt really happy because she'd finally passed her driving test.</u>
Which happened first:
• *feeling happy?* • *passing her driving test?*
Which action does the Past Perfect describe? Why?

c <u>By the time he's thirty-five, John Hughes will have seen 10,000 films.</u>
How old is John Hughes now:
• *under thirty-five?* • *over thirty-five?*
When will he see his 10,000th film?
• *before he's thirty-five?*
• *when he's thirty-five?*
• *after he's thirty-five?*
What tense is *will have seen*?

**2** All perfect tenses link two times. Which of the sentences above:
• links the past and present?
• links two points in the past?
• links two points in the future?

***Now read Language summary A on pages 151-152.***

## Practice

**1** Read the sentences. Tick (✓) the ones that are true for you, and write a cross (✗) next to the ones that are false. If the sentences do not apply to you, mark them like this (–). Compare answers with a partner.

a I've been at this school for more than a year. ☐

b The lesson had already started when I arrived at school today. ☐

c I'll have finished my studies by the time I'm twenty-six. ☐

d I'd never heard of John Hughes until this lesson. ☐

e I'd already heard of the Future Perfect before today's lesson. ☐

f I haven't done much studying recently. ☐

g By the time I'm twenty, hopefully, I'll have passed my driving test. ☐

h I'd learned to ride a bicycle by the age of eight. ☐

i By this time next year, I'll probably have moved house. ☐

j I'll probably have gone to bed by midnight tonight. ☐

k I've made more than three phone calls so far today. ☐

l I've been abroad this year. ☐

**2** Write:

a Three more things that you hope you'll have done by midnight tonight.

b Three more things you hope you'll have done by the end of the year.

**Compare your answers with a partner.**

........................................................

### Follow-up task

**1** Work in groups. Together, write twelve sentences similar to those above about the past, present and future achievements and experiences of people in the group. Six sentences should be true, and six false:

By the age of five / twelve *Mariko had already ...*

By the end of the year / month, *Juan Carlos will have become an uncle*

In the next (six months / five years, etc. ) ....
*Lucy hopes she will have ...*

**2a** Work with a student from a different group and read out your sentences. Your partner should decide if they are true or false.

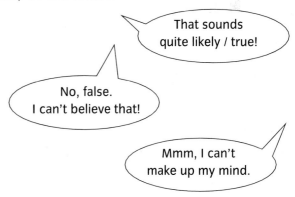

That sounds quite likely / true!

No, false. I can't believe that!

Mmm, I can't make up my mind.

**b** Give your partner a point for every correct guess. Did anyone get twelve correct? Did you discover anything surprising about other students?

**3** What are your proudest achievements? Why? Tell the other students in your group.

........................................................

# Language focus 2

## More about the Present Perfect Simple and Continuous

Which sentence describes each picture best?

① 
a He's stood on one leg for thirty-six hours.
b He's been standing on one leg for thirty-six hours.

②
a They've been learning about nuclear physics.
b They've learned about nuclear physics.

③
a She's won an Olympic medal.
b She's been winning an Olympic medal.

④
a They've painted their ceiling.
b They've been painting their ceiling.

⑤
a She's made over twenty phone calls.
b She's been making over twenty phone calls.

⑥
a He's owned the restaurant for fifty years.
b He's been owning the restaurant for fifty years.

# Analysis

1 **Similarities between the Present Perfect Simple and Continuous**
Both forms link the past and present. How are all the actions in the pictures above related to / important in the present?

2 **General differences between simple and continuous forms**
In Module 3 you looked at general differences between all simple and continuous tenses. Find one example above of the following:
- the continuous form used to show duration.
- the simple form used to show an action that is instant or complete.
- the continuous form not being used with state verbs.

3 **More specific differences between the Present Perfect Simple and Continuous**
a Because they have duration, Present Perfect Continuous verbs sometimes continue into the present. For example .......... above.
b Because they show duration / repetition, Present Perfect Continuous verbs often describe 'general activities' (they answer the question *How has this person spent his time?*). For example .......... above.
c Because they tend to show complete actions, Present Perfect Simple verbs often describe results (they answer the question *What has this person achieved?*). For example .......... above.
d Because they tend to show complete actions, Present Perfect Simple verbs are used to give the number of things you've done. For example .......... above.

*Now read Language summary B on page 152.*

## Practice

1 Choose the best verb form in each sentence. Can you explain why it is the best?

a Look outside: *it's snowed / it's been snowing*!

b Oh no! *I've left / I've been leaving* my credit card at home!

c I'm exhausted! *I've rushed around / I've been rushing around* all day!

d Ow! *I've cut / I've been cutting* myself!

e Sorry, but *I've changed / I've been changing* my mind. Could I have the chicken instead, please?

f *Has Sam spoken / Has Sam been speaking* to you about babysitting on Saturday night?

g Hi! *I haven't seen / I haven't been seeing* you for ages. How are you? What *have you done / have you been doing*?

h *My sister's made / My sister's been making* a lovely chocolate cake. Would you like a piece?

### Pronunciation

When you use the Present Perfect tenses in speech, you use contractions and weak forms for *has / have* and *been*. However, you should not omit these auxiliary verbs altogether.

[5.2] Practise saying the sentences above pronouncing the weak forms and contractions correctly.

/ ɪts bɪn snəʊɪŋ /
It's been snowing.

2 **a)** Look at the pictures on the right. In pairs, discuss what you think is happening in each story.

**b)** Decide what the characters are saying in each picture. Pay attention to the verb forms.

**c)** [5.3] Listen and compare your answers with the conversations on the cassette. What are the differences in:
- the story?
- the language you used in the conversations?

**d)** Choose one of the stories to act out in pairs. Write a few more lines to complete the story in the most interesting way you can.

① Paul was flat hunting. When he went to view Mr and Mrs Jones's apartment one evening, everything seemed fine at first ...

interesting ... ... how long / live here?

sixty years ... ... wife and I / very happy here

why decide / move?

wife / unwell... ... not sleep / behave strangely

decide / move somewhere quieter

you said / three bedrooms / only see two / other one?

② Jayne knew her flatmate was having boyfriend problems, so it was no surprise when she came home one evening to find Cindy looking red-eyed and unhappy ...

Hi! What happen / Cindy! cry...?

Fine / just watch / really sad film / that's all.

hear from Nick today...?

not care about Nick any more / not think about him all day / forget what / look like

good

actually / not the truth / phone him all day / leave about six messages on answerphone / not phone me back

**59**

# Writing skills

## Describing a film or book you have enjoyed

**1** Read the review of the film *Kolya* and complete the gaps with the appropriate phrase from the box below.

(a) ............................. is Kolya. What's unusual about it is that it's a film from the Czech Republic, and it's nice to have a change from American movies!
(b) ............................. because it won an Oscar for Best Foreign Film so I thought it must be
(c) ............................. (d) ............................. by a man called Jan Sverák, and (e) ............................. a Czech actor Zdenek Sverák, as well as a young Russian child actor, Andrej Chalimon.
The film (f) ............................. Prague, the capital city, and the action begins in the late 1980s, just before The Velvet Revolution, when communism was replaced by democracy. (g) ............................. of Louka, a musician with the state symphony orchestra, who suddenly loses his job, and is forced to play music at funerals in order to make a living. Eventually, he meets and marries a Russian woman, but unfortunately, she is only interested in getting citizenship, and immediately after the wedding she flees to Germany, leaving Louka to cope with her five-year-old son (h) ............................. by Andrej Chalimon. The film follows the relationship between the man and the boy, and the way they eventually learn to adapt to each other's way of life. Although (i) ............................., and a little slow-moving at times, there were a number of things I really liked about it. (j) ............................. the acting, which I thought was excellent (particularly Sverák and the boy), and I also liked the touches of humour, which were very subtle and gentle. (k) ............................. how people live their lives in such a different culture from mine.
(l) ............................. this film to anyone who is interested in seeing something different from the usual action-packed Hollywood blockbuster, and also anyone who enjoys a good cry!

| worth seeing | it stars | It tells the story of |
| --- | --- | --- |

worth seeing    it stars    It tells the story of
I particularly wanted to see it
On the whole, I'd certainly recommend
I was especially impressed by    It's directed
One of the best films I've seen this year
the film is a little sentimental    brilliantly played
I also found it very interesting to see    is set in

**2** Complete the table using information from the review.

| Title | a |
| --- | --- |
| **b** *Reason for going to see it* | • a change from American movies<br>• because it won an Oscar for Best Foreign Film |
| **Director** | c |
| d | Zdenek Sverák<br>Andrej Chalimon |
| **Where / when the film is set** | e |
| f | A musician with the state symphony orchestra loses his job. While working as a musician at funerals, he meets ... |
| **Positive points about the film** | g |
| h | • a bit sentimental,<br>• slow-moving at times |
| **Who I'd recommend it to** | i |

# Wordspot

*up*

**1** **a)** 🔊 [5.4] Can you think of a phrase with *up* to complete the conversations?

1   A:  Lee, could you .......... these files .......... to the accounts office on the sixth floor?
   B:  Sure.

2   A:  Have we got any more washing powder? I've .......... the old packet.
   B:  I think there's some more in the cupboard under the sink.

3   A:  I don't understand this photo.
   B:  I'm not surprised – you're looking at it ..........!

4   A:  It's freezing in this house!
   B:  I know, I've .......... the central heating. It'll soon .......... I'm sure.

5   A:  Why's everyone looking so serious today? ..........?
   B:  Apparently they're going to announce more redundancies this afternoon.

6   A:  Where do you want to go tomorrow night?
   B:  .......... – it's your birthday!

7   A:  Are you still ..........? It's one o'clock in the morning!
   B:  I know, but I've got to get this essay finished.

8   A:  Can I have some ice cream for pudding, Mum?
   B:  Not unless you .......... all your vegetables.

9   A:  Did you know that Rachel and Bob have ..........?
   B:  Oh no, that's really sad after all these years. What happened?

**b)** Put the phrases with *up* in the correct place on the diagram.

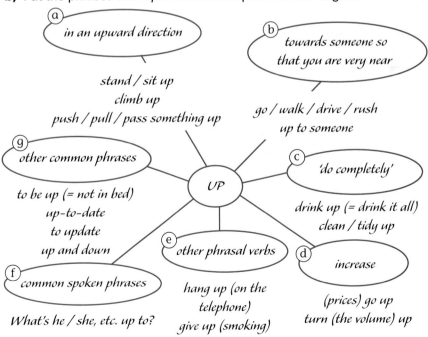

**3** Make a similar table about a film or play you have seen recently, or a book you have read. Which sections do you need to change if you write about a book? Complete your table with as much information as possible.

**4** Use the table to write your own account of a film, play or book you have enjoyed. The other students are going to read your review, so make sure that it is clear and accurate.

**5** Display the reviews on a wall or desk. Which of the films / plays / books have you already seen / read? Do you agree with the writer's comments? After reading the reviews will you read / see any of the films or books? Which ones?

**2** Work in pairs. Student A looks at the card on page 143, and Student B looks at the card on page 146. Read out the sentences on your card and stress the phrases in **bold**. Your partner changes the stressed words to a phrase with *up*.

**For example:**
A: We need to **modernise** our communications systems. They're very old.
B: We need to **update** our communications systems.

**61**

# Do you remember?

**Think of a famous person, or someone you know personally who:**

- has won an important award or prize.
- has raised a lot of money for charity.
- has had to cope with a lot of personal problems recently.
- has shown a lot of stamina.
- has had to overcome a lot of difficulties to achieve what they have.
- has broken a world record.
- has made a lot of sacrifices for the sake of their family or job.
- has achieved something really worthwhile, in your opinion.

**Compare answers in groups. If necessary, explain why you have chosen this person.**

**Complete the table with the correct form of the words. Mark the stress, as in the example.**

| verb | noun |
|---|---|
| to invent | • invention |
| to develop | _____ |
| to _____ | spread |
| to discover | _____ |
| to _____ | liberation |
| to achieve | _____ |
| to _____ | award |

**Complete the sentences with *has been*, *had been* or *will have been*.**

a) In December, Doris .......... with the company for forty years, so we've decided to have a party to celebrate.

b) David knows the way to our house, surely – he .......... here before.

c) I'm getting really fed up with Sonia – she .......... late every morning this week.

d) I lived with my grandfather until he died when I was fifteen. He was a very interesting man. He .......... all over the world and knew lots about everything.

e) Just think! At the end of this holiday, we .......... to three different continents!

f) Tony and Rosa got married about ten years ago, but I think she .......... married before.

**a)  The verbs in bold are commonly used in either the Present Perfect Simple or the Present Perfect Continuous. Explain why one or the other verb form is used in each sentence.**

1) I **haven't been sleeping** very well.

2) I**'ve been trying** to phone you all day.

3) I**'ve finished** my essay.

4) I**'ve left** my wallet at home.

5) You**'ve been driving** for ages.

6) It**'s been raining**.

7) I**'ve torn** the page of my book.

8) He**'s been working** really hard.

**b)  In pairs, create five short conversations using one of the phrases above in each.**

**a)  What does *up* mean in each diagram?**

| 1) | use tidy drink | — up — | your bedroom your coffee the rest of the packet |
|---|---|---|---|

| 2) | climb take it run | — up — | the stairs a steep hill to your room |
|---|---|---|---|

| 3) | turn put speak | — up — | a little bit the volume on the television the price |
|---|---|---|---|

| 4) | drive go walk | — up to — | a house a stranger a crossroads |
|---|---|---|---|

**b)  Use each diagram to make three common phrases with *up*.**

**For example:** *drink up your coffee*

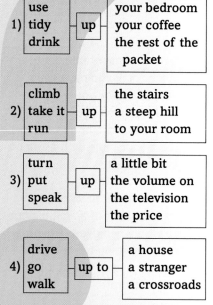

# module 6

## Getting it right

### Part A  **Task**

Reading and vocabulary: how to pass exams
**Preparation for task:** match the advice to the topic
**Task:** make a list of tips on
*How to…*

## Reading and vocabulary

### How to pass exams

**1** Discuss the following questions in groups.

- Are you the sort of person who loves or hates exams? How do they make you feel?
- What's the most difficult exam you have ever taken? Why?
- Have you got any 'exam horror stories' (times when you or one of your friends missed exams, were ill during exams, etc.). What happened?

**2 a)** Read the list in the box and check the meaning of the phrases in **bold** in your mini-dictionary or with your teacher. Tick (✓) the things you should do when preparing for an exam, and write a cross (✗) next to the things you should avoid.

**b)** In groups, discuss which things you personally do / don't do when you are revising for exams. Do you have any other useful advice?

| |
|---|
| **draw up** a revision timetable and **stick to it** ☐ |
| **set** yourself tough **goals** for your revision each day ☐ |
| meet a friend and study together ☐ |
| spend a lot of time with your friends **moaning** about your exams ☐ |
| **get** easily **distracted** ☐ |
| only study for about thirty minutes at a time ☐ |
| **take** regular **breaks** ☐ |
| **give up** your social life during the weeks before the exams ☐ |
| **stay up** late studying the night before the exam ☐ |
| arrive at least an hour before the exam starts ☐ |
| compare what you've revised with other students just before the exam ☐ |

**3 a)** Read the article and mark each piece of advice as follows:

1 a really useful piece of advice
2 good advice, but hard to follow in practice
3 true, but pretty obvious
4 I don't agree. Bad advice!

Compare answers in pairs.

> This is a good idea. I hadn't thought of that before.

> I know in theory you're supposed to … but in practice … usually happens!

> I don't agree with this at all.

**b)** Which do you think is the best piece of advice? Does the writer disagree with you about any choices you made in Exercise 2?

**4** Find the phrases in box A in the article. Without checking in your mini-dictionary, try to guess from the context what each one means. If necessary, use the definitions in box B to help you.

---

**A**

1 to **sail through** an exam (4)
2 to **stretch your legs** (53)
3 to **wind down** (59)
4 the **trickier** (questions) (92)
5 to **pace yourself** (99)
6 to **gear yourself up** for exams (11)
7 to **hinder** your performance (57)
8 **snatched** (72)
9 to **tackle** a question (93)
10 to **retake** an exam (107)

---

**B**

a to make it difficult for someone to do something
b to go for a walk, especially after sitting for a long time
c to make a determined effort to do something difficult
d to succeed very easily in a difficult challenge
e to rest or relax after a lot of hard work or excitement
f to do an exam again
g to do something at a controlled, steady speed
h to prepare yourself for something you have to do
i taken quickly
j difficult, complicated, needing great care to do well

---

# There is a technique to just sailing through, so make sure you don't just count on good luck.

It's that time of year again when students across the country are gearing themselves up for exams. If you feel you've left your revision too late, don't despair. Follow our guide and start today.

## Before you start

• Get organised: draw up a revision timetable of topics to cover. Stick to it and let friends and family know that you are serious, so they don't interrupt your studies. ❑

• If you find it difficult to concentrate, don't study at home where you will be easily distracted; go to your library instead. ❑

# HOW TO PASS EXAMS

• If motivation is a problem, arrange to meet a friend and 30 study together. But don't let it turn into an excuse for a social chat or a moaning session! ❏

• Remember what you are 35 studying for. Why do you need these exams? Keeping your long-term goal in mind will help maintain your motivation. ❏ 40

Studying tactics

• Go with your body clock: if you're slow in the morning, use that time to do some background reading. Do the 45 weightier work in the afternoon. ❏

• Don't study for more than thirty to forty minutes at a time. Take regular breaks to 50 get enough fresh air and stretch your legs. ❏

• Don't study too late, especially the night before your exam. Tiredness will 55 hinder your performance the next day. Always make sure you wind down before you go to bed. ❏

• It's important to maintain a 60 happy, positive frame of mind, so don't let revising take over your whole life. Give yourself something to look forward to after a day's 65 studying: meet friends for a drink, or relax in a warm bath. ❏

• Eat well; have a proper meal rather than snacks 70 snatched at your desk. ❏

On the day

• Allow plenty of time to get to the exam, but don't arrive too early or you'll sit around 75 getting nervous. ❏

• Resist the temptation to compare what you've revised with other students while waiting. ❏ 80

• Do read the paper thoroughly before starting. It's time well spent. It's very easy to misunderstand simple instructions when you're 85 under a lot of pressure. ❏

• On multiple-choice exam papers, go through and do all the easy questions first then go back to the beginning and 90 try the trickier ones. ❏

• On essay papers, tackle the questions you feel happiest about first, so you can build up your confidence. ❏ 95

• Work out how much time you have for each question and pace yourself accordingly. You have nothing to gain from 100 finishing early. ❏

• Always keep things in proportion. The worst thing that can happen is that you'll fail. If necessary, 105 you can usually retake an exam. ❏

From *Cosmopolitan*

## Personal vocabulary

# Task: make a list of tips on *How to...*

### Useful language

**Do's**

"Always remember to ..."

"Think about ..."

"Practise ..."

"Allow plenty of time for ..."

**Don't's**

"Avoid ..."

"Resist the temptation to ..."

"Don't let ... happen / Don't allow ... to happen."

**Both**

"It's important (not) to ..."

"Make sure that you (don't) ..."

"Be careful (not) to ..."

"You should always / never ..."

"Make an effort (not) to ... / try (not) to ..."

"If / Unless you ..., ... will / might happen."

## Preparation for task

**1** The pieces of advice below are all taken from *How to ...* books. Match the advice in the box to the appropriate book titles. Do you think they give good advice or not?

• How to choose the right career
• How to learn a foreign language
• How to get fit
• How to meet new people and improve your social life
• How to be well-dressed
• How to manage your personal finances
• How to give up smoking
• How to travel on a low budget

a Work out a realistic monthly budget and stick to it, and always allow a little extra for emergencies, such as your car breaking down, or an unexpected bill.

b Start by making a list of the things in your present life that you most enjoy doing and the things that you least enjoy doing.

c Don't appear too keen or over-friendly, this can put people off.

d Invest in one or two good quality, classic items that will form the basis for the rest of your wardrobe.

e Take every opportunity you can to use what you have learned, without worrying too much if you make mistakes.

f Choose the right moment in your life to do it. If you are under stress, or starting a new job, for example, you are less likely to keep it up.

g Be careful not to overdo it – you could easily injure yourself if you're not used to taking exercise.

h Keep out of the tourist areas for eating, shopping and places to stay – they are invariably the most expensive.

**2** Think of one more piece of advice for any of the books. Read it out to the rest of the class, and see if they can guess which book you chose.

## Task

**1 a)** Work in pairs or groups. Choose from the list in Preparation for task, Exercise 1 and spend about fifteen minutes thinking of good advice for people in that situation, including any of the ideas you mentioned before.

**b)** Make a list of at least four more do's and four more don't's for the topic you have chosen. Ask your teacher for any words or phrases that you need, and write them in your *Personal vocabulary* box.

**c)** Look at the phrases in the *Useful language* box to help you express your ideas.

| Do's | Don't's |
|------|---------|
|      |         |

**2** Form new groups with students who have worked on other topics. Tell them about your list of advice, and find out if they have any ideas to add.

**3** Explain very briefly to the rest of the class which topics you have discussed. Tell them about the best piece of advice you have heard, and any advice that you really disagreed with.

# Part B **Language**

Use and non-use of articles
**Writing skills:** listening and taking notes
**Real life:** different ways of emphasising what you say

## Language focus

### Use and non-use of articles

**1** Read the text *Improving your memory*. If necessary, check the meaning of any words in your mini-dictionary or with your teacher. What suggestions are made in the text? Do you think they will work?

**2** Read *Improving your memory* again and underline:

- all the articles (*a, an, the*).
- all the nouns which do not have an article in front of them.

**3 a)** There are many rules about the use of articles in English, but many of them may be the same in your language. Work either in pairs or individually. Complete the rules in Part 1 of the quiz with examples from the text above.

**b)** Now read *Language summary A1* on page 153. Underline any rules that you did not already know.

**4 a)** Look at Part 2 of the quiz and complete the gaps with *a / an / the* or *ø* (= nothing).

**b)** Now read *Language summary A2* on page 153. Underline any rules that you did not already know.

### Improving your memory

A recent article in *Psychology* magazine suggests that exam students can improve their memory by studying with the help of unusual smells. The author, Dr Rachel Herz of the Chemical Senses Center in Philadelphia, claims there is a strong link between our memory for facts and our memory for odours. In the experiment she describes, students were asked to memorise a text in a number of rooms scented with peppermint, violet and pine. Smell association helped them improve their memory by twenty per cent. 'Go to a perfume department,' says Dr Herz, 'pick out something you have never smelled before, put it on your desk while you're studying for a test, and then bring it with you a few days later when you are doing the test. It really works.'

# What do you know

**PART 1**  **Five basic rules you need to know**

**1** We use *a / an* when 'we do not know which one' because:
- there are many of these — it is not unique and
- it has not been mentioned before.
  **For example:** *a recent article*
  **a** another example .................................................

**2** We use *the* when 'we know which one' because:
- it has been mentioned before **b** for example
  ................................................
- it is defined by a phrase or **c** for example
  clause which follows ................................................
- it is unique or unique **d** for example
  in that context ................................................

**3** We use **no article** when we make **generalisations** using plural or uncountable nouns:
  **For example:** *exam students can improve their memory ...*
  **e** another example .................................................

**4** We normally use **no article** with the names of people or places (but there are many exceptions to this rule, see Part 2 question 1 below):
**For example:** *Dr Rachel Herz*
**f** another example .................................................

**5** We use *the* with set phrases with **noun + of + noun:**
**g** for example .................................................
except with many expressions of quantity:
**For example:** *a number of rooms*
**h** another example .................................................

---

**PART 2** **Five areas that often cause problems to learners**

**1** With *prison, college, church, home, hospital,* etc. (institutions) When you talk about the **normal purpose** of institutions, rather than a particular building, you use **a** *a / an / the / ø*:

**4** Normally with phrases of time there is **no article** but sometimes we use *the* with:

| | |
|---|---|
| dates: | *on* **a** .............. *25th December* |
| meal-times: | *at* **b** .............. *lunch* |
| days / parts of days: | *on* **c** .............. *Wednesday afternoon* |
| | *at* **d** .............. *Christmas* |
| *next / last / yesterday / tomorrow:* | |
| | **e** .............. *last week* |

**5** Generally there is **no article** with place names, but sometimes we use *the* with:
continents: *in* **a** .............. *Africa*
countries: *in* **b** .............. *Bulgaria*
states: *in* **c** .............. *Florida*
regions: *in* **d** .............. *northern France*
cities: *in* **e** .............. *Warsaw*
towns: *in* **f** .............. *Brighton*
roads / streets: *in* **g** .............. *Oxford Street*
parks: *in* **h** .............. *Hyde Park*
shops: *to* **i** .............. *Harrods*

# about using articles in English?

**b** to be in .................. *Ø* .................. jail
**c** to leave .................................. school
**d** to start .................................. university
**but** when you are talking about a **specific** building you use
**e** *a / an / the / ø*:
**f** .................................. university is outside the town centre
**g** .................................. village church is 300 years old

**2** We use **a** *a / an / the / ø* with **jobs**:
**b** She's .................................. engineer.
**c** He's .................................. professional singer.

**3** You use **a** *a / an / the / ø* in **superlative phrases**:
**b** .................................. biggest study ever done
**c** one of .................................. most respected experts in the world

restaurants: *to* **j** .............. *Nico's*
theatres / cinemas: *to* **k** .............. *National Theatre*
hotels: *at* **l** .............. *Apollo Hotel*
mountains: *up* **m** .............. *Mount Everest*
mountain ranges: *to* **n** .............. *Andes*
lakes: *by* **o** .............. *Lake Geneva*
seas: *across* **p** .............. *Atlantic*
rivers: *on* **q** .............. *Danube*
canals: *through* **r** .............. *Suez Canal*
names with *of*: *in* **s** .............. *South of France*
*from* **t** .............. *Republic of China*
*at* **u** .............. *Palace of Versailles*

## Practice

**1** Work in pairs or groups. Look at the cards from a general knowledge quiz game. Unfortunately, there was a problem and they were all printed without any articles!

**a)** Check the questions, and complete them with *a / an* and *the* where necessary.

**b)** Answer the questions.

① If a* person cannot remember anything, he / she is suffering from:
a insomnia  b amnesia  c influenza  d anorexia

② Delhi is:
a in north of India  b in centre of India  c in south east of India  d in south west of India

③ If you are 'discharged', you:
a leave prison  b leave university  c leave hospital d leave homee

④ Lake Victoria is:
a biggest lake in North America  b second biggest lake in North America  c third biggest lake in North America d none of these

⑤ Ladybird is:
a exotic plant  b African bird  c attractive young woman d red and black insect

⑥ If you are 'pastor', you are:
a priest  b nurse  c gardener  d lawyer

⑦ Thanksgiving day is:
a on fourth of July  b at end of October c last weekend in September  d in November

⑧ Which of the following is not in UK?
a Isle of Wight  b Glasgow  c Scilly Isles d River Shannon

⑨ Prague is capital of:
a Czech Republic  b Slovakia  c Poland  d none of these

⑩ Lizards are:
a trees  b insects  c reptiles  d shoes

⑪ Macey's, most famous department store in New York, is:
a opposite Statue of Liberty  b opposite Central Park c opposite Brooklyn Bridge  d none of these

⑫ 149.6 million kilometres is:
a distance from Sun to Earth
b distance from Moon to Earth
c distance from Sun to nearest star  d none of these

**2** [6.1] Listen to the questions and check your answers. Give yourself **two** points for every correct article you put in. You lose **one** point for every incorrect article, and for every time you put in an article where it was not needed.
Which group got the highest score (possible total 76 including the example)?

**3** Work in groups. Write three more multiple-choice quiz questions of your own like the ones in Exercise 1. Pay attention to the use of articles, asking your teacher's help where necessary. Read your questions out for the other students to answer.

## Pronunciation

When articles appear before vowels, they link onto the word which follows:

an insect   the Earth

This means the pronunciation of *the* changes to /ðiː/. Sometimes there is a small /j/ sound between the words:

the Earth
/j/

[6.2] Listen to the noun phrases below and practise saying them, linking the articles.

**1** an insect   an animal
an exotic plant
an African bird
an attractive young woman

**2** the Earth   the East
the Alps   the Atlantic
the end of October

# Writing skills

## Listening and taking notes

**1 a)** Here are some common ways in which people often waste time, or manage their time badly. Work in groups. Add some more ideas to the list.

- chatting for hours when you should be working
- putting things off
- not sticking to deadlines
- day-dreaming and being easily distracted

**b)** Do you organise your time efficiently, or do you often waste time? How?

**2** Look at the notes someone took during the first part of Alice Kretowicz's lecture.

**a)** Which of the problems from the list in 1a above was she dealing with in the first part of the lecture? What reasons does she give for this problem? What suggestions does she make?

**b)** Look through the notes and find an example of:

1 clear headings to show where the notes come from (a book, a lecture, etc.) and the date.
2 highlighting the most important ideas by using headings, underlining, circles, colours, arrows, etc.
3 missing out words which are obvious (such as articles) and using abbreviations for common words:

*(for example > eg, including > inc.)*

4 including your own opinions, thoughts and doubts, but distinguishing them from the actual notes (for example by using a different colour).
5 including any memorable or amusing quotations.

**3** 🔲 [6.3] Listen to the second part of Alice Kretowicz's lecture. Use the information from the lecture to complete the 'skeleton notes'.

**4** 🔲 [6.4] Listen to the third part of the lecture in which she talks about using the telephone efficiently. Make your own notes. Use any ideas above which you find helpful.

**5** Work in groups. Choose one of the following topics for step four of the lecture.

- organising and storing your personal possessions
- getting ready for a business trip or holiday
- being on time

Imagine what she said and make some notes. Give your notes to another group. Can they follow them?

Alice Kretowicz is a time management and personal organisation expert in the USA. She organises workshops and lectures on time management for business corporations and educational institutions.

Alice Kretowicz: Marconi Lecture Hall 22.7.99

<u>Finding the time: how to gain control of your time in four easy steps</u>

'Organising your time is a skill like learning to tie your shoelaces. Anyone can do it.'

<u>Four steps to control:</u>
<u>Step One: Stop Putting It Off</u>

Warning signs, e.g. Christmas shopping the day before, sending birthday cards late, putting off visits to doctor / dentist. (Do I do these?)

Why?

- job too difficult
- hope 'problem' will go away
- fear of failure

4 ways to stop putting it off

Make a 'to do' list + stick to it!

Do the hardest job 1st — the rest will be easy

Break big projects into small parts

Set deadlines and stick to them!

3 practical things to do to avoid interruptions:

(i) .................................................................................

.................................................................................

(ii) ................................................................................

.................................................................................

.................................................................................

(iii) ...............................................................................

.................................................................................

Useful phrase to deal with interruptions:

.................................................................................

.................................................................................

71

## *Follow-up task*

Write an article similar to the one on pages 64-65 called *You can organise your time better!* Include both Alice Kretowicz's ideas and your own from Exercise 5. Divide your article into headings (for example the ones in Exercise 5) and use bullet points in the same way as the article on pages 64-65. Ask your teacher for any words or phrases you need.

# Real life

## Different ways of emphasising what you say

**1** **a)** Read the conversation. What are Hannah and Dan discussing?

HANNAH: Oh this is annoying. Where did I put my car keys?

DAN: Not again! Have you looked on the kitchen table?

HANNAH: I've looked everywhere.

DAN: Hannah, you're hopeless!

HANNAH: Hmm, thank you. Oh look, here they are under this magazine!

DAN: Well, that just shows you need some kind of system for where you put things. You're always losing things, it's ridiculous.

HANNAH: You've got a nerve! You lost all your credit cards the other day, and I found them for you!

DAN: Yes I know, and I'm grateful to you, but you need to get yourself organised with keys.

**b)** [6.5] Listen to the conversation on the cassette. It is almost the same, but there are a few small differences in the way things are phrased. What is the effect of this?

**2** **a)** Listen again and mark the differences between the conversation in Exercise 1 and the one on the cassette, as in the example.

**b)** All the changes that you have marked are used to give special emphasis to what the speaker is saying. Make a list of all the different ways this is achieved. Now read *Language summary B* on page 154.

**3** [6.6] Match the words in column A with a reply in column B. Then think of a way to make the part in **bold** more emphatic. (In some cases, more than one answer is possible.) Listen and check your answers. Compare your answers to the ones on the cassette.

| | A | | B |
|---|---|---|---|
| 1 | They should have been here hours ago. | a | No, I can't, **it's important** that I speak to her right away. |
| 2 | **Did you invite** Linda's ex-boyfriend to the party? | b | **You need to** buy a more up-to-date model. |
| 3 | Could you wait till this afternoon? | c | Nothing! **I didn't** make the mess! |
| 4 | He's a typical politician. | d | I promise, **and I mean** it this time. |
| 5 | **What have you** been doing? | e | Actually, **I need** a nice cold drink. |
| 6 | Promise you'll never do it again. | f | **Where can they be?** |
| 7 | You look **exhausted**. Would you like a nice cup of coffee? | g | No, in fact **I wanted to see you**. |
| 8 | I just can't get this computer to do what I want! | h | Yes, but **how** was I to know he'd behave like that? |
| 9 | I suppose you've come to see Liz. | i | Oh, I don't know. He **seems to believe** in what he's saying. |

## Pronunciation

**1** Look at the tapescripts on page 169. As well as the ways of emphasising things above, you can use special stress:

> They should have been here <u>hours</u> ago.

> Yes, I know. Where on <u>earth</u> can they be?

**2** [6.6] Listen to the conversations again, marking the words that are specially stressed, as in the example. In pairs, practise the conversations copying the voices on the cassette. Practise the conversation between Hannah and Dan, paying attention to stress.

# Do you remember?

## 1

**Discuss the following in pairs.**

Dan and Ben have both been working for the same company for six months. Dan is a model employee, who will probably soon be promoted. Ben is not doing very well: if he's not careful he'll be fired soon. **Which things in the box do you think each of them does?**

Dan probably …
Ben probably …

a) always sticks to deadlines
b) puts everything off until the last possible moment
c) stays up late every night with his friends
d) has an early night if it's work tomorrow morning
e) fails his professional exams and has to retake them
f) passes all his exams the first time
g) moans about his boss all the time
h) wastes a lot of time chatting to his colleagues
i) is easily distracted from his work
j) sets himself goals and achieves them
k) doesn't take a lunch break
l) takes a cigarette break every half an hour

**Who would you prefer to work with? Why?**

## 2

**Find the mistakes in the use of articles (*a*, *the* or no article) in these sentences and correct them.**

a) My brother's social worker.
b) I hate the rudeness – it really annoys me.
c) What did you have for the lunch?
d) His birthday's on twenty-first of August.
e) Look, that's our house, at a top of the hill over there.
f) Do you want this one, or other one?
g) I hate thought of leaving you.
h) The new bridge will be longest in world.
i) In the modern society, even children sometimes suffer from the stress.
j) Have you got few minutes? I need to speak to you.

## 3

**Put the end of the sentences in the correct order, then practise saying them. Pay attention to the stress.**

a) Why are you complaining? *here / you / wanted / it / come / was / who / to*
b) You look really tired and fed up. *nice / you / cup / what / is / of / a / need / coffee*
c) If you want to apply for the job, *and / phone / an / get / form / application*
d) A: Have you been to that new Turkish restaurant yet?

B: Yes, don't you remember *was / me / recommended / who / it / you / to / it*
e) Okay, everyone, can you listen for a minute. *finish / what / I / this / exercise / want / homework / for / to / is / you / do / to*

## 4

**Practise the following conversations with a partner, taking turns to be A and B. Which word in B's part is specially stressed in each case? Mark it like this:**

(a) A: Your flat's on the third floor, isn't it?

B: No actually, it's on the fifth floor.

(b) A: Do you understand this exercise?

B: Not really, do you?

(c) A: Did you enjoy the concert the other night?

B: I didn't enjoy it much, but I think Laura did.

(d) A: You don't like tea, do you?

B: No, I loathe it.

(e) A: Are Jill's parents still alive?

B: Her mother is.

(f) A: Thank you very much for everything you've done.

B: Not at all, thank you.

(g) A: Have you read any of those books I lent you the other day yet?

B: I've read the first one – it's really good.

# module 7

## Big events

### Part A  **Task**

Listening and vocabulary: celebrations and festivals
**Preparation for task:** celebrations and festivals in your country
**Task:** describe an important festival or celebration in your country

Diwali

Christmas

Bull running, Pamplona

1st May

## Listening and vocabulary

### Celebrations and festivals

1 Look at the pictures. Which of the following can you see?

crowds waving flags    floats
special decorations    a procession
a military parade    spectators
special customs    participants
people in fancy dress
people in traditional dress
people dressed up in their best clothes
a lively, exciting atmosphere

Notting Hill Carnival

Beth Neher is a teacher from the West Coast of the USA. She has lived in London for ten years.

Claire Holder came to Britain twenty-eight years ago. A former lawyer, she has been the chief organiser of the Notting Hill Carnival for ten years.

3 📟 [7.1] On the cassette, in part A Beth Neher talks about Thanksgiving, and in part B Claire Holder talks about the Notting Hill Carnival.

*Either:* listen to one of them speaking and (✓) the topics below that you hear mentioned.

*or:* work in two groups, Group A listens to Beth Neher, and Group B listens to Claire Holder. Tick (✓) the topics below that you hear mentioned.

a   when the celebrations happen ❑     f   other entertainment ❑
b   what is being celebrated            g   food and drink ❑
    and its history ❑                   h   giving presents and
c   the people involved ❑                   sending cards ❑
d   any interesting statistics or       i   the personal feelings
    other facts ❑                           of the speaker ❑
e   music, dancing and
    costumes ❑

4 Listen again and make notes about the points above that they mentioned. Check the following words and phrases in your mini-dictionary to help you understand the details better.

| *For Beth Neher* |
| --- |
| survival / to survive    settlers    Native Americans    food-oriented |
| cranberry relish    pumpkin pie    to harvest    to be commercialised |

| *For Claire Holder* |
| --- |
| a bank holiday    ancestors    freedom    slavery    multi-cultural |
| a masquerade    a steel band    a sound system    a calypso    senior citizens |
| the interest rate    to choose a theme    spontaneous |

Thanksgiving

2 Discuss these questions in groups.

• The festivals and events shown in the pictures are internationally famous. Do you know anything about what happens at each one?

• Which would you most / least like to take part in? Why?

5 Work in pairs. If you listened to the same speaker, compare answers. If you listened to different speakers, tell your partner what you learned. Would you enjoy the celebrations you heard about? Why? Why not?

**75**

## Personal vocabulary

# Task: describe an important festival or celebration in your country

## Useful language

**Saying why the event is important**

"It's important to a lot of people because ..."

"It's a time for (families / remembering ...)"

**Describing customs**

"In the olden days, people used to / people would ..."

"Nowadays, people tend to ..."

**Describing how you feel about it**

"One of the best things about it is ..."

"What I object to is ..."

**Questions**

"Can you tell us (a bit more) about ...?"

"What exactly happens?"

"Does everyone get involved?"

"How did it originate?"

"How do you feel about it personally?"

## Preparation for task

**1** Complete the table with the most important events and celebrations in your country. Which are celebrated the most?

| Personal | *weddings* | *funerals* |
|---|---|---|
| Religious festivals | *Easter* | *Ramadan* |
| Celebrations of historical or political events | | |
| Days of remembrance | | |
| Other important celebrations and festivals | | |

**2** Complete the gaps with the name of one appropriate event for your country. If necessary, check the meaning of the words underlined in your mini-dictionary or with your teacher.

It's a time for families and friends to get together. .............................................

It's a national holiday, and shops and offices shut down. .............................................

It commemorates an important historical event. .............................................

Almost everyone joins in the celebrations. .............................................

People give each other presents and cards. .............................................

People get dressed up in their best clothes. .............................................

There are various special customs and rituals. .............................................

It's not celebrated as much as it used to be. .............................................

People let their hair down and go a bit wild. .............................................

People tend to spend too much money and overeat or drink too much. .............................................

It's got rather commercialised. .............................................

It goes on for too long. .............................................

## Task

**1** **a)** Imagine that you are going to appear on a radio programme called 'Celebrations and events around the world'. Choose one of the events you listed in Preparation for task, Exercise 1, and spend about ten minutes planning what you will say. Use the topics in Exercise 3 on page 75 to help you.

**b)** Decide whether you are going to give a short talk or be interviewed. Ask your teacher for any words or phrases you need, and write them in your *Personal vocabulary* box. Make notes about important points, but do not write out the whole talk.

**2** Spend a few minutes, individually, thinking about exactly how you will describe the event in English to someone who has never experienced it before. Look at the phrases in the *Useful language* box to help you express your ideas.

**3** *Either:* work in pairs. Student A is the radio interviewer, and Student B is a guest on the programme 'Celebrations and events around the world'. Act out the interview for the rest of the class. Listen to the other students' interviews, and notice any words or phrases that are useful if you have to describe this event to someone who has never experienced it before.

*or:* give a short talk to the rest of the class about the event you chose. Listen to the other students' talks and ask questions about anything you would like to know more about.

**4** If possible, record your interviews and talks onto a cassette to make a real radio programme of your own. Either your teacher or another student can briefly introduce each interview or talk.

# Part B **Language**

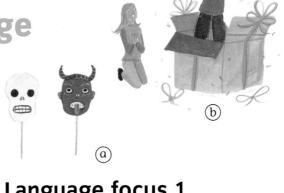

Relative clauses
Quantifiers, and *some* and *any*
Reading and vocabulary: history in the making
Real life: awkward social situations

## Language focus 1

Relative clauses

**1** The texts describe unusual customs from around the world. Read the texts and match them to an appropriate picture.

**1**
**Surprise, surprise!**

At Christmas time in Sweden, young men sometimes give themselves to their girlfriends as presents. They are delivered at their girlfriends' homes in huge boxes, (a) which ........... . However, not all giant-sized parcels contain human gifts. Less fortunate young women receive *Junklapp* instead – small presents (b) which ........... .

**2**
**Easter soaking**

On Easter Monday ◯(c) which .......... ◯Hungarian men splash their girlfriends with water until they are rewarded with coloured Easter eggs. In big cities, this old-fashioned custom has changed: women are instead sprinkled by their boyfriends with a few drops of perfume ◯(d) which .......... according to tradition.

**3**
**Feasting with the dead**

November 2nd, according to legend, is the 'Day of the Dead' in Mexico ◯(e) on which .......... . It is a national holiday, and many people picnic by gravesides on an unusual selection of foods: coffins ◯(f) which .........., skulls and skeletons ◯(g) which .......... ◯and wreaths ◯(h) .......... !

**2** 🖭 [7.2] Listen and complete the gaps. Which of these customs do you find the strangest? Which sounds most fun?

## Analysis

**1 Relative clauses with and without commas**
All the gaps that you completed in the texts are relative clauses with *which*. Look at the two relative clauses in Text 1.

a  Which relative clause gives you <u>information that you need</u>, in order to explain the first part of the sentence?

b  Which relative clause gives you <u>extra information</u> about the first part of the sentence?

c  Which type of relative clause has a comma before *which*?

d  Can you substitute *that* for *which* in the relative clauses with commas or those without?

e  Look at Texts 2 and 3, and decide which of the circles need commas and which do not.

**2 Participle relative clauses**
Some relative clauses can be shortened:
   *coffins which are made of chocolate   >*
   *coffins made of chocolate*
a  Can you find any other clauses above that you could shorten in the same way? Can you find any examples that are already shortened?

b  Shorten the following sentence with a present participle in a similar way:
   *Before Christmas, the shops are full of people who are rushing round buying presents.*

***Now read Language summary A, B and C on pages 154-155.***

## Practice

**1 a)** Before you do the exercise, check the meaning of the words in **bold** in the box.

| |
|---|
| a **witch**    a **wizard**    to **cast** a **spell**    a **bonfire** <br> to **play** a **trick** on someone        to **give** someone a **treat** <br> to **dress up** as (a witch)        to **blow** a place **up** |

Join each group of sentences together to make one long sentence using relative and participle clauses. Remember to put in commas where necessary.

**For example:**
Halloween and Guy Fawkes' night are two important celebrations in Britain. They take place in autumn.

*Halloween and Guy Fawkes' night*

*are important celebrations in Britain,*

*which take place in autumn.*

  *Halloween and Guy Fawkes'*

*night, which take place in autumn,*

*are important celebrations in Britain.*

1  Halloween is a night. Witches and wizards are supposed to come out. It takes place on 31st October.
2  A witch is a woman. She can cast magic spells.
3  A wizard is a man. He can do the same.
4  Children get dressed up as witches or wizards. They go round knocking on people's doors, asking for a 'trick or treat'.
5  This means that if you don't give them a treat they will play a trick on you. The treat usually consists of sweets or money.
6  Guy Fawkes' night celebrates a time 400 years ago. It takes place a few days after Halloween. At that time the British Houses of Parliament were nearly blown up.
7  People build bonfires and burn 'guys'. Guys are models. They are made of old clothes. They are stuffed with newspapers.
8  The guy represents a man. He was called Guy Fawkes. He was responsible for trying to blow up the Houses of Parliament.
9  In the days before Guy Fawkes' night you often see children. They are walking around with guys. They have made the guys. They are shouting, 'Penny for the guy'.

**b)** 🔲 [7.3] Listen and check your answers.

---

## Pronunciation

1  We normally show that we have finished what we are saying by going down at the end of the sentence. When the relative clause comes in the middle of the sentence, you show that you have not finished by going up at the end of the relative clause:

  *(= not finished)* ↗
  *Halloween and Guy Fawkes' night,*

   *(= not finished)* ↗
  *which take place in autumn,*

    *(= finished)* ↘
  *are both important celebrations in Britain.*

Practise reading the sentence, paying attention to the intonation.

2  Practise reading the other sentences in Exercise 1a, paying attention to the intonation. (The tapescript on page 170 has intonation arrows to help you).

**2 a)** You are going to do a general knowledge quiz. Team A looks at the questions on page 143, and Team B looks at the questions on page 146.

**b)** Before you do the quiz you must rewrite the questions where possible using participle clauses so that they sound more natural. (The correct answer to the question is the one underlined on the question card.)
**For example:**

| |
|---|
| *What kind of pie, ~~which is~~ made from a winter vegetable, do Americans traditionally eat on Thanksgiving Day?* <br> **a** *potato pie*  **b** *turnip pie*  **c** *pumpkin pie* |

**c)** Take turns to ask and answer the questions in teams. The other team scores four points for answering the question without the multiple choice answers, and two points for answering the question correctly with the multiple choice answers.

A:  What kind of pie, made from a winter vegetable, do Americans traditionally eat on Thanksgiving Day?
B:  *Pumpkin pie.*
A:  Correct - four points.

A:  *We don't know.*
B:  Is it **a** potato pie, **b** turnip pie or **c** pumpkin pie?
A:  *Pumpkin pie?*
B:  Correct - two points.

# Language focus 2

Quantifiers and *some* and *any*

**1** Discuss the following questions in groups.

- What are your favourite foods?
- Are there any foods you particularly hate?
  What are they?
- Are there any foods you cannot eat?

**2** Work in pairs. Read and discuss the statements, and mark the box as follows:

**a / b** if one of these pairs of sentences is true for you.
**n** if neither of them is true for you.
**?** if you're not sure what the sentences mean.

1 a I'm allergic to certain types of seafood. ☐
   b I'm allergic to all types of seafood.
2 a I don't like any type of beer. ☐
   b I like some types of beer.
3 a I don't like some types of chocolate. ☐
   b I like any type of chocolate.
4 a I can cook anything. ☐
   b I can't cook anything.
5 a I know little about Chinese cooking
     – it's not something that interests me. ☐
   b I know a little about Chinese cooking
     – I can cook several dishes quite well.
6 a There are very few vegetarian
     dishes that I like. ☐
   b There are quite a few vegetarian
     dishes that I like.
7 a I eat plenty of fruit and vegetables. ☐
   b I eat enough fruit and vegetables.
8 a Yesterday, I ate too much. ☐
   b Yesterday, I ate just the right amount.

## Analysis

**1 *Some* and *any***
Read the rules, then explain the differences between the two sentences in 2, 3 and 4 of Exercise 2:

*Some* refers to **certain but not all** of a group of things. We usually use it in positive sentences, but we can use it with negatives and questions.

*Any* refers to all of a group of things. We usually use it with negatives and questions, but we can use it in positive sentences.

**2 Small and large quantities**
a Why do the sentences in 5 end differently?

b Put the following in order from the least (1) to the most (5):
  *a few    very few    quite a few    several    few*

c Order the following from the least (1) to the most (7):
  *plenty    enough    too much / many
  not enough    lots    far too much / many
  not nearly enough
  just the right amount / number*

**3 Countable or uncountable?**
Put the quantifiers above into three groups:
C = used with countable nouns only
U = used with uncountable nouns only
U / C = used with both

***Now read Language summary D on page 155.***

## Practice

**1** Look back at the sentences in Exercise 2 that you marked either **n** or **?** and rewrite them using a quantifier to make them true for you.

**2** Choose the best construction from box A to describe your feelings about the things in box B. Explain to a partner why.

I like any ice cream. It's my favourite food in the world. I like some opera music, but I find a lot if it boring.

| A | I like some | I like any | I don't like any | I don't like some |

| B | ice cream    seafood    kinds of fruit    rock music |
|   | opera music    jazz music    babies    dogs    rodents |

**3** Find the things in the box in the picture. Make a sentence about each using the best phrase from the *Analysis* to describe the quantity.

**For example:**

*There are quite a few paper cups.*

cold meat   soft drinks   cutlery   paper cups   an ashtray
paper plates   crisps   olives   salad   other nibbles

**4** **a)** The food in the picture above is for Tom's twenty-first birthday party. He has invited thirty guests and they include:

• six vegetarians
• several people who are trying to lose weight
• five young cousins under the age of ten
• six people who can't drink alcohol
• ten smokers

Which of the following sentences do you agree with?

*There are far too many crisps.*

*There are very few soft drinks.*

*There aren't nearly enough hot dogs.*

**b)** Write eight more sentences like these of your own. Read them out to the other students, and find out whether or not they agree.

**c)** If you were organising a birthday party for thirty guests, would you provide this type of food and drink or not? What else would you give your guests?

*I'd definitely have some ... and plenty of ... and lots and lots of ...*

# Reading and vocabulary

**1** **a)** Discuss the following in groups or as a class.

- What have been the most famous events in your country over the last ten or twenty years?
- What about in the rest of the world?

**b)** Look at the pictures. Which world-famous events do they show? What do you know about them? Read the introduction to each text to check what you know.

**2** **a)** You are going to read accounts written by people who were there at the time. From the pictures, what do you imagine the atmosphere was like? How do you think you would have felt if you had been there yourself?

**b)** Work in threes A, B and C. Each person reads one of the descriptions and answers the following questions:

1 Where exactly was the eye-witness and why were they there?
2 What did they see?
3 How do they describe the atmosphere and their feelings? (Use your own words.)

Tell your partners about what you read.

**3** Read all three texts, and find as many words and phrases as you can to describe:
- the atmosphere / feelings of the author
  *worried, excited*
- sounds, smells, movements, and things that were visually striking
  *the scent of flowers*
- the way the people behaved
  *everybody was embracing each other*

If necessary, check the meaning of the words or phrases in your mini-dictionary. Compare your answers in pairs.

**4** What is your own reaction to each of the descriptions? Which do you find most moving? Why? Which event would you have been most interested to be present at?

(a)

### *I saw history in the making*

*On 9th November 1989, following a growing number of protests and demonstrations across the country, the East German government finally reopened the borders with West Germany, and for the first time in over forty years people were free to cross from East to West Berlin. Carmen Blazeweski and Andreas Höntsch were determined to see for themselves.*

'We just couldn't believe it, then we saw pictures on television showing people at the border crossing ... they were waving ... it seemed impossible. The next day, we bundled our sleeping daughter into the car and drove to the border. We were worried it might be closed again before we could get there, but when we reached it we were waved through. People were getting out of their cars and giving flowers to the guards. It was a very peaceful sight. Someone greeted us with a bottle of sparkling wine, and chocolate for the child ... we were in the West. I was shaking, I was so excited ... the streets were full of people, and everybody was embracing each other ... there was a feeling of great joy.'

From *The People's Century*

(b) On 11th February 1990, Nelson Mandela, later to become President of the new South Africa, was released after twenty-seven years in prison. Tens of thousands of people waited outside the Victor Verster prison to greet him: journalist Ann Leslie was one of them.

For me and thousands of others – black and white, young and old – who had gathered outside the bougainvillea-clad buildings on a small rural road, it had been a long, hot walk. The crowd passed the time singing freedom songs, 'Listen, we are calling you, Mandela,' in exquisite harmony, as 150 or so sweating and impassive policemen grouped round the front of the prison gates.

Then suddenly the crowd stiffened, like a huge dusty animal, sniffing something in the air. 'He's coming. Mandela! Mandela! Viva! Viva!'

As 'Comrade Mandela' walked towards us, lifting his right arm in the clenched fist salute of the ANC, his wife by his side, the crowd boiled over with the madness of unbottled joy and ecstasy. I was swept forward in a maelstrom of flailing limbs and sweat, dust and screams. My shoes were ripped from my feet and I felt my blood, warm and sticky, on the hot tarmac. Through the mass of sweating heads and Mandela T-shirts, I could see the blue uniforms of grim-faced white policemen linking arms with ANC marshals screaming, 'Get back! Get back!'

Then suddenly, the hysteria was over – for the moment. The crowd, realising that their hero had been whisked away in a motorcade, began the slow shuffle towards the distant roadblock. They stretched ahead for at least two miles as I began to trudge, shoeless and bleeding, with them, along the road.

From *The Daily Mail*

(c) *On 6th September 1997, the funeral of Diana, Princess of Wales, was held at Westminster Abbey in London. It was the biggest televised event ever, watched by between one and two billion people worldwide. Debbie Frank – Diana's personal astrologer – was one of the guests inside the Abbey that day. She wrote this eye-witness account.*

I felt that for one last time I was in Diana's presence. You had to be there to take in the scent of the flowers, or see the white lilies gently quiver on top of the coffin, to hear the gentle fall of the guardsmen's boots as they carried the coffin, to feel the sorrow of the massive crowd outside. Sunshine cast magnificent prisms of light inside the Abbey, bathing Diana's coffin in a golden, radiant glow. It was an experience so beautiful and so unreal that I had to stop watching the television monitors. I had to watch everything through my own eyes to make sure I was really there. I wanted to take in every little nuance, every scent, every tear and every breathtaking moment. It was only when Diana had left that I felt once again that emptiness I've felt all week. Suddenly the Abbey was cold, and sombre and sad. It wasn't just the scent of flowers that left us, it was Diana's very soul.

From *The Sun*

## Follow-up task

**1** You are going to produce an eye-witness account of an important event. Choose one of the following:

- A description of an important event or celebration in your country or abroad that you have attended (for example, one of the events from Preparation for task on page 77).
- A description of one of these events written from the point of view of a stranger, a foreign visitor, or even a visitor from another planet!
- A description of an important / famous historical event written from the point of view of someone who was there.
- A description of an important / famous historical event written as if you were there yourself.

**2** Make notes about what you will include in your description and plan what you will write using these headings to help you. Ask your teacher about any words or phrases you need.

> atmosphere   people   events
> people's behaviour / customs, etc.
> sights / sounds / smells

**3** *Either:* write your description.
*or:* record your description for your teacher to listen to and mark.

# Real life

## Awkward social situations

**1** In the pictures, Bella finds herself in some difficult social situations. Why? What would you say?

**a** *I'll explode if I have any more!*

Go on, have a bit more. It'll do you good! Go on, I insist. Have the last piece, Bella!

..................................

Oh dear, how clumsy of me! I'm really sorry, let me get a cloth.

..................................

**b** *Oh no, my best new shirt. I can't believe it!*

**c** *Vera? Vera who? Oh, where on earth do I know her from?*

You know Vera, don't you Bella?
- Hi there, Bella. Of course she knows me. How are things with you then?

..................................

You must try some of this spinach salad, Bella. It's their speciality!

..................................

**d** *Yuck, I hate spinach, it makes me feel sick just thinking about it!*

**e** *A whole day with Uncle Geoff and Auntie Mary. Help!*

It's been lovely to see you again, Bella. You must come and spend a day with us some time, mustn't she, Mary? I tell you what, how about the weekend after next for Sunday lunch?

..................................

**2** 📇 [7.4] Listen and write what Bella actually said. What do you think of the way she responded?

---

# Pronunciation

**1** 📇 [7.5] If you want to sound polite, your intonation is even more important than the phrase you use. Listen to some polite phrases Bella used again. You will hear each phrase twice. Decide which version is politer, A or B.

1 No, really I'm fine thank you. It was lovely, but I couldn't possibly manage any more! | A / B |
2 Don't worry it doesn't matter in the slightest! | A / B |
3 How lovely to see you again. It seems ages since we last met! | A / B |
4 Actually I'm afraid I can't eat spinach, it doesn't agree with me. | A / B |
5 I'd love to come, but I don't think I'll be able to make it. | A / B |

**2** 📇 [7.6] Listen to the polite versions again and copy Bella's intonation. If you find it difficult, start by humming the phrase like this:

MM MM-mm mm MM MM-mm >
*No, really, I'm fine thank you.*

**3** Here are some similar situations. Make dialogues of your own, using some of the phrases above. Act out your dialogues.

- You are out shopping. Someone taps you on the shoulder and says 'hello' and your name. It is obvious that they remember you, but you can't remember their name, or how you met.
- You are visiting your future in-laws for the first time. You are offered a coffee, but you are so nervous that you immediately spill it over the white carpet.
- Your future mother-in-law has been offering you biscuits, sandwiches and cakes every five minutes. Your girl / boyfriend doesn't seem to have noticed that you find the situation embarrassing.
- A foreign acquaintance takes you to a restaurant which serves food from his country. He urges you to order a liver casserole, which is his favourite dish. You can't stand liver – even the sight of it makes you feel ill.
- A colleague from work (who you are not very keen on) invites you to a party at her house next Saturday evening. You haven't got anything planned for that evening, but you don't really want to go.

# Do you remember?

## 1

Work in pairs. Can you explain the difference between:

a) a **participant** and a **spectator**?
b) a **procession** and a **display**?
c) wearing your **best clothes** and wearing **fancy dress**?
d) a **flag** and a **decoration**?
e) a **celebration** and an **event**?

## 2

Put the words in the box into the correct column, according to the stress pattern. Mark the weak /ə/ sounds, as in the example.

festival  carnival  event  display
atmosphere  parade  celebration
costume  historical  military
commercialised  religious

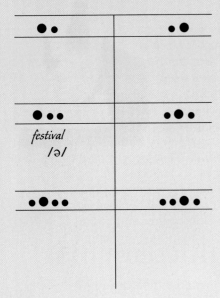

## 3

Complete each sentence with the best ending from the box.

get involved   shut down   overeat
get together   joined in   went wild

a) At lunchtime in some countries, all the shops and banks …
b) If you don't want to put on weight, be careful not to …
c) After the exams had finished, we had a big party, let our hair down and …
d) We'll give you a call and arrange a night out. It would be lovely for all of us to …
e) The atmosphere at the carnival was amazing; everyone was dancing in the street and even some of the policemen …
f) If Joe and Allan start arguing again, I'm going home. I don't want to …

## 4

Some (but not all) of these sentences need a relative pronoun (*who*, *that*, *which*, etc.). Where necessary, put in the pronouns and any commas that are needed.

a) Tomorrow three men will appear in court charged with the theft of the jewels.
b) The President will be eighty next month has announced that he is going to retire.
c) Did you get the message I left you?
d) Sorry, the person was dealing with it has now left.
e) A well-dressed man pointing a gun was walking slowly towards me.
f) The accident took place around midnight was caused by drink-driving.
g) Bill's father died when he was very young.

## 5

In each of these sentences cross out (✗) the alternative which is wrong. Explain the difference between the two correct possibilities.

a) We've got *plenty of* / *enough* / *any* time for lunch before the meeting.
b) My uncle had *several* / *quite a bit of* / *enough* money, but he was very mean.
c) There was *too much* / *too many* / *just the right amount* of food for everyone.
d) Alexia can understand *anything in English* / *much English* / *some English* now.
e) There were *very few* / *quite a few* / *plenty* people I knew at the party.

## 6

Work in groups. Think of situations in which you might do the following:

sweat a lot   bleed   scream
shake   have tears in your eyes
sniff something   embrace someone
shuffle along slowly

# In the public eye

## Part A **Task**

> **Reading:** famous people who go into public life
> **Vocabulary and speaking:** quiz – *Are you a political animal?*
> **Preparation for task:** interview with an eco-warrior
> **Task:** present your views on an issue

## Reading

**1** Look at the photographs. These people are all celebrities, at least in their own countries. Do you recognise them? What do you know about them?

**2** Read through the text briefly and find out what these people have in common. What does each picture show?

**3** Read the text again. In pairs, answer the following questions, where possible.

a  What political positions have these people stood for? Which of them were actually elected?

b  What are / were their policies? What are they for and against?

c  What has each of them achieved:
   • in their original careers?
   • in politics?

d  In which career has each of them been most successful, do you think?

e  Did you discover anything else surprising or interesting about any of these people?

Originally an actor, Ronald Reagan served two terms as President of the United States in the 1980s, but he always remained an actor at heart. When he won the election for Governor of California, Reagan was asked what he planned to do when he took office. 'I don't know,' he replied, 'I've never played a governor.' And at the 1987 Economic Summit in Venice, Italy, the leaders of the world's industrial nations were surprised to see Reagan reading his lines off specially written cards: not just at important meetings, but even at informal cocktail parties! But Reagan is not the only one who has used his fame to make an impact in the political world ...

The star of such films as *A Fistful of Dollars* (1964), *Dirty Harry* (1971) and *Sudden Impact* (1983), Hollywood actor Clint Eastwood took time off from his film career to serve two years as mayor of Carmel, California (population 4,800) in the 1980s, at a monthly salary of just $200. Frustrated by petty bureaucracy and regulations, Eastwood entered politics insisting that his concern was strictly with Carmel and that he had no larger ambitions, 'I approached it from a business point of view, not a political one.' His slogan was simple, 'Bring the community together', and the proudest achievement of his two years in office was the construction of a new children's annexe at the local library.

Until 1997, 46-year-old Rosemary Scallon was famous for one thing only: at the age of eighteen, as Dana, she had become the first Irish winner of the Eurovision Song Contest with a naive little song entitled 'All Kinds of Everything'. Twenty-eight years later, now living with her husband and four children in the United States, Rosemary Scallon stood for the Presidency of Ireland on a non-party platform. She launched her campaign claiming, 'There's nothing in the Constitution to say I can't sing as President'. At first her candidacy was widely seen as a joke, but in the end her campaign, based on traditional Christian values and morals, gained her fourteen per cent of the vote and established her as a force to be reckoned with in Irish politics.

In a career lasting more than twenty-five years, Romanian tennis star Ilie Nastase won fifty-

Clint Eastwood

Rosemary Scallon

Ilie Nastase

Ronald Reagan

**86**

seven titles, and was rated the world's number one player in 1973. For all the brilliance of his play, he was also known for his flashes of temper and eccentric behaviour: once, he left the court during a doubles rally to chat to a blonde woman in the front row of the crowd. When his furious partner asked him why he hadn't finished the point, Nastase replied, 'There'll be another point in a minute ... there might never be another woman like that.' After retiring in 1985, he became a successful businessman, with homes in Romania, France, and the United States. In 1996 – apparently shocked at the poor state of the city's roads – he decided to run for mayor in his childhood home of Bucharest, 'I tell my opponents they are ugly, lining their own pockets, and don't have a clue how to fix the city's most serious problems,' he said. Nastase failed to secure a majority, however, and left politics almost as quickly as he had entered it.

Irene Saez

Irene Saez is Venezuela's most popular politician and a likely President of the future. In 1981, she was crowned Miss Universe, but turned down lucrative Hollywood offers to finish her graduate studies in political science. In 1995, she entered politics and won election as the mayor of Chacao, a district in Venezuela's capital city, Caracas. She managed to sort out the financial deficit, restore public buildings and even cut the crime rate. Proof of her popularity came when she was re-elected with ninety per cent of the vote. Although cynics might assume her success has something to do with her looks (indeed an Irene Saez doll is a big seller in the country) her supporters believe that she is that rare thing – a politician who really makes a difference to people's lives. The fact that she has the looks of a movie star is just an added bonus.

**4** Discuss the following questions in groups.

- Are there any celebrity politicians in your country? What about other famous people who have become involved in political issues?
- Do you know anything about what they believe in or how they became involved?
- Do you think it is a good idea for celebrities to become involved in politics? Would you be more or less likely to vote for a celebrity than an ordinary politician?

## Vocabulary and speaking

**1** What is your attitude to politics? How much do you know about current affairs? If necessary, check the meaning of the words and phrases in **bold** in your mini-dictionary. Then work through the quiz with a partner. In part B, give examples to support your opinions.

### Are you a political animal?

**A How many of these questions can you answer?**

- How often are **general elections** held in your country?
- How many ex-presidents or prime ministers of your country can you name?
- Who is the current **foreign minister** of your country? How many other ministers can you name?
- At the moment, is your country generally considered to be experiencing an economic **boom**, an economic **recession**, or neither?
- Name two important **policies** of the current government of your country.

**B Mark the statements below as follows:**

1 = I completely agree

2 = not sure

3 = I completely disagree

- In my opinion, the average politician is **corrupt** and only **'out for him or herself'**.☐
- I would take part in a **political demonstration, strike** or protest **march** if I felt strongly enough about the issue.☐
- I think the majority of people are **disillusioned** or **apathetic** about politics.☐
- I believe that **environmental** and **human rights issues** are more important than economic issues like **unemployment, taxation**, etc.☐
- I believe that everyone has a duty to **vote** in elections – the political **party** you choose can make a big difference to your life.☐

**2** Is your partner a political animal or not?

**87**

## Personal vocabulary

# Task: present your views on an issue

## Useful language

### a Describing beliefs and policies

"We believe that ..."

"We are (strongly) in favour of / opposed to ..."

"It is our intention / aim to ..."

"We would encourage people to ... (by doing ...)"

"We will / won't allow (people to) ..."

"We would make it legal / illegal to ..."

### b Asking for more information

"What would you do if ... happened?"

"What about the issue of ...?"

### c Agreement / disagreement

"I think you're right about ..."

"I support what you say about ..."

"Yes, but have you thought about ...?"

"I see your point, but ..."

## Preparation for task

**1** As people in many countries become disillusioned with politicians, there have been a growing number of 'single issue' campaigns. Look at the photos. What are the people campaigning about? Are there any campaigns like this in your country?

**2** Read about Tony Cripps below. Which of these campaigns has he been involved in? What kind of things has he done? If necessary, check any new words in your mini-dictionary.

Tony Cripps, an ex-soldier, has been an environmental campaigner, or 'eco-warrior', for a number of years. He has campaigned against the live export of veal calves, against the building of new roads, and against the building of a second runway at Manchester airport. To draw attention to these causes, at various times he has boarded ships at sea, abseiled down cliffs, lived in trees, and spent weeks at a time living in tunnels underground. He has been forcibly evicted from these places by bailiffs many times, and has been arrested on a number of occasions.

## Task

**1** Look at the list of single issue parties below. In groups, think of at least one policy that each of these parties has. Ask your teacher about any words or phrases you need to express your ideas. Compare your ideas with other students.

- the 'ban cars in cities' party ☐
- the 'animal rights' party ☐
- the 'women's rights' party ☐
- the 'men's rights' party ☐
- the 'better rights for working mothers' party ☐
- the 'smokers' rights' party ☐
- the 'job opportunities for young people' party ☐

**2** Work in pairs or individually. A national television channel is giving single issue groups two-minute programmes to put across their views and policies. *Either:* choose one of the parties above that you agree with
*or:* invent your own party to promote another issue you feel strongly about.
You have about twenty minutes to prepare your programme. You should include:

- your four or five main aims / policies.
- the reasons behind these policies / your beliefs.

Ask your teacher for any words or phrases you need and write them in your *Personal vocabulary* box.

**3 a)** Spend a few minutes practising what you will say. Remember you have only two minutes, so make sure you put your views across concisely. Look at the phrases in the *Useful language* box to help you express your ideas.

**b)** Think about any arguments people might have against your ideas, and how you will respond to these criticisms.

**4 a)** Listen to each others' talks. As you are listening, note down the main opinions and policies of each group and think about whether or not you agree with them. When they have finished, ask questions and give your opinions about what they suggest. Look at the phrases in the *Useful language* box to help you.

**b)** Vote for the party whose arguments most impressed you (you cannot vote for your own party). Which party won the election in your class?

**3** 🎧 [8.1] You are going to listen to some extracts from an interview with Tony Cripps. In part A he talks about his experiences during the campaign against the second runway at Manchester airport. Listen and mark the following statements (T) true or (F) false, according to what he says.

a Many wild animals and trees were destroyed when the second runway at Manchester was built.
b The protesters wanted to close Manchester airport.
c They built tunnels underground and locked themselves to trees.
d Their aim was to stay there as long as possible and cost the building company a lot of money.
e Living underground is very exciting.
f At night in the tunnels, they lock lots of doors in case anyone tries to evict them.
g It becomes very difficult to breathe after you've been locked into the tunnels for a while.
h The eco-warriors don't stay in there all night because it is so claustrophobic.

**4** In part B of the interview, Tony explains **why** he campaigns. Listen and tick (✔) the things that he mentions below.

a The world used to be a very beautiful place.
b Today we are destroying that beauty.
c People treat the environment very stupidly.
d We won't have such a good quality of life if we don't change the way we do things.
e The way we drive cars and use hairspray are examples of what we do wrong.
f People are terribly cruel to animals.
g It is wrong to abuse animals to test new products.
h There is no hope for future generations.
i We must look after the world for future generations.

Do you think it is acceptable to do illegal and dangerous things to draw attention to a cause you believe in? Would you ever do anything like this?

# Part B **Language**

Infinitive forms
Infinitive or gerund (*-ing* form)?
**Writing skills:** linking ideas and arguments
**Wordspot:** *about*

## Language focus 1

Infinitive forms

**1** Read the quotations on the right about public life. In pairs, discuss what they mean. If necessary, check the meaning of any words in your mini-dictionary or with your teacher.

**2** Which do you think is: the wisest; the wittiest; the best?

Do you have any favourite quotations? Can you translate them into English?

### Analysis

**Different infinitive forms**
Read the quotations again, and underline all the examples of infinitives. Find examples of:
a infinitive with *to*
b infinitive without *to*
c negative infinitive
d perfect infinitive
e continuous infinitive
f passive infinitive

***Now read Language summary A on page 156.***

---

### Wit and wisdom

1 'There is only one thing worse than being talked about, and that is not being talked about.'
(Oscar Wilde, Irish writer)

2 'Politics are too serious a matter to be left to the politicians.'
(Charles de Gaulle, former President of France)

3 'A celebrity is a person who works hard all his life to become well-known, then wears dark glasses to avoid being recognised.'
(Fred Allen, American humorist)

4 'Politicians are like nappies, they should be changed often, and for the same reason.'
(US journalist)

5 'A politician is an acrobat – he keeps his balance by saying the opposite of what he does.'
(Maurice Barres)

6 'It is impossible to work out what he believes in. He agrees with whoever he happens to be speaking to at the time.'
(journalist describing US President, Bill Clinton)

7 'When it is not necessary to change, it is necessary not to change.'
(Lucius Cary, English royalist politician)

8 'Money can't buy friends, but you get a better class of enemy.'
(Spike Milligan, Irish comedian)

9 'Tis better to have loved and lost
   Than never to have loved at all.'
(Lord Tennyson, English poet)

10 'Failure is not falling down, it is not getting up again to continue life's journey.'
(Richard Nixon, former President of the US)

---

### Practice

Choose the best infinitive form to complete these sentences. In some cases, more than one form is possible.

1 Celebrities say it's annoying *to be stopped / to have stopped / to be stopping* in the street by fans, but I'm sure the time *to worry / to have worried / to have been worried* is when no one recognises you any more!

2 Gerald Ford is thought *be / to be / to have been* the only US President *to work / to have worked / to be working* as a model.

3 What a shame I missed the Prime Minister's speech on TV last night. I'd like *to have seen / to see / see* it. It's sure *being repeated / to repeat / to be repeated* this evening, though, I suppose.

4 The ex-dictator is thought *to have escaped / to be escaped / not to have escaped* during the revolution in 1995, and is now believed *to live / to be living / to have lived* abroad, but nobody knows for sure what happened.

5 John Lennon is perhaps the most famous celebrity *to have murdered / to have been murdered / to murder* by a so-called fan.

# Language focus 2

Infinitive or gerund (-*ing* form)?

## Analysis

1  Look back at the quotations and underline all the examples of the gerund (-*ing* form) that you can find. Complete the general rules about the use of gerunds and infinitives, using examples from the quotations.

   a  To express the purpose of an action you use the infinitive / the -*ing* form.
      For example: .............................

   b  It is common for adjectives (and nouns) to be followed by the infinitive / the -*ing* form.
      For example: .............................

   c  When an action is the subject or object of a sentence (instead of a noun or pronoun), you normally use the infinitive / the -*ing* form.
      For example: .............................

   d  After prepositions, you always use the infinitive / the -*ing* form.
      For example: .............................

2  Many verbs are followed by gerunds or infinitives, but these have to be learned individually.
   For example:
   **avoid + gerund:** *He wears dark glasses to* **avoid being** *recognised.*
   **happen + infinitive:** *... whoever he* **happens to be** *talking to.*
   Think of three more verbs that take each of these constructions.

*Now read Language summary B and C on page 156.*

## Practice

1  Complete the gaps with the appropriate gerund or infinitive form of the verbs in brackets. (You may need to use passive, negative or perfect forms.) If necessary, check the meaning of any words or phrases in your mini-dictionary or with your teacher.

> **Tax scandal forces Valentino to quit**
> Mr Tony Valentino, leader of the New Democratic Party, shocked his followers earlier today by (a) .......... (*announce*) his resignation. He said he was retiring in order (b) .......... (*spend*) more time with his family, and refused (c) .......... (*comment*) on recent newspaper reports about his financial affairs. Mr Valentino is accused of (d) .......... (*avoid*) up to $10 million in taxes over the last five years, but has always denied (e) .......... (*do*) anything illegal. Mr Valentino said he was happy for his financial affairs (f) .......... (*investigate*) and was willing (g) .......... (*co-operate*) fully with the tax authorities as soon as he returns from a four-week (h) .......... (*ski*) holiday at a secret location abroad.
> Mr Valentino seems (i) .......... (*begin*) his holiday already, as his private helicopter was seen flying away from his luxury villa this afternoon. 'We are very sorry indeed (j) .......... (*lose*) Mr Valentino as our leader and are confident that he will be able (k) .......... (*prove*) his innocence,' said deputy leader Jayne Belowski. 'It is far too early (l) .......... (*talk*) about (m) .......... (*choose*) a successor, although of course, if I am asked (n) .......... (*stand*) as leader it would be foolish (o) .......... (*not do*) so – I have a duty (p) .......... (*serve*) the party as best I can.'

2  ▭ [8.2] Listen to the same story and check your answers.

## Pronunciation

1  Listen again to the first sentence of the story. What kind of words are stressed? What kind of words are weak (not stressed)?
   /ə//ə/ /ə/
   *Mr* <u>Ton</u>*y Valen*<u>ti</u>*no,* <u>lea</u>*der of the* <u>New</u> *Demo*<u>cra</u>*tic Party,* <u>shocked</u> *his* <u>follow</u>*ers* <u>ear</u>*lier to*<u>day</u> *by an*<u>nounc</u>*ing his resig*<u>na</u>*tion.*

2  Listen to the next sentence and mark the stressed and weak words in the same way.
   *He said he was retiring in order to spend more time with his family, and refused to comment on recent newspaper reports about his financial affairs.*

3  Practise saying the sentences above, paying attention to the stressed and weak forms. Sometimes it is easier if you start by mumbling, like this:
   mm-mm MM-mm mm-mm-MM-mm, MM-mm

4  Imagine that you are a newsreader. Practise reading the whole story aloud. Ensure that it is clear and easy to follow by using the stressed and weak forms correctly.

### Follow-up task

**1a** Would you like to be someone rich and famous? Close your book and work in groups. Think of as many arguments as you can for and against.

**b** Read the extract. How many of the same topics did you mention? What do you think would be the worst aspect of fame? Has the article changed your attitude to being rich and famous at all?

**Ten things to worry about if you're rich and famous ...**

- Whether your friends like you for yourself or just because you're famous.
- Being followed by the *paparazzi* to the most fashionable parties and restaurants.
- Fans ruining your holiday by asking for autographs and photos.
- Fashion editors criticising your dress sense.
- Ex-lovers selling their story to the newspapers.
- Whether or not your children will be able to have a normal childhood.
- Finding a reliable chauffeur, cleaner and cook.
- Whether or not your accountant is secretly cheating you.
- Finding the ransom money if one of your relatives is kidnapped.
- Your investments, the state of your yacht, and whether or not to sell your third home.

**Ten things to worry about if you're not rich and famous ...**

- Why all your friends seem to be more successful than you are.
- Never going to any fashionable parties or restaurants.
- Whether you'll have enough money to go on holiday this year.
- Whether people will notice you haven't bought any new clothes for over a year.
- Ex-lovers telling your friends how boring you are.
- Whether you'll ever be able to afford to have children in your financial position.
- How on earth, before eight o'clock this evening, you are expected to drive to the shops, clean the house and cook dinner.
- Whether or not the woman in the supermarket is deliberately short-changing you.
- Finding the money for your nephew's birthday present.
- Your debts, the fact that your motorbike isn't going to last much longer, and whether or not to sell your old books.

**2a** Work in groups. Each group chooses one of the following topics and thinks of five things to worry about / five things not to worry about if:

- you're a genius
- you're very tall
- you're exceptionally good-looking
- you're single
- you're under twenty-one

*One good thing about being ...   Another thing is ...*

*If you're ... it's much easier to ... / more difficult to ...*

**b** Tell the rest of the class what you discussed, and see if they can add any more points to your lists. What would / wouldn't you like to be?

## Writing skills
### Linking ideas and arguments

**1 a)** The sentences describe some of the advantages and disadvantages of being rich and famous. In each sentence, underline a word or phrase that is used to link the ideas together.

1 Rich people may not have to worry about paying their bills every month. <u>However</u>, wealth brings other worries of its own.

2 The rich have different financial problems from the rest of us: whereas most of us worry about not having enough money, rich people may worry about what to do with all their money.

3 Although being famous means you often get special treatment, you lose a lot of your privacy.

4 It is much more difficult to know who to trust if you are very rich or very famous. What is more, other people may not know how to react towards you. For this reason, many famous people find it difficult to make true friends.

5 Despite all their achievements, many successful people still feel very insecure.

**b)** Match the linking words above with the explanations:

1  to link arguments for and against *however* ...
2  to give more reasons for your argument ...
3  to explain the consequences of something ...
4  to compare two different situations ...

**c)** Add the words below to the lists in **b** above.

| furthermore   nevertheless   while |
| on the other hand   in spite of |
| besides   even though   therefore |

Now read *Language summary D* on page 157.

**2** **a)** Complete the student's composition with suitable linking words, paying attention to the punctuation and grammatical construction of the sentences. Use as many different linking words as possible.

**b)** Underline six more linking words in the composition.

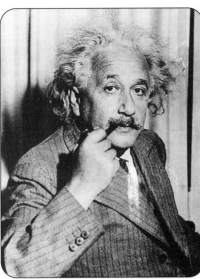

Genius can take many different forms, but tends to be most common in fields such as music, mathematics, poetry or art. Some geniuses emerge very young – Mozart started composing at the age of five; (1) ......... others are late developers – Einstein was apparently very slow at school! It is also interesting that there tend to be far more male geniuses than female ones – or perhaps they are just given more encouragement. So what would it be like to be a genius? Is this something that most people would really want?

Obviously, there are many advantages. To begin with, all those things that other people struggle with, such as passing important exams, would come very easily to you if you were a genius. (2) ......... most ordinary people spend hours studying and revising, you would be able to walk into exams and score top marks without even trying. Wouldn't that be wonderful! (3) ........., it would be clear what your talents were, and (4) ......... choosing a career, or direction in life, would probably be much easier than for most people. And (5) ......... you might behave in a strange way sometimes, people would always respect and admire you because of your abilities.

(6) ........., there are also important disadvantages. Because being so talented might make you feel special, you might find it difficult to relate to other people and (7) ......... find life a bit lonely sometimes. (8) ........., you might end up feeling very superior to the rest of the world, never learning to value and respect other people properly. And, (9) ......... being so brilliant in certain areas, you might not learn important practical skills that other people have to learn and might not (10) ......... develop into a well-balanced person. In fact, you could end up leading rather a sheltered life, cut-off from the real world, and all its ups and downs.

On the whole, I think ...

**3** Look at the model for writing a for and against composition.

Introduction:
points of interest – why the subject is interesting.

↓

Paragraph 1: arguments for.

↓

Paragraph 2: arguments against.

↓

Conclusion:
your own opinion and why you have reached it.

Which paragraphs was the student writing in Exercise 2? What could he write about in his conclusion?

**4** **a)** In pairs or individually, you are going to write a for and against composition. Choose a topic you have discussed in this module, or another topic which is controversial in your country and which interests you. Here are some possible titles:

The pros and cons of being rich and famous

Is being a politician a worthwhile job?

Which is better, being married or single?

Is it acceptable to break the law for a cause you really believe in?

The pros and cons of banning cars in cities

Should we bring back the death penalty?

Does modern technology do more harm than good?

**b)** Brainstorm ideas to include in your composition. Follow the model in Exercise 3. Remember to include arguments on both sides, saving your own opinion for the end. Ask your teacher for any words or phrases you need.

**c)** If you have time, write a first draft of your composition and correct it with your teacher. Then write a final draft for the other students to read.

# Wordspot

## *about*

**1** **a)** Which of the phrases in the box are missing from the mini-conversations? (You do not need all the phrases.)

| |
|---|
| give a speech about  travel about  argue about do something about it  It's about  I'm about to How about ...?  walk about  What about ...? laugh about  gossip about  he was about to rush about  write about  round about tell me all about it  Just about  worried about |

1 BOY: I'm going out now, see you later!

MOTHER: ............. your homework? I hope you've done it properly!

2 WOMAN: How many guests have they invited to the wedding?

MAN: I'm not sure ............. a hundred, I think.

3 GIRL: Have you finished your exams yet?

BOY: ............. . I've got one more left!

4 DOCTOR: Hello, what can I do for you, Mrs Lakes?

MRS LAKES: ............. my husband, Doctor. I'm really ............. him.

DOCTOR: I see, well try not to get upset, then you can .............!

5 MAN: Sorry to disturb you again, but it's the sink in the kitchen. I think it's blocked.

PLUMBER: Okay, I'll ............. when I've finished this. Just give me ten minutes.

6 MANAGER: Maggie, could you quickly type this letter for me?

SECRETARY: Actually, ............. go home. It's my daughter's birthday and I promised not to be late home for once.

7 MAN: What happens when we arrive?

GUIDE: Well first of all we'll have lunch, then you'll have an hour or so to ............. and look at the sights before we get back on the coach.

**b)** 🔊 [8.3] Listen and check your answers.

**2** Write the phrases above in the correct place on the diagram.

(a) dealing with a certain subject
*It's a book about dreams.*

(b) after verbs relating to communications / thoughts / feelings, etc.
*think about talk about*

(h) to fix / deal with
*to do something about (a leaking tap, etc.)*

ABOUT

(c) to introduce a topic
*It's about (my husband).*

(g) with verbs of movement (about = 'up and down' / in many different places)
*run about*

(d) to make a suggestion
*What about (meeting at my house first)?*

(f) to say that something will happen very soon
*The bell's about to ring.*

(e) approximately (with numbers and measurements)
*about twenty metres long*

**3** **a)** In pairs, discuss the following questions. Use a phrase with *about* in your answer.

1 What was the last film you saw at the cinema or on TV? What kind of story was it?
2 In general, what kind of books (fiction or non-fiction) do you most enjoy reading?
3 If you could write a book or make a TV programme, what would it be about?
4 How many people are there in your school / where you work / in your town?
5 Are there any domestic matters (for example, repairs) that you need to do something about?
6 When you go out with your friends, what do you talk about? Are there any topics that you never talk about?
7 Do you ever argue with your friends or family? What about?
8 What do you worry about?
9 Is anything interesting about to happen in your family / where you work / at your school?
10 Are there any important projects, or pieces of work, that you've just about finished?

**b)** Choose five phrases with *about* that you did not know before and write sentences with them. Use the questions in Exercise 3 a to help you.

# Consolidation
## modules 5–8

## A Use of articles

**Choose the correct article *a / an*, *the* or *ø* (= no article) to complete the two stories.**

### Britain's hardest-working man?

(1) _____ hardest-working man in (2) _____ Britain has decided to take life (3) _____ little easier. James McSporran has retired as (4) _____ only police constable on (5) _____ tiny *Hebridean island of Gigha in (6) _____ North-West of Scotland. However, he will continue to serve (7) _____ island's 200 inhabitants in (8) _____ number of other roles, for he is also (9) _____ postman, (10) _____ ambulance man, (11) _____ shop-keeper, (12) _____ taxi driver, (13) _____ school bus driver, as well as doing ten other jobs. (14) _____ police job wasn't that demanding he told (15) _____ *Times*. (16) _____ islanders are all either (17) _____ relatives or (18) _____ friends, so there isn't actually any crime!

*\* The Hebrides is the name of this group of islands*

### The new Bill Gates?

(1) _____ sixteen-year-old schoolboy has set up (2) _____ business with (3) _____ turnover of tens of thousands of dollars from (4) _____ home computer. Described as (5) _____ new Bill Gates, Tim Dunton designs (6) _____ websites for (7) _____ Internet. His company (8) _____ Gobal Gold Internet Services, also buys up (9) _____ names that (10) _____ companies might like for their websites. For example, he bought (11) _____ name Linkexchange for $120, and sold it to (12) _____ American company for $7,500.

## B Word combinations

**1 All the phrases in the box come from Modules 5–8. Sort them into the correct categories (some may fit into more than one category). Compare answers in pairs.**

> waving a flag   experiencing economic recession
> overcoming difficulties   getting dressed up
> taking part in a procession   voting in an election
> making sacrifices   putting things off   taking risks
> sticking to deadlines   experiencing an economic boom
> setting yourself goals   getting easily distracted
> coping with stress   making an effort   joining in the fun
> wearing fancy dress   joining a political party
> taking part in a demonstration

| celebrations | politics and economics | study / work | achievements |
|---|---|---|---|
|  |  |  |  |

**2 Test your partner. Read out part of the phrase and see if your partner can give you the word combination from above.**

risks → take risks

## C Record breakers: perfect tenses

**Choose the best verb form to complete the fascinating facts.**

### Record breakers!

**1 The world's oldest royal family**
The royal family of Japan *had occupied / have occupied* the Japanese throne for over 2,500 years.

**2 The President absent from his country the longest**
Before becoming President of his country in 1997, Valdus Adamkus, the President of Lithuania, *has been living / had lived / had been living* in Chicago in the USA for over fifty years. Political opponents complained that he had an American accent when he spoke Lithuanian.

### 3 The world's richest man

Bill Gates, born in the USA in 1955, is officially the world's richest man. It is estimated that by the age of forty-eight he *had made / will have made* over $1 million million, making him the first trillionaire in the world.

### 4 The youngest sportswoman to earn over $1 million

By the age of sixteen, in 1997, the Swiss tennis champion Martina Hingis, *had earned / will have earned* over $3 million in prizes and sponsorship.

### 5 The world's most often married celebrity

Zsa Zsa Gabor, born in Hungary in 1917, is generally considered the world's most frequently married celebrity. She *is married / has been married* at least eight times. She claims that she *married / has married* her first husband when she was thirteen.

### 6 The world's most patient fiancée

When Octavio Guillen from Mexico finally named the wedding day in June 1969, bride Adriana Marinez, eighty-two, *has waited / has been waiting / had been waiting* sixty-seven years. Guillen, also eighty-two, *has first proposed / had first proposed* to her in 1902!

### 7 Population explosion?

The population of the world in 1995 was calculated at 5.7 billion. It is estimated that by 2025 it *has reached / will have reached* between 7.5 billion and 9.5. billion. By then, some experts believe that the population of China alone *has reached / will have reached* 1.5 billion.

### 8 The world's richest teenager

Prince Abdul Aziz Bin Fahd of Saudi Arabia holds the record for being the richest teenager in the world. In 1987 at the age of fourteen, he was given a present of $300 million because his previous allowance *has not been / had not been* sufficient for his needs and he *has been running up / had been running up* large debts.

## D Relative clauses

**1 Insert the sentences from box B into the best places in box A using the correct relative pronoun. (You may need to omit other words to make them into correct relative clauses. Add any necessary commas.)**

---

**A** Toddler Aruw Ibirum (a) *who lives in Bradford* miraculously survived after a 38-ton lorry ran her over as she lay in her pushchair. The lorry driver (b) _____ pulled up after he heard an unusual scraping noise. Aruw (c) _____ was discovered with just a few cuts and bruises. An astonished elderly woman (d) _____ told reporters, 'You wouldn't have believed a child could have come out of that alive.'

---

**B** she saw the whole thing happen    ~~she lives in Bradford~~ Yorkshire    her pushchair had been dragged along for nearly a kilometre    he was unaware of what was happening

---

**A** An Australian man (e) _____ finally discovered the cause of his acute backache last week. It was due to a shark's tooth (f) _____ . Leo Ryan, sixty-six (g) _____ had been attacked by the shark as a teenager. In the accident, (h) _____ (i) _____ he also lost three fingers and part of his arm. 'That shark was determined to hang onto me,' he told reporters.

---

**B** it had been stuck in his spine for almost forty-eight years he has been suffering for years
it happened off the Gold Coast
he had been swimming there
he will be having an operation to remove the tooth

---

**2** 🔲 **Listen and check your answers. In pairs, practise reading the complete stories aloud.**

## E Speaking game

**1 Work either as a class or in groups. Each choose one of the topics and spend about five minutes preparing what you will say (you are going to speak about the topic for two minutes).**

a  What it's like to be famous.
b  What environmentalists are trying to achieve.
c  An amazing recent invention.
d  Protest marches and political demonstrations.
e  The political system in your country.
f  Common ways of wasting your time.
g  An event in modern history that everyone will remember.
h  A national holiday in your country, and what happens.
i  A typical procession or carnival.
j  How to pass your exams.
k  What food you would prepare if you were organising a party.

**2 Take turns to speak for two minutes about your topic. Listen to the other students and then say which topic they chose.**

# module 9
## Problems and oddities

## Part A  Task

Vocabulary: describing things
that are odd or unusual
**Preparation for task:** famous
mysteries
**Task:** solving mysteries and
problems

## Vocabulary

### Describing things that are odd or unusual

**1** Look at the picture for two
minutes and find eight things
which are odd or unusual.
Compare notes with a partner. Did
you notice the same things?

**2** If necessary, check the
meaning of the words in **bold**
in your mini-dictionary or with
your teacher. Look back at the
picture and find something which:

a  doesn't **make sense**
b  has got **a hole** in it
c  is badly **stained**
d  has got **something missing**
e  has **broken down**
f  is **inside out**
g  is **going the wrong way**
h  is **torn**
i  is **cracked**
j  is **in the wrong place**
k  has been **badly damaged**
l  is **upside down**
m  has **melted**
n  has **got stuck**

**3**  [9.1] Listen to someone
describing the picture. Find
six differences between the
picture and the way the speaker
describes it.

**4** Work in pairs. Describe the picture in the same way as the speaker
on the cassette, with at least five differences between your
description and the one on the cassette. Your partner closes his / her
book and tries to remember which parts of your description are wrong.

## Personal vocabulary

# Task: solving mysteries and problems
## Preparation for task

**1** The pictures relate to real life mysteries from around the world. What can you see? Where do you think the photos were taken? Read the captions to find out more.

# Real life mysteries

Three schoolchildren found this on an Australian beach in 1993.

Something unusual occurred in Hindu temples all over the world in 1995.

This photo was taken in Scotland in 1934. It appeared in newspapers and caused an instant sensation. Sixty years later, the secret was finally revealed.

## Task

2 The three boxes below contain key names, places and phrases for explaining what happened in each case. Check any unknown words in your mini-dictionary or with your teacher.

> **Picture A**   a smooth rock   a giant egg   a museum
> Madagascar   to pay $25,000   a flightless bird
> to be extinct   the ocean currents   400 years ago
> the children's families

> **Picture B**   marble statues   the god Ganesha   London
> the texture of the marble   to drink spoonfuls of milk
> twenty litres of milk   a traditional offering   to absorb
> to witness a miracle   scientists   to trickle down
> thousands of people   Hong Kong

> **Picture C**   Loch Ness   a huge prehistoric monster
> plastic wood   to be genuine   to be a fake
> a toy submarine   to really exist   to play a trick
> Duke Whetherill   Duke's children   the press
> to confess   to take a photograph

1 Work in groups. Decide what the mystery (and explanation) was in each case, using the key words in Exercise 2 to help you. Ask your teacher about any further words or phrases you need, and write them in your *Personal vocabulary* box.

2 **a)** Spend a few minutes planning how you will present your solutions to the rest of the class. Look at the phrases in the *Useful language* box to help you to express your ideas.

**b)** Listen to the other groups, and note briefly all the different solutions.

3 🔲 [9.2] Listen to the real solutions. Which group's explanations were closest to the real one in each case?

4 Do you know of any other real life mysteries like these? Tell the story to the rest of the class, and discuss what you think happened.

# Part B Language

Modal and related verbs –
present forms
Past modals
Reading and speaking: *It's all a conspiracy!*
Real life: saying what's wrong with things
Writing skills: formal letters and formal language

## Language focus 1

Modal and related verbs – present forms

**1** Read the text and answer the questions.

a What kind of events can be predicted from the behaviour of animals?
b Which animals are involved?
c Do you know of any similar cases?

**2** Look at the modal verbs in **bold** in the text. Which could be replaced by a verb from the box, without changing the meaning of the sentence?

| need to | have to | ought to | is / are (not) able to | could |

Rather than investing in expensive scientific equipment to predict earthquakes, perhaps scientists **should** spend more time watching their pets. Many researchers now believe that the behaviour of certain animals **might** help them to predict natural disasters. For example, Chinese scientists in the 1970s thought that reports of farm animals running around in circles, and of dogs barking all night **may** indicate an impending natural disaster. They decided to evacuate the city of Haichin, which shortly afterwards was hit by a huge earthquake. Thousands of lives were probably saved, as a result. Japanese scientists have also discovered that catfish become livelier several days before moderately strong earthquakes. Many scientists now accept that this **can't** be pure coincidence; they believe the explanation **may** be linked to slight changes in the Earth's magnetic field. Although human beings **can't** perceive such changes, it is thought that the sensitive nervous systems of some animals **must** be affected by them. Now scientists **must** discover exactly which animals are affected in this way, so that they **can** save more lives in the future.

## Analysis

**1** Find one or more verbs from Exercise 2 to complete each explanation.

a .......................................... mean(s) that something is a good idea or the right thing to do.
b .......................................... mean(s) that something is necessary, an obligation.
c .......................................... mean(s) that you are sure, logically, that something is true.
d .......................................... mean(s) either you are able to do something, or it is **generally** possible.
e .......................................... mean(s) you are not able to do something, or it is not logically possible.
f .......................................... mean(s) that something is possible in either the present or the future.

**2** Write *can't, could, may, might* and *must* in the correct place on the diagram.

| sure that it is true | perhaps it is true | sure that it is not true |

***Now read Language summary A on pages 157-158.***

## Practice

**1** Choose a verb from the *Analysis* to complete the sentences. In some cases more than one verb is possible. If so, is there any difference in meaning?

a  Scientists ..................... be completely sure how birds know where to migrate: some believe that they ..................... have a built-in compass that senses the Earth's magnetic field.

b  Some sharks ..................... go for up to three months between feeds.

c  According to experts, humans ..................... sleep for at least six to eight hours a day: elephants, however, sleep only two.

d  A beehive ..................... contain as many as 40,000 worker bees, but only one queen.

e  A flea ..................... jump more than thirty centimetres up into the air – the equivalent to a human jumping over a seventy-storey building.

f  Many animals, including elephants and tigers, ..................... become extinct unless action is taken to stop hunting.

**2** **a)** All the ideas in *Fact or myth?* below are commonly believed to be true, but only three of them really are! Read them and decide which are true. If necessary, check the meaning of any words or phrases in your mini-dictionary or with your teacher.

**b)** Compare answers in groups. Use the modal verbs of possibility to express your opinions, like this:

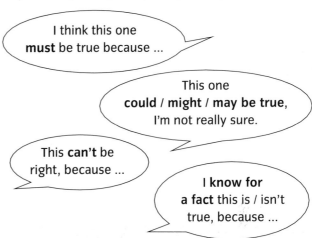

I think this one **must** be true because …

This one **could / might / may be true**, I'm not really sure.

This **can't** be right, because …

**I know for a fact** this is / isn't true, because …

**c)** 🎧 [9.3] Listen to the answers and find out if you were right.

# Fact or myth?

1  A sudden fright or profound shock can turn your hair white overnight.

2  Women have one more rib than men.

3  Newborn babies have more bones in their bodies than adults.

4  One bite from a tarantula is usually deadly.

5  Elephants are afraid of mice.

6  If you are struck by lightning, you will probably be killed.

7  Turkeys cannot fly.

8  Water going down the plughole travels in the opposite direction in the northern hemisphere to how it travels in the southern hemisphere.

9  When faced with danger, ostriches bury their heads in the sand.

# Language focus 2

## Past modals

Choose the best way to complete the sentences.

1   My niece was an
    exceptionally bright child.
    By the age of four, she
a   could read fluently.
b   can have read fluently.
c   could have read fluently.

2   The school's regime was
    extremely harsh. Pupils
a   should have got up at 4.30 every morning for
    prayers and exercise.
b   had to get up at 4.30 every morning for prayers
    and exercise.
c   must have got up at 4.30 every morning for prayers
    and exercise.

3   Last weekend we decided to drive into the city centre
    rather than taking the bus, but we got stuck in traffic
    and it took us ages to find a parking space so we
    hardly had time to do all our shopping. Perhaps we
a   should have left the car at home.
b   had to leave the car at home.
c   must have left the car at home.

4   When they got separated
    from the rest of the group,
    they were forced to find
    their own way down the
    mountain without maps
    or any protection from
    the extreme cold. It
a   had to be a terrifying
    experience for them.
b   might have been a
    terrifying experience
    for them.
c   must have been a terrifying
    experience for them.

5   Looking at the size of the
    footprints – which are
    roughly a metre across, far
    bigger than a man's foot,
    I'd say they
a   mustn't have been made
    by a human being.
b   may have been made by
    a human being.
c   can't have been made by
    a human being.

6   We had to drive all the way home in the dark
    without headlights. Fortunately there were very few
    cars on the road at that time of night so we got back
    without an accident, but really it was a very
    dangerous thing to do, we
a   could go off the road at any time.
b   could have gone off the road at any time.
c   were able to go off the road at any time.

## Analysis

1   Look at questions 1 to 3 and say which modal
    verb means:
    a   this person was able to do this ....................
    b   this was necessary ....................
    c   this was a good idea, but this person didn't
        do it ....................

2   Look at questions 4 to 6 and say which modal
    verb means:
    a   I'm sure this was true ....................
    b   perhaps this was true ....................
    c   I'm sure this wasn't true ....................

***Now read Language summary B on page 158.***

## Practice

1   Answer the questions using modal verbs.
    Compare answers in pairs or groups.

a   Write down two things that people **could** do a
    hundred years ago, and three that they **couldn't**.
b   Write down two things you **had to** do and two that
    you **didn't have to** do, when you were at nursery
    school / kindergarten.
c   Write down two things that you **should have done**
    last weekend, and two that you **shouldn't have
    done**.
d   Write down one thing that you think your parents
    or teachers **should have done**, and one thing that
    they **shouldn't have done**.

A hundred years ago,
people could travel by rail,
but they couldn't travel by air.

When I was at nursery
school, we had to stand
in the corner if we did
anything naughty.

2 Choose the best explanation on the right to complete the sentences.

a You might have left your glasses at work ⟋ I saw them on the kitchen table a few minutes ago.
You can't have left your glasses at work ⟍ I haven't seen them since you came home.

b Vera and Jack must have got lost — they've been here dozens of times before.
Vera and Jack can't have got lost — they phoned to say they were on their way hours ago.

c The murder must have happened after eleven — the victim was seen in a pub a few minutes before eleven.
The murder may have happened after eleven — the forensic evidence isn't clear.

d Annie can't have gone home — she said she had a bit of a headache earlier on.
Annie could have gone home — her car's still in the car park.

e Katie had to buy a lot of new clothes — she needed to look smart in her new job.
Katie must have bought a lot of new clothes — she's completely changed her image!

3 This story is grammatically correct, but many of the phrases underlined do not sound natural. Rewrite them using past modals to make them sound more natural.

# STEVE BRODIE'S STORY

A young man named Steve Brodie spent several months telling his friends that (a) he was able to jump off the Brooklyn Bridge into the East River without hurting himself. On 23rd July the day chosen for the great event, Brodie spent so long preparing himself in a nearby bar, that in the end (b) it was necessary for a friend to drive him to the middle of the bridge and leave him there. Some time later a passing policeman saw something fall into the river. Thinking that someone (c) had certainly fallen in by accident, the policeman sent a rowing boat to pick the poor victim out of the water. 'About time too!' said Brodie, indignantly. (d) 'It was possible for me to have drowned in here!'

Brodie became quite famous as a result of this, and eventually opened a saloon, where he never tired of describing his great deed. But there was never any real proof that he had done it, as no-one had actually seen him jump. Some said that Brodie (e) had faked the whole thing for sure – (f) it wasn't possible for anyone to survive such a huge leap. Certainly, Brodie always refused to repeat his feat, saying (g) it was unnecessary for him to prove himself again!

Follow-up task

### A real life whodunit

On 9th March 1929, the body of 31-year-old Isidor Fink was found in the back room of the laundry he owned on Fifth Avenue, New York. Fink was an immigrant who had very few friends. He had made the laundry into a kind of fortress: it was equipped with the best locks money could buy, and the windows were fitted with heavy iron bars. When the police finally found him, his body was lying ten metres from the doorway, with two bullet holes in his chest, and another in his left wrist. There was no gun in the room, and there was money in both Fink's pocket and in his cash register. But what made the case so strange was that the room was locked and bolted from the inside!

1 Read the real life mystery above. In groups, discuss possible answers to the questions.
a Why was Isidor Fink so worried about security?
b Was it significant that he was an immigrant with very few friends?
c Did he commit suicide?
d Did a burglar kill him?
e Why did he have a bullet hole in his wrist?
f Did the killer escape through the window?
g What is your theory about who killed Isidor Fink, and how he came to die in a locked room?

2 Present your group's conclusion to the class. Ask your teacher for any words or phrases you need.
(See page 144 for what the experts now think happened.)

# Reading and speaking

Singer Elvis Presley died in 1977, but there are still thousands of sightings of Elvis every year.

Actress Marilyn Monroe died in mysterious circumstances in 1961.

The TV series The X-Files follows the adventures of US federal agents Mulder and Scully and their encounters with the paranormal. It has been seen in over seventy-five countries worldwide.

**1** Read the definition of *conspiracy theory* taken from the *Longman Dictionary of Contemporary English*.

> **con·spi·ra·cy** /kən'spɪrəsi/ *n* [C,U] a secret plan made by two or more people to do something that is harmful or illegal.
> **conspiracy theory** (=the idea that an event was caused by a conspiracy) *conspiracy theories about President Kennedy's assassination*

**2** How are the pictures connected with the idea of a conspiracy? Discuss your answers with a partner, then read the text to check your ideas.

**3** Read the text again. Work in pairs or groups. Explain in your own words:

a why Mel Gibson was so popular in the role of Jerry Fletcher.

b three reasons why conspiracy theories became more widespread in the 1990s.

c what Freemasons and Communists have in common.

d what MJ12 is.

e the deal that (according to Milton William Cooper) MJ12 has made with the aliens.

f what the deaths of John F. Kennedy, Marilyn Monroe and Diana, Princess of Wales all have in common.

g what happened with the cartoon figure Pikachu.

h what the real purpose of Pikachu was, according to the conspiracy theorists.

**4** Discuss the following questions with the rest of the class.

• Do you know any more details about any of the conspiracy theories mentioned in the text? Do you know of any other famous conspiracy theories?

• Do you think there is any truth in any of these theories?

• Do you believe that aliens really have visited Earth? If not, what is your explanation for the sightings of UFOs?

## It's all a conspiracy!

In the 1997 film *Conspiracy Theory*, Mel Gibson plays Jerry Fletcher a New York cab driver obsessed with the idea of conspiracies — if it's not a plot to change thought patterns through water fluoridation, it's a secret plan to assassinate the President. The film was a box-office smash hit worldwide: perhaps a sign that there are many others who, even if they don't share Fletcher's extreme paranoia, at least identify with the idea that there is some kind of high-level conspiracy going on out there, and that we're all the victims of it. Access to the Internet, the international success of the paranormal thriller series *The X-Files*, which bases many of its stories around conspiracy theories, and acts of terrorism such as the Oklahoma bombing in 1995, have given conspiracy theories a wider audience than ever. Jonathan Vankin and John Whaler, authors of the best selling *Sixty Greatest Conspiracies of All Time* called the 1990s 'the conspiracy decade'.

Of course, conspiracy theories are nothing new: it's who is behind the conspiracy that changes with the times. Once upon a time it was the Freemasons, now seen by most people as a harmless semi-secret religious society, but two hundred years ago taken seriously enough to be banned all over Europe as an international conspiracy to overthrow monarchies and begin social revolution. In the United States in the 1950s, it was the turn of the communists, who were supposedly responsible for (among other things) rock and roll (a plot to destroy the moral health of young people), and turning Hollywood into a Soviet propaganda machine. And where would the James Bond movies be without a whole succession of all-powerful mysterious figures striving for world domination?

With the communist 'threat' gone in the 1990s, encounters with UFOs now provide conspiracy theorists with their richest source of paranoia. We have become used to hearing tales of alien landings, like the one in Roswell, New Mexico in 1948, the abduction of motorists on country roads late at night, and the inexplicable mutilation of cattle. This,

US President John F. Kennedy was assassinated in Dallas, Texas on 22nd November 1963. The exact motive for his killing, and the true identity of his assassin have never been finally established.

according to conspiracy theorists, all has a perfectly logical, if sinister, explanation.

According to former US intelligence man Milton William Cooper and his followers, there has been a kind of government within a government — the MJ12, or the Majestic Twelve — looking after the whole alien question since the 1950s, and keeping a whole lot of important information back from the poor ignorant public. The theory is — wait for it — that MJ12 has done a deal with one or more alien races. You may have thought our rapid technological advances over the last decades were due to a lot of investment, research and a bit of human cleverness. Sorry, all this technology was actually donated by grateful aliens to MJ12. And in return for what? Well, that's where the cattle mutilations come in. All over the United States and elsewhere, since the 1960s, there have been cases of cattle being found, their internal organs removed with surgical precision and their blood sucked out. This — according to Cooper — is our part of the bargain. The aliens are apparently afflicted with some mysterious illness and need these spare cattle parts to cure them.

If you find that one hard to believe, perhaps you'd prefer something a little closer to home. The mother of all conspiracy theories surrounds the assassination of John F. Kennedy in Dallas in 1962 (you can take your choice from the US Secret Service, the Mafia or even MJ12!), but similar theories have surrounded the deaths of Marilyn Monroe (possibly murdered at the orders of the US President), Elvis Presley (he didn't really die, he just wanted to live like a regular person again), and even Diana, Princess of Wales (supposedly a victim of MI6, the British Intelligence Service). It seems that any event nowadays can have a sinister explanation. When seven hundred Japanese children were reported to have suffered epilepsy-like symptoms as a result of watching a cartoon squirrel with flashing eyes known as Pikachu, conspiracy theorists immediately claimed this was a new mind-control weapon being tested on Japanese youngsters! But don't worry. Even If the conspiracy theorists are right, you won't become a victim of the great conspiracy just as long as you don't drive, eat, drink water, or watch TV. Better safe than sorry!

# Real life

## Saying what's wrong with things

1 Which of the problems in the box could be wrong with the things in the pictures?

| |
|---|
| it's the wrong **size**     it doesn't **suit** you     it's **chipped** it's **scratched**     it doesn't **work**     the colour has **run** it's not what you **ordered**     it's got a **hole** in it it's got a dirty **mark** on it     it's **over-cooked** it's got a **crack** in it     it's **split**     it's **shrunk** in the wash it's not cooked properly     one of the parts is **missing** |

2 📼 [9.4] You are going to hear four conversations in which people are talking about one of the items above. Complete the table below.

| what the item is | what's wrong with it | how the problem is resolved |
|---|---|---|
| 1 | | |
| 2 | | |
| 3 | | |
| 4 | | |

3 Prepare a similar short conversation (about twelve lines) using these ideas to help you.

| where it happens / the speakers | what the problem is | how it is resolved |
|---|---|---|
| shop | • meal no good | • goods exchanged |
| restaurant | • wrong goods delivered | • refund |
| over the phone | • object doesn't work • present that went wrong | • customer gives up / admits mistake |
| in an office argument | • student put in wrong class | • huge argument |
| at a language school | • garment doesn't fit | |

# Writing skills

## Formal letters and formal language

**1** Jane phoned the manager of ElectroWorld to complain about a television she had bought there. Look at some extracts from her conversation and the letter she wrote afterwards. What differences do you notice in the language?

(a) It's about a portable TV I bought from your shop a couple of months ago.

(b) I'd only had it for a couple of weeks when it went wrong.

(c) They told me that someone would come and see to it the following day.

(d) The repair man told me I needed a new valve.

(e) He said it would only take a couple of days to get it.

(f) That was eight weeks ago. Since then nothing's happened.

(g) I'm absolutely fed up with this.

(h) I've tried phoning the helpline dozens of times. All I get is a recorded message telling me to try again later.

(i) Please can you sort this out straightaway.

**2** **a)** Read Jane's letter and underline the formal phrases which mean the same as the informal phrases in the speech balloons. The first one is done for you.

```
                              24 Princes Street
                                          Holt
                         Manchester MN9 6RD

                              24th April 1999

Mr Clark
The Manager
ElectroWorld Superstore
Knowsley Way
Manchester M60 3BY

Dear Mr Clark,
     Following our telephone conversation, I am writing to
complain about the Dekon UX-95 portable TV I purchased
from your store on 8th February 1999.
     I had only had the set for approximately two weeks
when it developed a fault. When I finally received an
answer from one of your helpline staff, I was told that
an engineer would attend to the fault the following day.
Two days later, when the engineer finally appeared, he
informed me that the original valve was faulty, and that
a new one would be required. He assured me that the part
would be ready within two or three days. Eight weeks
later, I am still waiting for the part.
     I need hardly point out that I am extremely
dissatisfied with the service you have provided. I have
phoned both your helpline and your office on a number of
occasions, only to be told to try again later as all the
lines are busy. I feel the way my problem has been dealt
with has been absolutely appalling, and that I am
entitled not only to an apology, but also a replacement
portable TV. I would ask that you give this matter your
most urgent attention and expect to hear from you by the
end of the week.
     Yours sincerely,

     Jane Mitchell

     Jane Mitchell
```

**b)** Find formal expressions in the letter for the words in the box.

| buy a couple of weeks it went wrong come and see to it |
| I'm fed up dozens of times Can you ... sort it out |

**For example:**
buy    purchase

**3** **a)** Look at the position of the following features in the letter. Are there any differences from formal letters in your own language?

- names and addresses
- the sign-off (*Yours ...*)
- the sender's signature
- the greeting (*Dear ...*)
- the date

**b)** Circle any other phrases you think are useful for writing other letters of complaint. Look at the suggestions on page 144, then write a similar letter of complaint.

# Do you remember?

## 1

Look at the items in the pictures. For each picture, cross out (X) the phrase which cannot be used to describe it.

a

it doesn't suit you
it doesn't fit
it's cracked
it's inside out

b

it's chipped
it doesn't make sense
it's upside down
it's torn

c

it's melted
one of the parts is missing
it's shrunk in the wash
it's badly damaged

d

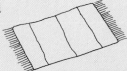

it's badly stained
it's got a hole in it
it's got a dirty mark on it
it's in the wrong place

## 2

Are the pairs of sentences the same or different?

a) I can't help you – you need to speak to the manager.
   I can't help you – you have to speak to the manager.
b) You don't have to tell anyone about the meeting.
   You mustn't tell anyone about the meeting.
c) Jan may know where it is.
   Jan might know where it is.
d) You must try this sauce – it's fantastic!
   You should try this sauce – it's fantastic!
e) They should have gone home after the lesson finished.
   They must have gone home after the lesson finished.

## 3

Complete part B in the conversations. Use *should (have), must (have), can't (have), ought to (have)*, etc. and the suggestions given.

For example:

A: Oh, no! I can't find my passport anywhere!
B: • (in your briefcase)
     *It might / could be in your briefcase.*
   • (leave it at work)
     *You must have left it at work.*
a) A:  David was late on his first day in his job!
   B: • (be really embarrassed)
      • (have problems because of the train strike)

b) A: Have I told you about my friend Flavia? She's twenty-seven, and she's going to marry a man who's nearly seventy.
   B: • (be in love with him)
      • (think about it carefully)
c) B: Did you have a good lunch at that new restaurant?
   A: Yes, we ended up having five courses!
   B: • (feel full)
      • (bill be expensive)
d) A: Richard's still smoking, even though the doctor's told him to stop because of his heart.
   B: • (be difficult to give up after all these years)
      • (cut down, even if he can't stop completely)

## 4

Find phrases which mean the same in the box. Which phrase is formal, which is informal / neutral? Write them in the correct column like this:

| formal | informal / neutral |
| --- | --- |
| *purchase* | *buy* |

absolutely fed up   ~~buy~~   attend to it
I think you should say you're sorry
develop a fault    come and see it
sort this problem out    go wrong
~~purchase~~   extremely dissatisfied
give this matter your most urgent
attention    dozens of times
I feel I am entitled to an apology
on a number of occasions

# module 10

## Getting together

### Part A  Task

Vocabulary and reading: co-operation and competition
**Preparation for task:** organise an international sporting event
**Task:** organise an international event

## Vocabulary and reading

Co-operation and competition

**1** We are all aware of the importance of communication and co-operation in bringing together people from different countries peacefully. Here are some ways to achieve this. Add at least five more ideas to the list, using the pictures to help you.

- political organisations like the UN
- scholarships and educational exchange visits
- international peace-keeping missions or humanitarian aid
- ................................................
- ................................................

**2 a)** Look at the list below. If necessary, check the meaning of the words in **bold**, in your mini-dictionary or with your teacher. Which of these things are positive (+), and which are negative (–)?

- it **broadens** people's **minds**
- people work together for their **mutual interests**
- it enables people to **communicate face-to-face**
- it brings many **economic benefits**
- it brings exciting new **opportunities**
- it leads to **conflicts, rivalries** and **petty squabbles**
- it **makes** people more **aware of** each other's culture and beliefs
- it's all about **cheating** and **bending the rules**
- people **compete against** each other **in a spirit of friendship**
- people become **anti-social** and **ignore** the people around them
- it creates **a sense of community** and **comradeship**

**b)** Which of these ideas describe the things you listed in Exercise 1? Discuss answers in groups.

**3** Four people are talking about their experiences of these activities and saying what they think about them.

**a)** Which forms of international co-operation are they talking about?

**b)** Do they believe these activities help to promote co-operation and communication or not? Why? Why not?

**4** Work in groups and discuss the following questions.
- Do you agree with the arguments or not? What is the other side of the argument in each case?
- What do you think are the best ways of bringing about co-operation and communication between people of different cultures?

①

"The dream of the Olympics used to be for the youth of the world to come together to compete in a spirit of friendship, but nowadays there's no getting away from the fact that all these big sporting events are not really about fair play, but about winning at all costs ... and if that means cheating or bending the rules in whatever way you can, then people will do it because of the pressure they're under from the public and the sponsors. People only want to see winners, they're not interested in anything else."

Richard Cooke, former Olympic rower

② "The more people travel, the more they get to know other cultures, how other people live ... and you can only learn to appreciate ways of life which may be different from your own if you see for yourself. There were sixty-four million visitors to Spain last year ... that can only be a good thing; just think of the economic benefits, not just for the Spanish economy, but for Europe as a whole. Travel doesn't only broaden the mind, it enriches all of us culturally as well as economically."

Marta Salas, travel agent

③ "Forget the hype about the Internet creating a global village and all those things about bringing people together – we're in danger of producing a society where people spend their lives in front of a screen, and become unable to communicate face-to-face. People spend their lives talking on their mobile phone and ignore the people around them. In the end all this technology is destroying our sense of community. Remember that society got along just fine before we had mobile phones, faxes, e-mails and such, maybe better because people had more time for each other."

Robert Moses, US journalist

④ "People were against monetary union, but it happened anyway ... so what about political union? If we have a single currency, it's only a matter of time before we have a single government not only in Europe, but also in other areas like Latin America and Asia. I think it makes sense, as it's the best way to avoid local conflicts like they had in former Yugoslavia. We need to put aside national differences and think of ourselves as Europeans, Latin Americans, whatever, otherwise politics will just fragment into petty squabbles and local rivalries."

Alice Kaltzer, student

# Task: organise an international event
## Preparation for task

**1** Next year, the World Student Games are going to be held in your town. You are on the organising committee, which is holding a meeting to discuss a number of important issues.

**a)** Below is the agenda for the meeting. Before you read it, check the meaning of the words in **bold** from the agenda in your mini-dictionary.

| |
|---|
| to **broadcast** something **on television**      **live television coverage** to charge **a fee**     to give a **speech**     a **ceremony** a **display** (of dancing, etc.)     the **highlight** of an event     a **procession** **stunning** (adj)     **simultaneous** translation     a **participant**     a **spectator** |

**b)** Read quickly through the agenda. Which four issues are being discussed?

## Useful language

**Describing your decisions**

"We've decided to ..."

"We're going to ..."

"We'd like to ..."

**Explaining your decisions**

" ... will make a lot of money for ..."

" ... will be far too expensive ..."

" ... makes better sense financially ..."

" ... will attract a lot of publicity / television coverage / people ..."

"We think / don't think people will appreciate / enjoy ..."

"It's fairer / unfair to ... (students / local people, etc.) if we ..."

" ... if / when we ... , ... may / will happen ..."

## WORLD STUDENT GAMES

### Agenda for next committee meeting

**1  Who will give the opening speech?**

The speech will last about ten minutes and be given to a crowd of about 50,000 people. It will be broadcast on live television around the world, with simultaneous translation, if necessary. Options to discuss:
- a famous national or international sporting personality, for example .............................. (normal fee about $40,000)
- the local mayor (no fee)
- a famous national or international politician, for example .............................. (probably no fee required)
- other .............................. (fee depends)

**2  What will be the highlight of the opening ceremony?**

This will be very important in influencing the amount of television coverage the games attract. Television contracts bring in tens of thousands of dollars, as well as important publicity. Options to discuss:
- A procession of all the student athletes, dressed in their national colours, carrying their national flags, and accompanied by brass bands playing music, etc. This option is quite cheap, and will involve relatively little organisation.

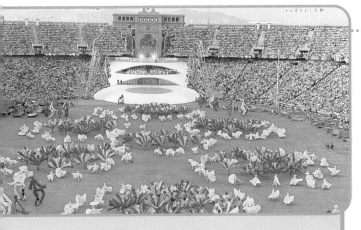

- A human flower arrangement produced by thousands of schoolchildren dancing and holding up coloured paper. This will be stunning when filmed by television cameras from the air, but less interesting for those watching in the stadium. It is the most expensive option and will require the most organisation.
- A display by local folk dancers and musicians. This will be the cheapest option, since they only charge a small fee, but a lot of organisation will be required.
- Other ...............................

## 3   New event

The games already include all the usual events, athletic, gymnastic, swimming and water sports, but it is traditional each time the games are held to bring in one new event. Options to discuss:
- Rollerblade racing
- synchronised swimming
- a sport from your country which is less well-known internationally, for example ...............................
- Other ...............................

## 4   Free concert

It has already been agreed that a free concert will be provided in a large park at the end of the games for the participants in the games, spectators, and local people. This may also possibly be broadcast on television around the world (bringing in tens of thousands of dollars) depending on who performs.
Options to discuss:
- an internationally famous rock group, for example ........................... ...............................
  (fee up to $100,000)
- a famous singer from your country, for example ............................... (fee up to $40,000)
- a world-famous Italian tenor has offered to perform for free because of his interest in promoting sports for young people, and his fondness for your town
- a selection of local / student rock and folk bands, who will perform for free
- other ...............................

**2 a)** Work in groups. Your teacher will give each of you one of the roles on the committee.

- Chairperson, see page 141.
- Director of Finance, see page 142.
- Publicity and Marketing Director, see page 143.
- Student Representative, see page 144.
- Local Mayor, see page 145.
- International Representative, see page 146.

**b)** Read your card carefully. Spend a few minutes thinking about what your priorities will be when making your decisions.

**3 a)** Read the agenda again, and decide which of the options you favour, bearing in mind your priorities. If necessary, decide which sporting personalities, singers, etc. you would like to suggest for the opening speech and free concert, or any alternative suggestions that you have.

**b)** Think about how you will present your arguments to the other members of the committee. Ask your teacher for any words or phrases you need and write them in your *Personal vocabulary* box.

## Task

**1** Work through the agenda as a group, making sure that everyone has the opportunity to put forward their point of view. The chairperson should decide when it is time to move on to the next item.

**2** Imagine that your committee has to present its conclusions (and the reasons for them) to a press conference. Spend a few minutes preparing what you will say. Look at the phrases in the *Useful language* box to help you.

**3** Listen as a representative from each group presents their decisions. Were they the same or different to your own? Do you like any of their ideas better than those of your group?

# Part B **Language**

Review of basic future forms
Listening and speaking: an interview with a communications expert
Future Continuous and Future Perfect
Writing skills: formal and informal messages
Real life: dealing with problems when telephoning

## Language focus 1

Review of basic future forms

**1** James and Richard are arranging a trip to an ice-hockey game. Read their telephone conversation.

**2 a)** Look at the future forms in the conversation, and cross out (X) the alternatives that are wrong in each case.

**b)** 🔲 [10.1] In some cases, both forms are possible. Is there any difference in the meaning? Listen and compare your answers to those on the cassette.

| | |
|---|---|
| JAMES: | Hello? |
| RICHARD: | Hi James, it's Richard. |
| JAMES: | Richard, hi, how are things with you? What's new? |
| RICHARD: | Oh, nothing much. Listen, the reason I'm calling is that (1) *I'll take / I'm going to take* Sam, my nephew, to the hockey game on Saturday. (2) *Are you going / Do you go?* |
| JAMES: | I want to, the only problem is that we (3) *are having / are going to have* lunch at my mom's this Saturday, but if the game (4) *starts / will start* later on, (5) *I'll probably go / I probably go.* |
| RICHARD: | It (6) *starts / will start* at five – I've just phoned to check. Do you think your mother (7) *'ll mind / minds* you leaving a bit early? |
| JAMES: | I don't think so – not if I tell her it's something really important! |
| RICHARD: | Well what could be more important than a hockey game? |
| JAMES: | Yeah, (8) *it's going to be / it'll be* one of the biggest games of the season. Apparently they've already sold over 10,000 tickets. |
| RICHARD: | Yeah, I know. So who do you think (9) *'ll win / is going to win?* |
| JAMES: | Well Buffaloes (10) *won't win / aren't going to win*, not with all the injuries they've had this season, and the way they've been playing! Saints are definitely the favourites! |
| RICHARD: | Mmm, I really hope you're right! By the way, do you want me to collect you? (11) *I've decided to drive / I'm going to drive* there, it'll be easier with Sam. |
| JAMES: | Yeah, that would be great if it's no trouble. |
| RICHARD: | No, no problem. Let me think, what time do we need to be there? |
| JAMES: | About half four to buy the tickets? |
| RICHARD: | Yeah. Okay then, (12) *I'll collect you / I'm going to collect you* at four – we'd better leave plenty of time in case the traffic (13) *'s / 'll be* bad. Is that okay? |
| JAMES: | Yeah, great. See you on Saturday, then. |
| RICHARD: | Yeah, see you then. |

# Analysis

## Plans and decisions

**1** Why is *going to* used in **a** and *will* in **b**?
   a *I'm going to take my nephew to the hockey game.*
   b *I'll pick you up at four.*

**2** Is there any difference between these two sentences?
   a *We're going to have lunch at my mom's this weekend.*
   b *We're having lunch at my mom's this weekend.*

## Present Simple to express the future

The use of the Present Simple to express the future is very limited in English. Why is it correct in these examples?
   a *It **starts** at five – I've just phoned to check.*
   b *We'd better leave plenty of time in case the traffic's bad.*

## Predictions

Is there any difference between these two sentences?
   a *It'll be one of the biggest games of the season.*
   b *It's going to be one of the biggest games of the season.*

## Other phrases that express future ideas

There are many other phrases used to express the future.
**For example:**
   *I've decided to drive there.*
Can you think of any others?

*Now read Language summary A, B, C and D on pages 158-159.*

# Practice

**1** Write sentences about the ideas below, thinking carefully about the future form you use. Compare answers in pairs.
a   Any plans or arrangements you've made for later this week.
b   Your predictions about the winners of any important sporting events in the next few months.
c   Some of the things you believe / hope will happen in your country in the next few years.
d   Some circumstances in which you won't be able to come to the next class.
e   Anything major that you're planning to buy this year.
f   The times and arrangements for any classes, concerts or other events you are attending, or journeys you are making in the next week or two.

**2** Work with a partner. Act out some short conversations based on these situations.
a   Your partner phones you to ask if you are going to a sports game in your town next weekend. Like Richard and James, you discuss the game and make arrangements for getting there.
b   Your classmate asks you to join him / her and some others for a coffee after class. At first you accept, but then when you think about it, you decide you'd prefer to go home.

c   A classmate mentions that he's got to catch the bus home, and you know the buses only run every half hour. Your classmate lives near you, and your car's waiting outside, but you have one or two errands to do on the way home.
d   You and your partner are trying to arrange to meet up next weekend to study together for an exam, but both of you have already made some arrangements. You have to find a time that is convenient for both of you.
e   Your friend is travelling to Africa next month. She wants to know what health / safety precautions she should take. Give her advice, explaining why, in each case.

**3** Act out some of your conversations. Your teacher and the other students will listen to the future forms you use for correction / discussion afterwards.

## Follow-up task

**1** Your class has decided to arrange an excursion for the day to celebrate the end of term. In groups, decide how you will spend the day. Think about the following:
- where you will go (make sure it is somewhere that appeals to everyone, and bear in mind the weather at this time of year).
- places to stop on the way.
- the best day for the trip so that everyone can come.
- travel arrangements.
- the arrangements for food / drink.
- any money arrangements.
- who exactly is responsible for doing / bringing what.

**2** Report back briefly to the class on the arrangements you have made.

# Listening and speaking

## An interview with a communications expert

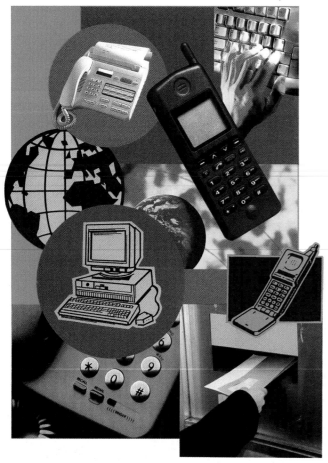

**1** Look at the list of methods of communication in the box. Which of them do you use yourself in what circumstances and why:

a in your personal life?

b for your work / studies?

> letters and postcards   fax machine   a mobile phone
> an ordinary phone   an answering machine   e-mail
> notes and memos

**2** 🖳 [10.2] Robert Emsworth has written a book about how communication technology has changed over the last 150 years. Listen to a radio interview with him and number the topics in the order that they are discussed. (One is not mentioned.)

a the advantages of e-mail ☐

b why e-mail doesn't always work ☐

c problems with telephone answering machines ☐

d what the 'communication revolution' is ☑

e the introduction of the telegraph ☐

f video telephones ☐

g the use and misuse of fax machines ☐

h the global impact of the modern telecommunication system ☐

**3** **a)** Listen again. Summarise the ideas in the interview by completing the sentences:

1 The 'communication revolution' is having a profound effect on life in developed countries. But ...

2 The great advantage of e-mail is that ...

3 However, the problem can be that ...

4 Telephone answering machines can be  ...

5 John Tawell had good reason to regret the introduction of the telegraph because ...

6 One prediction about telecommunications in the future which hasn't come true is that ...

**b)** Discuss the following questions in groups.

1 How have these changes in telecommunications affected your life?

2 What changes do you expect to see in the future?

3 Do you ever have problems with technology?

# Language focus 2

## Future Continuous and Future Perfect

## Analysis

**1** Tick (✓) the best explanation for the sentences.

a *In twenty years time, ordinary telephones will have disappeared.*

- This will happen in exactly twenty years.
- This will happen in less than twenty years.
- It will be more than twenty years before this happens.

b *By 2020 we will all be using videophones.*

- This will start happening before 2020.
- This will start happening in 2020.
- This will start happening after 2020.

**2** Match the time lines with an example above.

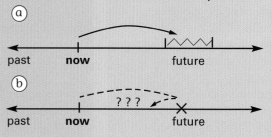

**3** Notice that we also use the Future Continuous for things that will happen because of arrangements we have already made.

*We've got a meeting tomorrow, so **I'll be seeing** Jane. I can give her the message then.*

***Now read Language summary E on page 159.***

## Practice

**1 a)** 🔊 [10.3] Match a line from box A with a line from box B. Listen to the conversations and check your answers.

**A**
1 So when can I speak to Mr Hammond?
2 Debbie said you can't come to the party on Friday.
3 I'm just going out to get some lunch. I won't be long.
4 So what time do you want us for dinner tomorrow night?
5 (on the phone) So see you in about half an hour. I've just got to go out and buy some coffee.
6 So, same time, same place next week?
7 Is it okay if I have the car tomorrow?

**B**
a Yeah, no problem. Matt's giving me a lift to work this week, so I won't be using it.
b I won't be here next week, I'm off on holiday! Hopefully, this time next week I'll be lying by the pool in the sunshine.
c Could you just post this for me? You'll be passing the post box, won't you?
d If you try again about half past two, he'll have come back from his lunch by then.
e Oh don't bother, I'll get it. I'll be driving right past the supermarket. What sort do you want?
f No. I'm on late shifts, so I'll be working, I'm afraid.
g Say about half past eight? The kids'll have gone to bed by then, so it'll be a bit more peaceful.

**b)** Explain in your own words the use of the Future Perfect / Future Continuous in each conversation.

### Pronunciation

**1** Listen to the conversations again, and notice the weak pronunciation of the auxiliary verbs in the Future Continuous, and Future Perfect.

I'll be /bɪ/ working unfortunately.
He'll have /həv/ come back from lunch hopefully.

**2** Practise saying the sentences above paying attention to the weak forms. Start with the main verb first and add on the weak forms.

```
     •              •                  •
working ...    be working      I'll be working
```

**2 a)** Mingle and find someone in your class for whom each of the statements below is true.

**b)** Before you start, plan your questions. Ask the simplest question possible to get the information, and pay attention to word order. Where appropriate, ask further questions, like this:

*What will you be doing in a couple of hours' time?*
*— I'll probably be travelling home on the train.*

*Oh, how long does it take you?*
*— About half an hour.*

**Find someone who . . .**

1 will be doing a lot of driving this weekend.

2 will probably be sitting on a bus or train in a couple of hours' time.

3 won't be eating at home tonight.

4 will probably have moved house by this time next year.

5 won't be coming to the next lesson.

6 will have taken some important exams by the end of the year.

7 won't be celebrating their birthday at home this year.

8 thinks they'll have got married by the end of next year.

9 doesn't think they'll have got married by the end of next year.

10 will definitely still be studying English this time next year.

# Writing skills

## Formal and informal messages

**1** Look at the texts and decide which is:

- a business fax.
- a telephone message.
- a congratulations card to a friend.
- a memo to a colleague (informal).

**2** **a)** Complete the gaps with these phrases.

- Regards
- When can we celebrate
- Liz called about
- Much love
- Maybe we can have the meeting next week instead?
- No. of pages (including this one)
- We're all delighted for you
- Could you call back
- If she doesn't hear from you
- Sorry to inconvenience you
- We look forward to meeting you in August. Best wishes
- There are one or two matters concerning your travel arrangements which I would like to finalise with you.

**b)** Which message(s):

1 do not use unnecessary words (pronouns, prepositions, articles, etc.)?
2 uses a lot of capital letters and exclamation marks for emphasis?
3 is the most formal in style?

**3** Choose two situations and write an appropriate message for each.

- You've just heard that an old friend who you haven't seen for a while is getting married in three months' time. Send her a card congratulating her on her engagement and suggesting a meeting before the big day.
- You have to send a fax giving travel and accommodation arrangements for a visitor to your town / city who is attending an international conference.
- Send a memo to a colleague in your company arranging a meeting for one afternoon next week. Suggest a time, and a place, and say what the meeting will be about.
- Your flatmate's friend has telephoned with details of the time and place where they're meeting this evening, leaving a number to phone if this isn't convenient. Leave a message for him / her.

**① ** Lucy

(a) _____ tickets for concert on Sat – only £25 tickets left – do you and Joe still want one? (b) _____ before 8 if possible?
(c) _____ she'll get 4 tickets anyway. O611 O8O 254 (mobile). Also can you let her know where to meet?

Matt

**②**

**To:** Dr Peter Kerr (07441 81 7649)
**Date:** 23rd April
**From:** Teresa Graham
**Cc:** Lisa Vincenti
**Subject:** SOLENT Annual Conference
(a) _____: 1

Dear Dr Kerr
Lisa Vincenti from our Manchester office has confirmed your participation at the SOLENT Annual Conference to be held in Manchester on 24th-26th August. We are very pleased that you will be able to attend. (b) _____
We suggest that you arrive the day before the Conference (23rd August)  on the 10.15 British Airways flight, or on the 13.20 Delta Airlines flight. Please let me know which flight you prefer. There is only one flight on Sunday 25th (the day after the conference) so we hope it will be convenient for you. It leaves Manchester at 15.40 and arrives in New York at 18.25.
(c) _____

Teresa Graham
Marketing Department

**③** Chris

I just checked in my diary and saw that I'll have to reschedule our meeting on Thursday, as I've got to be out of the office for a few hours on that day.
(a) _____ Give me a call and we'll arrange a time.
(b) _____
(c) _____

Jackie

**④** Claire

Just heard your great news!
CONGRATULATIONS!
(a) _____! (Mind you, it is about time!) (b) _____?
Let's fix something up soon.
(c) _____

Lauren

# Real life

## Dealing with problems when telephoning

**1** Discuss the questions in small groups.

- Do you spend a lot of time on the phone? Do you enjoy chatting, or are your calls usually short and to the point?
- Do you ever get annoyed or frustrated when you are making phone calls? What causes this? Have you had any difficult or annoying experiences on the phone recently?

**2** 📼 [10.4] You will hear three telephone conversations. Listen and complete the table.

| | speakers / relationship | what the problem is / how resolved |
|---|---|---|
| 1 | | |
| 2 | | |
| 3 | | |

**3 a)** 📼 [10.5] Listen to extracts from the three conversations again, and complete the gaps.

1 _____ time?
2 Could _____ ? _____ line.
3 I _____ .
4 Oh no, _____ !
5 I _____ .
6 I _____ half an hour when _____ .
7 What _____ ?
8 It's _____ Rome — I _____ .
9 Perhaps _____ name and number then _____ in ten minutes.
10 Sorry, _____ ?

**b)** Discuss with your partner when you would use these phrases. If necessary, check the meaning of any words or phrases in your mini-dictionary or with your teacher.

**4** Work in pairs. Prepare a conversation of your own, using the diagram to help you. Practise your conversation so that you can act it out for the rest of the class.

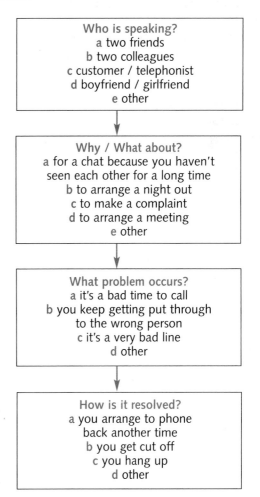

Who is speaking?
a two friends
b two colleagues
c customer / telephonist
d boyfriend / girlfriend
e other

↓

Why / What about?
a for a chat because you haven't seen each other for a long time
b to arrange a night out
c to make a complaint
d to arrange a meeting
e other

↓

What problem occurs?
a it's a bad time to call
b you keep getting put through to the wrong person
c it's a very bad line
d other

↓

How is it resolved?
a you arrange to phone back another time
b you get cut off
c you hang up
d other

**5** Listen to the other students' conversations, and answer the questions in Exercise 4 for each.

# Do you remember?

## 1

Which of the ideas in box A do you associate with the situations in box B? Discuss your answers in groups.

**A**

a lot of petty squabbles
conflicts and rivalries
cheating and bending the rules
people being very aware of each other's feelings
people competing against each other
exciting opportunities
a sense of community
people working together for their mutual interests
economic benefits
a spirit of comradeship

**B**

professional sport   family life   war
the business world   school life

## 2

Match words from columns A and B to make phrases that you have met in Module 10.

| A | B |
|---|---|
| give | good sense |
| attract | financially |
| broadcast | your mind |
| charge | publicity |
| broaden | a speech |
| communicate | a football match live |
| make | a fee |
| | face-to-face |

## 3

Choose the best alternative in each situation. Explain your answers in pairs.

a) Which of the following best describes your holiday plans for this / next year? Explain why.
   • I'm not having a holiday.
   • I'm having a holiday.
   • I'll probably have a holiday.

b) From what you know …
   • It's going to rain tomorrow.
   • It might rain tomorrow.
   • It's not going to rain tomorrow.

c) Which of the following would you say about a man who is single and wants to ask his girlfriend to marry him? Explain why.
   • He's getting married in the near future.
   • He's going to get married soon.
   • He'll probably get married before long.

## 4

Complete the following sentences in your own words. Compare answers with the other students in the class.

a) In a hundred years' time, I think a lot of people will be … -ing …
b) In twenty years' time, I hope I will be … -ing …
c) In twenty years' time, I hope I won't be … -ing …
d) Before I get old, I hope scientists will have …
e) Before I get old, I hope the government will have …

## 5

Who would say the following on the telephone to whom, and why? Discuss your answers in pairs.

a) Your voice sounds very faint – could you speak up a bit, please?
b) Could you put me through to Adam Hunt, please?
c) I'll just transfer you to the accounts department.
d) Am I calling at a bad time? Shall I call back later?
e) If I can take your name and number, I'll look into it, and call you back in ten minutes.
f) Don't just hang up, Louise, listen to what I've got to say, please.
g) Oh no, we've been cut off!
h) I'm calling regarding your advertisement in the local paper.

# module 11

## Modern medicine

### Part A  Task

Vocabulary and speaking:
scientific and medical advances
**Reading and speaking:** the
wonders of modern medical
science
**Preparation for task:** some
difficult cases of medical ethics
**Task:** make the right decision

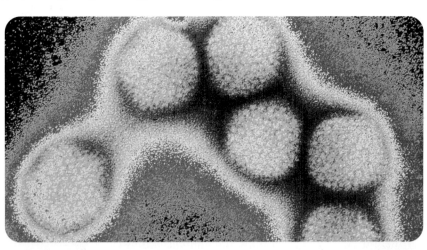

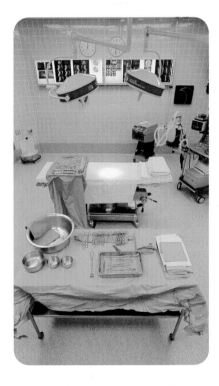

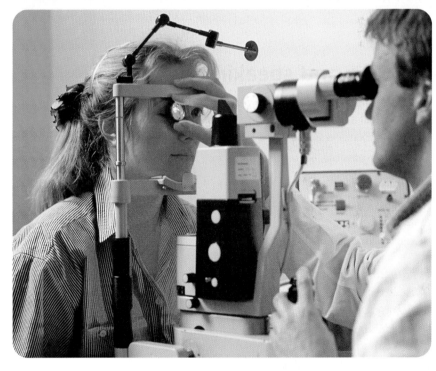

## Vocabulary and speaking

Scientific and medical advances

1  **a)** Work in groups. Think of examples of recent
advances in two of these scientific fields. Ask
your teacher for any words or phrases you need.

computer technology   medicine   surgery
fertility treatment   genetic engineering   laser technology

**b)** Compare answers with the rest of the class. What
future advances in these fields do you expect
to see?

2 Which of these things are already possible? Which will soon be possible? If necessary, check the meaning of the words in **bold** in your mini-dictionary. Compare answers.

a   the **cloning** of plants / animals / human **cells** / human **organs**

b   **kidney transplants** / ear transplants / head transplants / the transplant of animal organs into human beings

c   the **replacement** of **hips, elbows** and other **joints**

d   an **effective vaccine** to **eliminate** AIDS / cancer / tuberculosis

e   **treatment to prevent the spread of** AIDS / cancer in the patient's body

f   a successful **cure** for AIDS / cancer

g   a cure for **baldness** / **colour-blindness** / **snoring** / the common cold

h   a cure for **deafness** and **blindness**

i   the **implanting** of microchips into animals' brains / the human brain

# Reading and speaking

1 Read the text then work in pairs. Divide the medical achievements in Vocabulary and speaking, Exercise 2 into three groups:

a   already possible, according to the text.

*The cloning of plants*

b   likely to be possible in the next few years.
c   not possible.
d   not mentioned in the text.

2 Read the text again and answer the questions.

a   Will it ever be possible to produce exact copies of human beings? What are the possible advantages of cloning human beings?

b   Why do some people criticise the idea of head transplants?

c   What are the disadvantages of the new drugs that have been produced to treat AIDS?

d   What are the possible uses for microchips implanted into the human brain?

3 Discuss the following questions with the rest of the class. Which ideas in the text do you think:

•   are positive steps forward?
•   are worrying, from an ethical point of view?
•   should be prohibited?

Explain why.

# Five key questions about modern medical science

**What exactly is cloning and do I need to worry about it?**

Cloning is 'making a copy of a plant or animal by taking a cell from it and developing it artificially'. There is nothing new about this — plants were cloned in Ancient Greece over 2,000 years ago, and the first cloned frog appeared in 1968. But interest in cloning grew in 1997 when Dr Ian Wilmut and his colleagues from Edinburgh University announced the birth of the world's first cloned sheep, Dolly (some people pointed out that since all sheep look identical anyway, how could anyone tell?). However, many people were worried: what if the same techniques were used for some rich, elderly person to reinvent himself; or if an evil dictator produced hundreds of copies of himself in order to take over the world; or grieving relatives used cloning to bring their loved ones back to life?

The truth is that there is no chance that any copy of a human being would be identical either physically or mentally, any more than children are identical to their parents. The possible benefits of cloning, however, are numerous, for artificially producing human tissues and organs for transplant, and for preserving endangered animal species to name but two. Biologists have already genetically engineered headless frogs so it may in future be possible to clone headless humans whose organs could be used for transplants. But would we want to?

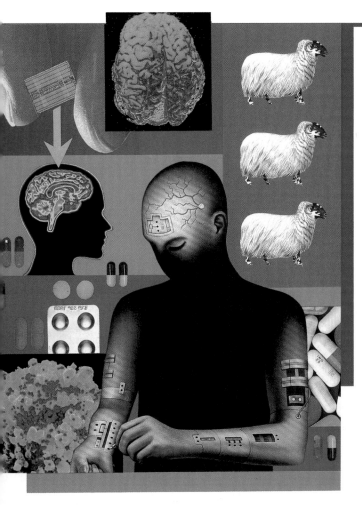

## How can transplants from other animals help humans?

In one famous case, a British girl born with a rare bone condition that left her with only one ear, had a new one grown for her at the Massachusetts Eye and Ear Infirmary in the USA. By taking cells from her existing ear and transplanting them onto the back of a mouse, scientists grew her another one, which could then be transplanted back. American scientists have also used sheep blood cells to make a universal blood which could be given to any patient, regardless of their blood group while British scientists are close to manufacturing artificial blood, with the aid of milk from genetically-altered cows and sheep. Scientists have also transplanted monkeys' heads on to new bodies, paving the way for head transplants to be performed on humans. The monkeys were able to eat, drink and sleep normally. Robert White, head of neurosurgery at Case Western Reserve University in Ohio said the operation could be available to humans within thirty years, but the experiment has been condemned as an example of 'the disastrous route Western medicine is taking, in which prolonging individual life takes precedence over everything'.

## Are we any nearer a cure for cancer or AIDS?

Although a definitive cure for cancer seems as elusive as ever, scientists have produced an impressive list of things that might help prevent it: green tea, green salads, brazil nuts, spinach, kidneys, mushrooms, and even lipstick. And although no cure has yet been found for AIDS, extraordinary advances have been made in its treatment. Drugs called protease inhibitors can halt and perhaps even reverse the progress of the virus in the patient's body, so it may be that AIDS will soon no longer be an incurable disease. The problem is the expense: a course of treatment costs many thousands of dollars, and so will do nothing to stop the epidemic in poor countries, where the money would be better spent on preventing malaria, cholera and tuberculosis.

## So what <u>can</u> we cure nowadays?

If you're a grey-haired, balding, colour-blind man who snores, there may be good news on the horizon. A doctor in England has announced that by adding a small amount of pigment to an ordinary pair of glasses he has been able to cure colour-blindness (though he admits he has no idea why it works!). A drug has been tested on dogs which stimulates muscles in their upper airway, thus stopping them from snoring. If it works for them, why not on humans? To prevent grey hair, a special shampoo has been developed that fools pigment cells into producing melanin, which gives hair its colour, and there may now even be a cure for baldness: a pill which reduces levels of the hormone dihydrotesterone, although there may be a less desirable side effect of a decreased interest in sex.

## Why would anyone want to implant a computer chip into a human brain?

Could it be possible for all the things you need to know to be implanted in your brain on a silicon chip? Doctors at the Max Planck Institute for Biochemistry in Germany claim to have found a way of connecting nerve cells to a silicon chip. Such implants — which have so far only been successful in rats — could be used to restore vision to people who have become blind or repair nerve damage after a stroke, but also to increase human intelligence. In theory, chips could be programmed to include all the knowledge a human being is likely to need during their life, so eliminating the need for school work!

## Personal vocabulary

# Task: make the right decision

**1** _____

Treatments now exist which can decide the sex of a baby according to the parents' wishes, but most doctors continue to feel that whether the child is a boy or a girl is a decision best left to nature. Mr and Mrs Schwarz are a married couple (a) _____. They have five healthy children – all (b) _____ – and are a happy, unified family. They are now planning a sixth child, but they are desperate to have a (c) _____ this time. Mrs Schwarz says she would rather have an abortion than have (d) _____; Mr Schwarz is equally insistent, 'What possible harm can there be in granting us our dearest wish to have (e) _____?' he asks. However, allowing parents to choose the sex of their children could affect the delicate balance of the sexes. It is estimated that (f) _____ of parents in the West would prefer a (g) _____, with serious social consequences.

QUESTION: **should the Schwarzes be granted their wish, or should nature be allowed to take its course?**

**2** _____

Scientists at the University of Texas (USA) believe they have discovered the key to stopping the ageing process — a simple chemical called telomerase which is produced naturally by (a) _____. Telomerase enables human cells to divide and replace themselves, but after a certain age the body stops producing it and begins to age. An American drug company has now applied for a licence to produce a drug containing large quantities of telomerase which, it is claimed, will enable takers to live for up to (b) _____ years. No harmful side effects have been identified after (c) _____ years of laboratory tests, though some scientists are concerned that there may be a small risk of (d) _____. With (e) _____ of the population of the USA already over sixty years old, the implications for the worlds of health and work are enormous.

QUESTION: **do you allow the drug company to produce the drug Telozan?**

**3** _____

In 1996, the papers were full of the story of L. , an (a) _____ girl paid by a Mr and Mrs R., a (b) _____ couple, to be a surrogate mother for their baby, using (c) _____ eggs and sperm donated by Mr R. In return for bearing it and then handing it over to its new parents, L. received $ (d) _____. All seemed well until (e) _____ after the birth of baby M., when L. refused to hand over the child, claiming that Mr and Mrs R. were not suitable parents and that, as the child's natural mother, she had the right to keep her. Although she had no (f) _____, L. claimed she would work to repay the money (which she had spent) rather than hand the baby back. The Rs said they had no interest in the money, but only wanted their baby, and took L. to court to get the child back. The judge ruled in their favour and, at the age of (g) _____, baby M. went to live with the Rs. L. was not allowed to have any contact with the child which was legally not hers.

QUESTION: **did the judge make the right decision?**

## Useful language

**Describing possible consequences**

"He / She should / shouldn't ... because ..."

"He / She should / shouldn't have ... because ..."

"This could / would affect ..."

"There are serious implications for ..."

**Weighing the arguments for and against**

"It's a question of whether or not ..."

"The most important issue is ..."

"We also need to think about the possibility of ..."

"On one hand ..., but on the other hand ..."

"You could argue ..., but then you could argue ..."

## Preparation for task

1 **a)** The stories describe difficult cases of medical ethics. Read them quickly and match these titles to the stories.

Whose baby?
Choosing the sex of your child
Drug to prevent ageing

**b)** Check the meaning of the words in **bold** in your mini-dictionary or with your teacher.

> a **harmful side effect**    a **surrogate** mother    a **risk of** (cancer, etc.)
> to allow nature to **take its course**    the ageing **process** / to **age**
> to **apply for** a **licence**    the **implications of** something
> the **consequences of** something    to **bear a child**    to **grant** someone **a wish**
> to **hand** something **over**

2 **a)** 🔊 [11.1] Listen and complete the gaps in the stories.

**b)** In your own words, explain the key facts in each case (do not try to answer the questions yet).

## Task

1 Work in groups. Choose one story which interests you. Look at the question at the end of the story and make notes individually under the following headings:

| arguments for | arguments against |
|---|---|
|  |  |

Ask your teacher about any words and phrases you need and write them in your *Personal vocabulary* box. Look at the phrases in the *Useful language* box to help you.

2 Compare and discuss your list of arguments with the rest of your group. Try to reach an agreement about the right decision. Spend a few minutes individually thinking about how you will explain your decision (and the arguments for and against it) to the rest of the class.

3 Listen to the other groups' decisions, and their arguments for and against. Do you agree with them or not? Have any of their arguments convinced you to change your mind?

4 🔊 [11.2] Listen to three people discussing one of the stories and answer the following questions:

a Which case are they discussing?
b What are the main arguments for or against that each person gives?
c Who do you agree with?

# Part B **Language**

Talking about hypothetical situations
Talking about hypothetical situations in the past
**Real life:** giving and reporting opinions
**Wordspot:** *have*

## Language focus 1

### Talking about hypothetical situations

Read the text below and discuss the questions in groups.

- Do you see anything wrong with people having these treatments if they want to?
- Would you ever consider having any of them yourself?
- Should such treatments be provided free by the state?
- Do you know of any other cosmetic treatments now available?

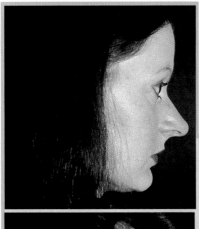

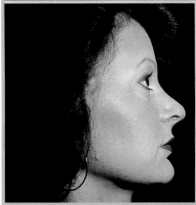

## Analysis

**1** Look at the verb forms in the tables and mark them:
(✔) if you know the verb form is grammatically possible.
(✗) if the verb form is grammatically wrong.
(?) if you are unsure and need to ask your teacher.

**a**

| If I | had | enough money, I | could | have cosmetic surgery |
| | would have | | might | on my teeth. |
| | | | would | |
| | | | will | |

**b**

| If only I | am | taller! Life | is | so much easier! |
| | was | | will be | |
| | were | | would be | |

**c**

| I wish | I wasn't bald! |
| | they could cure baldness! |
| | my hair would grow back! |

**d**

| Suppose that you | could choose | how intelligent your child | was. |
| Imagine that you | can choose | | is. |

**e**

| It's time people | change | their attitude to plastic surgery! |
| | changed | |
| | would change | |

**2** Look at the verbs underlined and choose the correct explanation for the use of the past form:
- they are talking about a past situation.
- they are talking about a hypothetical (imaginary) situation.
In each case can you explain why the situation is hypothetical?

**3** Look at the sentences where there is more than one correct possibility. What (if any) is the difference between these forms?

*Now read Language summary A on pages 159-160.*

# Interfering with nature?

As well as curing or preventing illness and disease, these days drugs and surgery can be used to alter or improve many more superficial problems too. The following treatments are either already available or soon may be:
- cosmetic surgery to reshape and rebuild your teeth.
- plastic surgery to alter the shape of your nose, cheekbones, stomach or breasts.
- injections to enlarge your lips or get rid of frown lines on your forehead.
- drugs to treat baldness and to stop you going grey.
- treatments to make you grow taller, or prevent further growth in people who are already tall.
- liposuction to remove fat from the thighs, stomach, etc.
- genetic engineering, enabling you to choose characteristics in your children such as hair colour, height or even their level of intelligence!

## Practice

**1 a)** Look at the picture. Match the balloons to the appropriate people.

I wish I could have a cigarette.

He's right, it really is time I gave up. I would give it up, if I could.

I wish he'd shut up.

It's time they banned smoking in public places.

**b)** Look at the pictures below. What are the people thinking or saying? Make sentences using:

| If | If only | I wish | It's time | Suppose |
|----|---------|--------|-----------|---------|

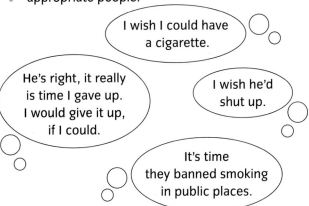

**2** Read the rules and then play the game *Imagine!*

## Imagine!

**1** Either: work in groups of three (A, B or C) or: work in three teams (A, B and C).

**2** Student A / Team A looks at the questions on page 144. Student B / Team B looks at the questions on page 145. Student C / Team C looks at the questions on page 146.

**3** Look at the questions and, if necessary, check the meaning of any words or phrases in your mini-dictionary or with your teacher.

**4** Take turns to read out your questions, starting with Team A / Student A.

**5** The other students have thirty seconds to think about their answer. They should think about:
- the possible consequences in each case.
- any new problems that would arise in those circumstances.
Be as original and imaginative as you can!

**6** After thirty seconds the person who read out the question chooses one student to answer.

**7** He / She speaks for thirty seconds about the topic. Afterwards, other students can add their ideas.

**8** Make sure that everyone in the group / class has an equal opportunity to speak.

### Follow-up task

**1** Which topics from the game *Imagine!* is the student writing about?

> I think it would change life more than we imagine. On the positive side, the economy would benefit; companies would save money because they would not waste so many days through sickness. The health service would certainly be better off: if doctors spent less time on people with minor illnesses, they would have more time for seriously ill patients.
>
> On the other hand, medicine companies would lose out, as people would buy fewer aspirin and other such drugs, causing unemployment. However, for me, the worst consequence would be that people would have no excuse for not doing things they didn't want to: no reason for the occasional day off work, or for missing a boring party. I think this would cause so many problems that before long, new ailments would appear to take the place in our lives of the ▓▓▓▓▓▓▓▓▓▓

**2** Choose one of the other topics discussed above. Write one or two paragraphs about the possible effects in a similar way. Ask your teacher for any words or phrases you need.

**125**

# Language focus 2

Talking about hypothetical situations in the past

Read about Sylvie's tattoo. Why did she have it done? How does she feel about it now?

At the age of nineteen, and to the horror of her parents, Sylvie had a heart tattooed on her shoulder. Eight years later, a lot has changed in Sylvie's life, but the tattoo is still there. How does she feel about it now?

" Well, one decision I now regret is getting this tattoo. I'd always liked the idea of having one. I really thought they looked good and some of my friends had them. I felt a bit scared about how much it would hurt, and I knew that my parents would hate the idea, but one day I got this done. It seemed like a really good idea at the time, my boyfriend really liked it and I think if he hadn't been so keen I wouldn't have done it. My parents were completely horrified, of course. I remember my dad saying he'd never seen a girl with a tattoo, and he hoped he never would again, but they sort of accepted it in the end. Now, I wish I'd thought more about it, especially the fact that you can't get rid of it, or it's incredibly painful and expensive anyway, so I suppose I'm stuck with it now. "

## Analysis

1 Find four examples of the Past Perfect tense in the text about Sylvie and underline them. Why is the Past Perfect used in each case:
   a to describe events **before** a point of time in the past?
   b for reported speech?
   c to talk about a hypothetical or unreal situation in the past?

2 Look at the verbs in **bold**. Do they refer to past or present time?
   a • *I wish I **had thought** about it more!*
      • *I wish I **didn't have** this tattoo!*
   b • *If (only) it **wasn't** so expensive and painful, I **would get** rid of it.*
      • *If (only) my boyfriend **hadn't been** so keen, I **wouldn't have done** it.*
      • *If I **had taken** more notice of my parents, I **wouldn't be** in this situation.*

*Now read Language summary B on page 160.*

## Practice

1 Here are four people who regret things they did or didn't do. Make sentences about them using the following phrases:

• Perhaps / probably if ...
• Perhaps he / she wishes ...

**For example:**

*Perhaps if Patrick hadn't got married so young, he and his wife wouldn't have got divorced.*

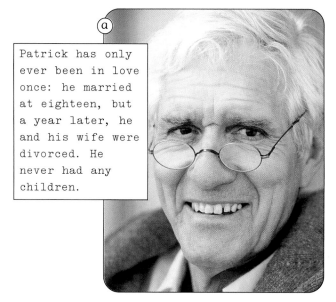

(a)

Patrick has only ever been in love once: he married at eighteen, but a year later, he and his wife were divorced. He never had any children.

(b)

> Charles left school at sixteen. Although he's now a successful businessman, he's sorry he never got a university education.

(c)

> Oona met a gorgeous Italian man while she was on holiday. He asked her to go out with him, but she was too shy and they never saw each other again.

(d)

> Two years ago, Elaine gave up her £70,000-a-year job as a company director to work for a charity for homeless people on a salary of £20,000 a year. As a result, she has changed her lifestyle a lot, including moving house, and selling her Porsche.

**2** Make at least eight true sentences of your own. Use the phrases below to help you. Compare answers.

a   I wish I could ... *sing better.*
b   If I could change one thing about my appearance, I ...
c   If only I had a ...
d   I wish I knew more about ...
e   I wish my husband / mother / boyfriend / sister / friend, etc. would / wouldn't ...
f   I really wish I / (*someone else*) ... hadn't ...
g   If I'd been able to see into the future when I was ... years old, I ...
h   If only this school / my boss / my parents / ...
i   It's time the government / people in this country / (*another group of people*) started / stopped ...
j   I bet ... (*a famous person*) ... wishes ...

# Real life

## Giving and reporting opinions

**1** ⌨ [11.3] Some people were asked their opinion about these issues:

a   Should smoking in the workplace be banned?
b   Should it be illegal to pay a surrogate mother?
c   Should experiments on animals be banned?

For each person, write in the table which issue they were asked about and their answer.

| No. | Which issue? | yes / no / not sure |
|-----|--------------|---------------------|
| 1 | | |
| 2 | | |
| 3 | | |
| 4 | | |
| 5 | | |
| 6 | | |

**2** Match the phrases in box A to the appropriate words in box B. Is each phrase used:

a   to introduce your own opinion?
b   to report someone else's opinion?
c   to say you're not sure about something?

| A | B |
|---|---|
| As far as ... | doubt that ... |
| Many people ... | honest ... |
| I'm absolutely ... | me ... |
| To be ... | I'm concerned ... |
| I've no ... | often said that ... |
| I haven't really ... | convinced that ... |
| If you ask ... | thought about it ... |
| It's ... | would say that ... |

# Pronunciation

**1** ⌨ [11.4] Write in the phrase that is used at the beginning of each sentence. Are any words particularly stressed?

a   _____ we should go ahead!
b   _____ , I don't care one way or the other.
c   _____ , there's nothing more to say.
d   _____ that what you say is true.
e   _____ the answer is obvious.

**2** Listen again and practise saying the sentences, copying the stress and intonation.

**3** Look at the tapescript on page 175 and underline other phrases for giving your opinion.

# Wordspot

*have*

**1** Put the phrases in the box into groups with a similar meaning / construction. There are three phrases in each group. Use the diagram in Exercise 2 to help you if necessary.

| | |
|---|---|
| have a dance | have your car repaired |
| have your coat on | have the window open |
| have an infection | have treatment |
| have your jacket cleaned | have a swim |
| have your bicycle stolen | have a look |
| have your house painted | have a strong influence |
| have the radio on | have your house burgled |
| have an important effect | have your car broken into |
| have serious consequences | have a pain in your chest |
| have a sore throat | have an operation | have surgery |

**2** Put the phrases in the correct place on the diagram. Add one more phrase to each group.

**3 a)** Why do you:

- take your car to the garage?
- visit the dentist?
- go to a plastic surgeon?
- go to the hairdresser's and beautician's?

Use *to have something done* in your answers.

**For example:**

*You might take your car to the garage to have the brakes checked.*

**b)** Rephrase the sentences in A using *have*. Start with the words in B.

**For example:**

*The hairdresser's doing my hair at 2 p.m.*    *I'm having my hair done at 2 p.m.*

| A | B |
|---|---|
| 1 At work, we listen to the radio. | At work, we usually .......................... . |
| 2 Shall we dance? | Shall we ..........................? |
| 3 Someone stole my car last week. | I .......................... . |
| 4 She was wearing a red hat. | She .......................... . |
| 5 His shoulder was painful. | He .......................... . |
| 6 They are going to operate on my hip. | I .......................... . |
| 7 The door of her bedroom was locked. | She .......................... . |
| 8 His throat felt sore. | He .......................... . |
| 9 The weather can affect your mood. | The weather .......................... . |
| 10 His uncle influenced him strongly. | His uncle.......................... . |
| 11 My bedroom window is always open at night. | I always .......................... . |
| 12 The consequences of this will be serious. | This will .......................... . |
| 13 I'm only joking! | I'm only .......................... . |

**4** Copy the diagram in Exercise 2 and make a poster for your classroom wall.

# Do you remember?

**How do you pronounce the following words? Practise saying them correctly.**

> blood  a cure  a disease  muscles
> surgery  a species  treatment
> a virus

**Work in pairs. Find the odd one out in the groups. Explain why.**

a) hips  joints  elbows  knees
b) deafness  blindness
   colour blindness  baldness
c) a side-effect  a disease
   an infection  a virus
d) organs  liver  kidneys
   heart
e) surgery  treatment
   prevention  cure
f) risks  consequences  effects
   implications

**Find mistakes in the use of the verb forms in two of the sentences and correct them.**

a) I really wish I could write better in English.
b) Imagine if you could eat whatever you wanted without putting on any weight! Wouldn't it be wonderful!
c) Come on – it's time we go home now, we need to get some sleep.
d) I wish I'd had as much confidence as her when I was her age!

e) If only we had a bit more time to do everything, it would be so much easier.
f) I wish Roberto would stop snoring – he's making a terrible noise!
g) If only the traffic hadn't been so bad, we would catch the 10.45 train like we planned to, and we wouldn't have had all these problems.
h) Just think how different your life would have been if you'd had children in your early twenties like Helena did.

**Answer the following questions with complete sentences, using phrases with *have*. Either write your answers or ask and answer in pairs.**

a) What clothes have you got on today?
b) Have you got the door or window open at the moment? Have you got any music on?
c) Have you ever had anything stolen, or had your house burgled?
d) Have you got any aches and pains at the moment? Do you have many colds and sore throats or not?
e) Have you ever had an operation? Would you ever consider having plastic surgery?
f) Who (apart from your parents!) has had a strong influence on you?

**Look at the verbs in the box. Are the noun forms of these words the same or different? Write down any nouns which are different and mark the stress.**

> to affect  to ban  to burn  to cure
> to discover  to grow  to influence
> to operate  to prevent  to remove
> to regret  to risk  to treat
> to transplant

| verb | noun |
|------|------|
| *to treat* | ●<br>*treatment* |

# module 12
# Media, money and power

## Part A  Task

Vocabulary and speaking: the media

Speaking and listening: the media game

Preparation for task: newspaper articles

Task: summarise and discuss the newspaper article

## Vocabulary and speaking

### The media

**1** Think of some examples of these forms of media in your country. Which are the most popular at the moment? Do you read / watch them yourself? Which are your favourites?

| |
|---|
| tabloid newspapers |
| serious newspapers |
| fashion magazines |
| game shows |
| television commercials |
| soap operas |
| violent crime series |
| television news bulletins |
| television documentaries |
| weather bulletins |
| real life dramas (such as emergency rescues) |
| cartoons |

**2 a)** If necessary, check the meaning of the words and phrases in **bold** in your mini-dictionary or with your teacher.

**b)** In groups, discuss which of these comments might be made about each of the forms of media in Exercise 1. Explain your reasons if necessary.

| |
|---|
| their approach tends to be very **sensational** and sometimes **irresponsible** |
| the reporting is very **biased** |
| the reporting is usually **objective** and **accurate** |
| they can be very **misleading** |
| they're **harmless** fun |
| the information they provide is usually **reliable** |
| they **are mainly aimed at** women / men / children |
| they can **influence** the way people think and behave |
| they **raise** important **issues** sometimes |
| they **make** people more **aware of** what's going on in the world |
| they can **cause** a lot of **harm** |
| they can be very **entertaining** |
| they really **annoy** me sometimes |

# Speaking and listening

**1** Work in groups of three or four. Play the game. You will need a dice, some coins and a watch. Who is the winner in each group?

| | | | | |
|---|---|---|---|---|
| **FINISH** | go back 4 spaces | miss a turn | Talk for one minute about news photographers. | go to FINISH |
| Talk for one minute about television documentaries. | Talk for one minute about the programmes you liked best when you were a child. | You have thirty seconds to list ten famous cartoon characters. | go on 2 spaces | Talk for one minute about the things you read / don't read in the newspaper. |
| Talk for one minute about sport on television. | miss a turn | go on 1 space | You have twenty seconds to list five famous television crime series. | Talk for one minute about the weather forecast on the television in your country. |
| Talk for one minute about violence on television. | go on 2 spaces | Talk for one minute about listening to the radio. | Talk for one minute about the advantages of having satellite television. | go back to START |
| go back 2 spaces | You have thirty seconds to name three stories that are in the news at the moment. | miss a turn | Talk for one minute about women's magazines. | Talk for one minute about television commercials that you really like or hate. |
| **START** | Talk for 1 minute about your favourite television programme. | Talk for 1 minute about your favourite newspaper or magazine. | go on 3 spaces | You have twenty seconds to list 4 different ways you can find out the news. |

**2** [12.1] Listen to some people talking about the topics in the game and answer the questions.

a  Which topics were they talking about?
b  What were the main points that they made?
c  Do you agree with them?

**Personal vocabulary**

## Task: summarise and discuss a newspaper article

**Who's the weaker sex now?**

**More women than men are becoming the main breadwinner. Is your partner coping with the sexual revolution?**

From *Bella*

**STUDY PROVES POWER OF TV ADVERTISING**

From *The Independent*

# A nation of shopaholics

One in five people are addicted to shopping

From *The Daily Mail*

### Useful language

**Phrases for summarising the article**

"This article is all about ... "

"This article describes ... "

"Basically, what happened is this ... "

"The main point it's making is that  ... "

"According to the article ... "

"The article claims that ... "

"Apparently ... "

**Questions arising from the article**

"The question that struck us is this ... "

"The main issue I think it raises is this ... "

"What interests me, is whether or not ... "

"I'd be interested to know what other people think about ... "

# Woman banker stole £100,000 for clothes

From *The Daily Mail*

## Preparation for task

**1** Look at the newspaper headlines. If necessary, check the meaning of any words in your mini-dictionary or with your teacher. Can you guess what each story is about? Compare answers with other students.

**2** The words and phrases in the box are important for understanding the articles. If necessary, check the meaning of any words, then discuss with your partner which article(s) they come from.

> peak time viewing / viewers    to authorise a loan
> your disposable income    a spending spree
> financial ruin    a purchase    consumer debt
> conclusive proof    to be unfulfilled

**3 a)** 🔲 [12.2] Listen to someone summarising the main points of one of the articles.

1 Which article had he read?
2 What else did you find out about the article?
3 What questions did he ask at the end?
4 What is your opinion about these issues?

**b)** Read the article he was summarising on page 141 and underline the points he mentioned. Did he mention everything in the article? Why not?

## Task

**1 a)** Work in pairs or groups. Your teacher will give each group an article to read (article 1 on page 143, article 2 on page 144, article 3 on page 145. Read it carefully, using your mini-dictionary to check any words if necessary.

**b)** Discuss the following with students who read the same article as you:
1 Who is the article about / What events does it describe?
2 What are the most important claims / suggestions made in the article?
3 Are there any important statistics or examples which illustrate these?

**2 a)** Your group is going to summarise the article for other students in the class, like the man on the cassette did. Remember, you do not have to include everything. Discuss with your partners what you will say. Ask your teacher for any useful words and phrases and write them in your *Personal vocabulary* box.

**b)** Think of one or two interesting questions arising from the article that you would like to discuss with other students. These can either be personal questions (like *Do you think advertising influences what you buy?*) or more general questions (like *If it has been proved that advertising works, should we ban adverts for harmful products like alcohol?*).

**3** Spend a few minutes, either individually or with your partner, practising how you will summarise your article for the class. Look at the phrases in the *Useful language* box to help you.

**4** Work in groups with students who have read different articles. Listen to a summary of each article and to the questions that the other students ask. Give your own opinions and responses.

# Part B **Language**

Reporting people's exact words
Verbs that summarise what people say
Wordspot: *speak* and *talk*

## Language focus 1
Reporting people's exact words

**1 a)** In groups, discuss the following questions.

- What do you know about Oprah Winfrey?
- Have you ever seen her show? What did you think of it?
- Do you have similar shows in your country?

**b)** Read about the famous court case in which Oprah Winfrey was involved after an interview on her show. Check any words in your mini-dictionary or with your teacher.

**2** The extracts on the right come from a newspaper article written at the end of the trial. Read them and discuss the following questions in pairs.

a   Which of the comments were made:
  - during the programme?
  - after the programme?
  - after the trial?
b   At the time of the programme, had there been any cases of BSE in the United States?
c   Which of Oprah Winfrey's comments do you think were especially damaging for the cattle farmers? Why?
d   Did the farmers win their case?
e   Who do you sympathise with, Oprah Winfrey or the cattle farmers?
f   In cases like this, why is it important that newspapers report exactly what the people said?

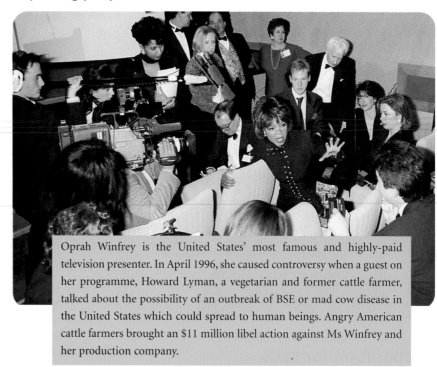

Oprah Winfrey is the United States' most famous and highly-paid television presenter. In April 1996, she caused controversy when a guest on her programme, Howard Lyman, a vegetarian and former cattle farmer, talked about the possibility of an outbreak of BSE or mad cow disease in the United States which could spread to human beings. Angry American cattle farmers brought an $11 million libel action against Ms Winfrey and her production company.

# Oprah triumphs over Texan cattle farmers

① Howard Lyman said that while there had been no documented cases of mad cow disease in the United States, it was bound to strike if it had not already.

② Ms Winfrey asked Mr Lyman if he believed that an outbreak of BSE in the United States would make AIDS look like the common cold.

③ He agreed that it would.

④ Ms Winfrey responded that Mr Lyman had just stopped her from eating another burger.

⑤ Angry Texan farmers accused Ms Winfrey of defaming beef, and claimed that the programme had sent beef prices to a ten-year low.

⑥ Ms Winfrey said the verdict was a victory not just for her and not just for free speech but for Afro-American civil rights and even for God.

⑦ The National Cattlemen's Association issued a statement saying it was disappointed with the verdict. 'In today's world of instant communication the impact of misinformation can be devastating,' the group told reporters.

⑧ Ms Winfrey remained defiant. 'I will continue to use my voice ... I refuse to be muzzled. I will not change the way I operate,' she told reporters.

From *The Independent* / *The Guardian*

# Analysis

**1** Find five examples of reported speech in the extracts. What were the person's words? What are the differences between reported and direct speech in the following areas:
a verb forms?   b word order of questions?

**2** Find two examples of direct speech. How can they be reported?

**3** Find four more verbs in the extracts used for reporting people's exact words.

*say* ____   ____   ____   ____

Use your mini-dictionary to check which constructions can be used after each.

**4** Look at how another newspaper reported one of the extracts. Why hasn't the tense changed?

> Oprah said afterwards that she will not change the way she operates.

***Now read Language summary A on pages 160-161.***

## Practice

**1** Here are some more statements reported from the Oprah trial. Are the following correct?

• the use of tenses and word order.
• what follows the reporting verb (*if, to, that*, etc.).

a Ms Winfrey asked Mr Lyman ~~did he know~~ *if he knew* of any cases of BSE in cattle in the United States.

b After Oprah Winfrey's show, many people said they will stop eating beef.

c During the trial, a lawyer asked Ms Winfrey did she realise the effect her remarks will have.

d Ms Winfrey told the court she was only exercising her right to free speech.

e Afterwards reporters asked Ms Winfrey how did she feel during the trial.

f The forewoman of the jury told to reporters that the jury hadn't liked what they had decided, but that they felt that legally they had no choice.

g Another jury member told journalists she felt that so many rights have disappeared in the United States that freedom of speech is the only one left.

**2** **a)** In everyday life people often report what others have said, but not always accurately!

• What is happening in the situations opposite?
• What does each speaker claim has been said?

① Earlier on I chatted to Tammy Beauregard, the star of the film, about rumours that she is pregnant. She told me this was nonsense and that she will never have children because of her career.

② Your mother phoned about half an hour ago. She said she'd call back tonight some time.

③ She said I'd taken some money from her purse!

④ Do you know what! My boss asked me if I wanted to go out for dinner with her tonight. I told her she must be joking!

⑤ It's my turn!

Mum said I can play for as long as I like and that you've got to wait until I've finished.

**b)** [12.3] Listen and correct what was said:

*Actually, she said ...*

You do not have to report every word, provided that the content is correct.

**135**

# Language focus 2

## Verbs that summarise what people say

Below are quotes from different people talking to the press. Who said what? Choose from the following:

1 a rock star.
2 the mother of a kidnap victim.
3 a politician.
4 the manager of a sports team.

a 'Please, please return our daughter to us safely. Please don't do anything to hurt her.' ☐

b 'Yeah, okay, it's true I have taken drugs, but I'm not the only one — everyone in this business takes them, you know that.' ☐

c 'The minister has lied to Parliament about his financial affairs. He has lied again, and again, and again.' ☐

d 'The economic mess this country finds itself in was caused by the misguided policies of the previous government.' ☐

e 'United deserved their success today, I can only say well done to them: brilliant, great result!' ☐

f 'No, I will not resign. Despite our poor results in recent matches, I will continue in this job as long as I can. I have no intention of resigning.' ☐

g 'If you journalists don't go away and leave me alone, I'll call the police!' ☐

h 'The government will investigate all allegations of corruption, I can assure you of that.' ☐

i 'I would ask the media not to interfere in our negotiations with the people who have our daughter. Our main concern is her safety, we don't want to put her life at risk.' ☐

j 'There is absolutely no truth in the allegation that I have shown favouritism towards certain players: it is complete and utter nonsense!' ☐

## Analysis

1 Look at the way the first two quotes were reported in the news. Why isn't every word quoted? Which verbs summarise what has been said? What construction is used after these verbs?

   a *The mother of the victim begged the kidnappers not to harm her daughter.*

   b *The rock star admitted having taken drugs, claiming that everyone in the rock music business takes them.*

2 a Match the other quotes to one of these verbs:
   *threaten   refuse   deny   promise blame   urge   accuse   congratulate*

   b Use your mini-dictionary to check the construction that follows each verb. Then make a sentence like the ones above reporting what was said. Omit any unnecessary phrases.

3 Use your mini-dictionary to check the meaning of these verbs and the construction used with them. Write down an example sentence using each verb showing the construction that it takes.
   *suggest   warn   insist   agree   persuade conclude   order   assure   offer   decide*

*Now read Language summary B on page 161.*

## Practice

**1** If necessary, check the meaning of these phrases in your mini-dictionary, then scan through the story and answer the questions.

> to play bingo    to win the jackpot    to split your winnings
> to be entitled to something    to take someone to court
> an unwritten agreement

a What was the relationship between Maureen Benn and Rosemary Morecombe?

b Why did they end up in court?

c Who won the case?

# Bingo! Bang goes a beautiful friendship!

Leeds Crown Court yesterday heard the story of Maureen Benn and Rosemary Morecombe, next-door neighbours and best friends, who played bingo together every Thursday night for over seven years. From the beginning, the two women (a *agree / split*) any money they won fifty-fifty, and this system worked perfectly until one evening, three years ago, Mrs Morecombe managed to win the National Jackpot — a total of over £42,000!
At first she (b *assure / friend / share*) the winnings as usual, and both women went home excitedly planning how they would spend the money. However, by the next day, Mrs Morecombe had changed her mind. She (c *offer / give Mrs Benn*) a quarter of the £42,000, but Mrs Benn (d *refuse / accept*) anything less than half. Mr Morecombe, attempting to keep the peace between the two angry women, (e *suggest / wife / give / friend*) a third of the money instead, but Mrs Benn still (f *insist / be entitled*) to an equal share. She (g *claim / they / have*) an unwritten agreement to share their winnings, and (h *threaten / take*) her neighbour to court, if she did not hand over the full amount.

**2** Use the words in brackets to complete the sentences.

**3** Do you think the judge was right? What would you have done in Mrs Morecombe or Mrs Benn's position?

> Husband Ronnie Benn, 34, tried to (i *persuade / his wife / accept/ Mrs Morecombe's offer*), but Mrs Benn (j *refuse / give up*) and so eventually this week the case appeared in court, although by this time Mr Benn had (k *decide / leave*) his wife, unable to bear the financial and emotional pressure of the lawsuit any longer.
> The judge, Annabel Archer QC, listened as Mrs Benn (l *accuse / former friend / cheat / her*) while for her part, Mrs Morecombe (m *deny / enter into / agreement*) with Mrs Benn. After hearing both sides of the story, Ms Archer (n *conclude / Mrs Benn be right*), there had been an unwritten agreement, and she (o *order / Mrs Morecombe / pay / Mrs Benn*) £21,000 plus £6,000 interest.
> Speaking to reporters as they left the court, Mrs Morecombe (p *complain / judge / treat / her*) unfairly and (q *confess / not know*) how she would repay the money which had all been spent on a new kitchen and holidays abroad. However, Mrs Benn a mother of three, who works as a supermarket cashier, (r *insist / she / suffer*) the most of the two, having lost not only her best friend, but also her husband, as a result of the dispute.

·········································

## *Follow-up task*

**1a** The article above is often described as a 'human interest' story. *Either*: find a similar human interest story in a newspaper or a magazine (the original story can be in your own language). Read it carefully and think about how you could summarise it in English for the other students in your class.
*or*: think about a similar story you know yourself, either a dispute involving money, or a dispute between neighbours (it could even be a personal story). Think about how you could tell the story in English for the other students in your class.

**b** Ask your teacher about any words or phrases you need to help you tell the story.

**2** Work in groups. Take turns to tell your stories. Listen to the other students' stories. What is your reaction to each? Who do you think was right in each case?

·········································

# Wordspot

## *speak* and *talk*

**1** Answer the following questions in pairs or small groups. If necessary, check the meaning of the phrases in **bold** with your teacher first.

a Which are the most popular **talk shows** in your country at the moment? Do you like them, or not?

b How many **English speaking** countries can you think of? What about **French speaking** ones?

c Name three languages you **don't speak a word of**.

d Do you have a loud voice, or do people often tell you to **speak up**?

e If someone asks you to do something that you don't want to do, are you the kind of person who finds it difficult to say no, or can you usually manage to **talk your way out of it**?

f Are you good at **talking** other people **into** doing things they don't want to do?

g Do you agree with the saying '**actions speak louder than words**'?

h Are you the kind of person who likes to **speak your mind**, or do you tend to keep your opinions to yourself?

i Are you normally good at **small talk**, or is it something you dread?

j Which public figures in your country do you think really **talk sense**? Which ones **talk rubbish** in your opinion?

**2** Add the phrases in **bold** from the questions to the diagrams. Check the meaning of any phrases on the diagrams that you don't already know.

**3** Work in pairs.

**a)** Student A looks at the card on page 144 and reads out the definitions. Student B answers using a phrase with *speak*.

**b)** Student B looks at the card on page 146 and reads out the definitions. Student A answers using a phrase with *talk*.

**4** Make a poster for your classroom wall using the diagrams in Exercise 2 to remind you of the uses of *talk* and *speak*.

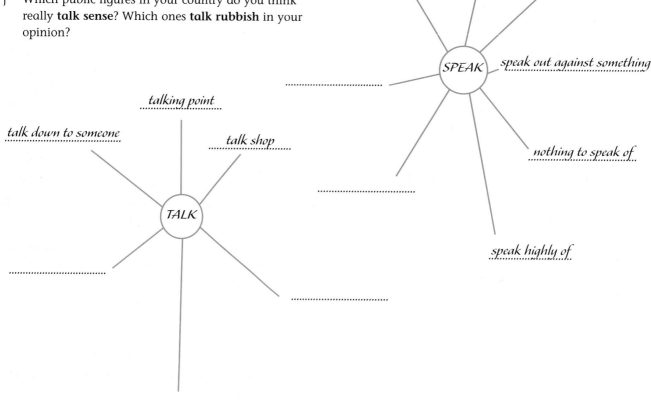

*talking point*

*talk down to someone*

*talk shop*

TALK

SPEAK

*speak out against something*

*nothing to speak of*

*speak highly of*

# Consolidation

## modules 9–12

## A Speaking: future forms

**1 Work in pairs. Each pair chooses a topic. You must include a sentence in your conversation which you will find on the page given next to the topic.**

### Conversation topics

**2 Practise your conversation in pairs, including the sentence as naturally as possible.**

**3 Act out your conversations for the class. If the other students can guess what the sentence was, they win. If they guess incorrectly, you win.**

## B Grammar and speaking: modals and hypothetical forms

**1 The speakers below are imagining themselves in the following situations. Read the texts quickly and say which situation each speaker is discussing.**

- a person who has won the lottery
- one of the first astronauts to go into space
- a person in prison for a crime he / she didn't commit
- a survivor of a terrible disaster like the Titanic

**1** I suppose at first they _must have been_ (be) incredibly relieved to be alive, but after that I imagine perhaps that they _might have felt_ (feel) guilty about the others who didn't survive. They (a) _____ (think) that they (b) _____ (do) more to help them, or that there were other people who deserved to survive more than they did. It (c) _____ (be) a terrible experience.

**2** It (d) _____ (be) unimaginably frustrating – the sense of unfairness, and helplessness. I think I (e) _____ (get) very depressed in that situation. I (f) _____ (go) a bit crazy, even.

**3** They (g) _____ (be) incredibly brave. There (h) _____ (be) an accident at any moment, and they (i) _____ (be) blown to pieces in space, with no chance of survival.

**4** It (j) _____ (be) very strange. I imagine that at first you (k) _____ (feel) fantastic, knowing that you can buy whatever you want, that you don't have to go to work, or whatever, but your life (l) _____ (change) an awful lot. Your friends (m) _____ (start) behaving differently towards you, and with all that money you (n) _____ (lose) your motivation and sense of purpose in life. You (o) _____ (end up with) a lot of problems.

**5** If I (p) _____ (be) one of their wives or children, I think I (q) _____ (be) terrified, knowing that the person you loved was all that distance away in such a completely unknown situation, and maybe I (r) _____ (feel) a bit angry too because they had chosen to put their life at risk like that.

**6** I think if it (s) _____ (happen) to a member of my family or a close friend, it (t) _____ (be) quite difficult. I (u) _____ (get) jealous, you just don't know. I (v) _____ (feel) as if I had a right to some of their money. Who knows what would happen to our relationship.

**2a Put the verbs in brackets into appropriate forms. There may be more than one possibility.**

**b** 🖳 **[1] Listen and compare your answers with what the people actually said.**

**3a Write sentences or short paragraphs of your own. Imagine that you are in an extraordinary situation. Either write more about some of the people in Exercise 1, or about some of these people.**

- Someone who became a superstar at a very young age (for example, Michael Jackson).
- A couple who, as a result of fertility treatment, have sextuplets.
- A person being harassed by a stalker.
- An ordinary person whose husband or wife suddenly became famous with thousands of fans.

- A footballer who missed a vital penalty for his country in an important World Cup match.
- A soldier coming home after a war.
- A person who has been deaf or blind all his / her life who is suddenly able to see or hear.

**b Think about how the person must feel, what they might do, and what other people involved in the situation might feel. Start your sentences like this:**

*It must / can't / might be / have been*
*They must / can't / might be / have been*
*If I was / had been, I would / would have*
*Perhaps they feel as if they should / should have*

**4 Compare and discuss your answers.**

## C Listening and grammar: reported speech

**1 Look at the pictures. What is happening in each picture? In which picture would you expect someone to:**

| | |
|---|---|
| promise to do something | refuse to do something |
| threaten to do something | insist on doing something |
| agree to do something | suggest something |
| persuade someone to do something | |
| apologise for something | deny doing something |
| blame someone for something | |

**2 ⌑ [2] Listen to the conversations. Use the verbs in the box to summarise what was said in each conversation. Use each verb at least once. (You can also use *say*, *tell* and *ask* if you prefer.)**

The hotel manager ...          The guest ...
The first driver ...          The second driver ...

## D Vocabulary: alphabet quiz

**1 Work in pairs. Complete the sentences with words from Modules 9-12. (The first letter of each word is given, and the number in brackets refers to the Module in which the word appears.)**

1 Most people nowadays are a _ _ _ _ of the link between smoking and cancer. (12)
2 The President's speech was b _ _ _ _ _ _ _ _ live on television and radio. (10)
3 Scientists have spent many years searching for a c _ _ _ for AIDS. (11)
4 The church was badly d _ _ _ _ _ _ in a serious earthquake three years ago. (9)
5 Nobody knows for sure why dinosaurs became e _ _ _ _ _ _ millions of years ago. (9)
6 This photo is rather f _ _ _ _ _ _ _ _ _ : she's much less attractive when you meet her in real life. (12)
7 Although many people are afraid of spiders, they are actually quite h _ _ _ _ _ _ _ . (12)
8 Immigration is one of the most controversial i _ _ _ _ _ facing the government. (12)
9 The case will be heard by a panel of j _ _ _ _ _ at the Court of International Law. (11)
10 The cause of death was acute k _ _ _ _ _ failure. (11)
11 Claiming that the newspaper article was full of lies, the minister has threatened to sue for l _ _ _ _ . (12)
12 It snowed during the night, but when the sun came out it soon m _ _ _ _ _ . (9)
13 This is a fantastic o _ _ _ _ _ _ _ _ _ _ ; it's always been my dream to visit India! (10)
14 The festival begins with a p _ _ _ _ _ _ _ _ through the streets, with everyone in fancy dress. (10)
15 There is an intense r _ _ _ _ _ _ between supporters of the two clubs – they desperately want to beat each other in the league. (10)
16 Unfortunately, my pullover has s _ _ _ _ _ in the wash, so it doesn't fit any more. (9)
17 Graham is off work today – apparently he's got a sore t _ _ _ _ _ _ . (11)
18 It was rather embarrassing that his painting was hung u _ _ _ _ _ d _ _ _ and no-one noticed! (9)
19 It's common for babies to be v _ _ _ _ _ _ _ _ _ to protect them from diseases such as measles. (11)
20 I w _ _ _ _ _ him about the dangers of hang-gliding, but he refused to listen! (12)

**2 Work in pairs. Find five more words and write clues for them. Take turns to read out your clues and see if the other students can remember the words.**

# Communication
## activities

## Module 1: Exercise 3, page 7

### Student A

| | |
|---|---|
| a | How have cars changed since they were invented? |
| b | How have computers and technology changed since you were younger? |
| c | How would you describe the role of women in society today? |
| d | How will the economic situation in your country change in the future? |

## Module 1: page 10

**ANSWERS**

**1a** Formula 1 driver **b** taxi driver **c** Present Simple (*I drive*) used for permanent situations; Present Continuous (*I'm driving*) used for temporary situations.

**2** Because they describe states. Some common state verbs are: *have; see; remember; believe; agree; want; love; hate.*

**3b** *He's being* very unfriendly. (= at the moment; it's not his usual state) **d** *What are you thinking*? (= what's in your mind at the moment? / *What do you think*? = what is your opinion?)

**4a** *she was ice-skating / we were sitting* **b** No. **c** Maybe.

**5b** Present Perfect shows past action which is still relevant in the present (her hair is different now).

**6** *She's worked…* with diagram **a** (action continues until the present). / *She worked…* with diagram **b** (action is finished / completed period in the past).

**7** *They'd known* each other for a long time shows an action **before a particular point in the past** so it must be completed with a past verb form (before they started going out). / *They've known* each other for a long time shows an action in the past which still continues in the present so it must be completed with a present verb (but they **don't get on very well**).

**8a** *I'll answer it.* You are deciding as you speak.
**b** *I'm having a party…* The party is already arranged.

**9a** *get* home / *can*, etc. **b** *phone* him / *speak* to her, etc. Verb in present after time words *as soon as, until, when,* etc.

**10** Sentences **b** and **d** really refer to the past. Both **a** and **c** refer to hypothetical situations in the present.

## Module 10: Exercise 2, page 111

**Chairperson**
It is your job to make sure everyone speaks, and the needs of different groups are balanced in the final decisions. You should make sure that the decisions are practical, and easy to organise. If the committee cannot agree, you make the final decision. Introduce the members of the committee to each other.

**Useful language**
• **For introducing people**
"This is … / I'd like to introduce … (name + role on the committee)."
• **For asking opinions / reaching agreement**
"Does anyone have anything to add?"
"Does anyone want to say anything else?"
"So I think we all agree that …"

## Module 12: Exercise 3, page 133

### Study proves power of TV advertising

Television advertising really does work, according to the most detailed study yet of the links between commercials and shopping habits.

Researchers claim to have found the first 'conclusive proof' that watching an advert makes you more likely to pick a particular product, after a hi-tech investigation into the influence of television. The survey found that people who watch the most television were most responsive to adverts on the box,* although even the lightest viewers were influenced by commercials.

The researchers also found that adverts shown during peak-time television had a bigger impact on people's shopping habits. This suggests that people concentrate more when watching peak-time soaps and films than at other times of the day.

The biggest impact was made when adverts were seen up to three days before a shopping trip, although they could still influence choices made fourteen days later. Repeat viewing of adverts had an effect, showing the value of those shown during popular shows on several times a week.

To reach their conclusions researchers used devices fitted to televisions in 750 homes to find out what adverts people had seen. This was then matched to a record of purchases of household items at the supermarket. Sue Moseley, a spokesperson for the company which carried out the research, said that the results of the study were fascinating. 'When people see adverts for a product, they will buy it at a greater rate than people who don't see them. It's conclusive evidence that advertising does have an effect.'

* a slang word for the television.

## Communication activities

### Module 1: Exercise 3, page 13

Student A

> a  If you guess the answer to a question, you might
>    ... or ...
> b  If you put a coin into a vending machine, it
>    might ...
> c  If a child at school is violent, he is sure to ...
> d  If you try to catch a mouse, it might ...
> e  If you saw in the newspaper that your best friend
>    had been arrested, you'd ...

### Module 1: Exercise 2, page 14

The mystery person is Mick Jagger.

### Module 2: Exercise 1, page 24

> annoyance   anger   happiness   hostility   fear
> low self-esteem   depression   guilty   relaxed
> stressed   embarrassment

### Module 3: Exercise 2, page 29

**Mostly A** You're obviously not the adventurous type! Take a risk
occasionally, 'Nothing ventured, nothing gained!'

**Mostly B** You're not a daredevil, but you're willing to take risks.
Your motto is probably 'Look before you leap'.

**Mostly C** No-one thinks you are boring! But be careful: you will
get into trouble if you don't control your reckless impulses.

### Module 10: Exercise 2, page 111

> **Director of finance**
> You want the games to make as much money as
> possible, with as little expense as possible.

### Consolidation: A, page 139

- I'll probably be watching it on TV.
- I'll have gone to bed by the time it finishes.

### Module 3: Practice, Exercise 2, page 37

Student A

> 1  Write down what you were wearing yesterday.
> 2  Write down two things that you definitely won't be
>    doing tomorrow evening at 7.30.
> 3  Write down how many years you've been living in
>    your present house.
> 4  Write down how many years you had been learning
>    English before this course started.

### Module 4: Quiz, 2, page 42

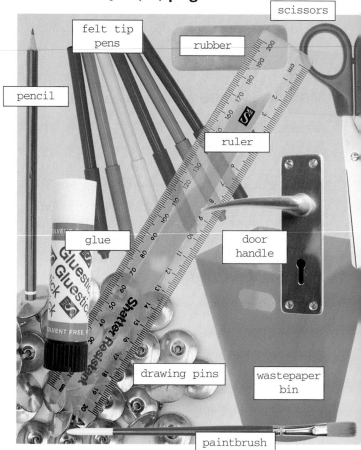

### Module 4: Exercise 2, page 45

Student A

> **Linguapack**
> - Over 500,000 Linguapacks sold worldwide.
> - One video, one CD-ROM, two audio-cassettes and
>   self-study booklet included in price.
> - Easy to use with answer key to exercises.
> - Cassettes with hundreds of real life conversations.
> - Ideal for use at home, in the office, in your car.
> - Certificate for all who complete the course.

## Module 5: Exercise 2, page 55

**Television / film:** In 1926, Logie Baird demonstrated the first television system. Television is now transmitted internationally through satellites. The Lumière brothers showed the first moving picture in 1895. The first 'talking' movie was made in 1927.
**Telephones:** In 1876, Alexander Bell invented the telephone. Nowadays, computer signals can be sent along telephone lines via modems.
**Microchip:** A microchip is a tiny integrated circuit. Microchips have made electronic equipment cheaper, more efficient and smaller.
**Penicillin:** The antibiotic penicillin was discovered by Alexander Fleming in 1929. Before this, thousands died from bacterial diseases.
**Rock and roll:** Rock music began in the mid-1950s in America. The Beatles appeared in 1962, and have influenced nearly all pop and rock musicians since.
**Aeroplanes:** The Wright Brothers made the first powered flight in 1903. Passenger flying developed after 1918. Today most long distance travel is by jet.
**Space:** Russia sent the first satellite into space in 1957. The first space station, Skylab, was launched in 1973. Passenger flights to the moon are the next stage.
**Spread of democracy:** In the late 1980s' popular revolutions in Eastern Block countries led to the end of Communism. China is now following a policy of reform and modernisation.
**Liberation of women:** New Zealand women won the right to vote in 1893. The struggle continues on education, property rights and equal pay.

## Module 5: Exercise 2, page 61

### Student A

> a   Lucy looks really depressed today. I wonder **what's the matter** with her?
> b   It looks as if petrol prices are going to **rise** by about five per cent this January.
> c   For a couple, staying together can seem difficult at times, but **separating** can be even harder!
> d   There you are! I've been looking for you two for ages. What **have you been doing**?
> e   We weren't able to find a taxi so late at night, so we **finished by** walking all the way home.

## Module 10: Exercise 2, page 111

> **Publicity and marketing director**
> You want to make sure that the games get as much media attention as possible, particularly international television coverage.

## Module 7: Exercise 2, page 79

**Team A**

**1** Thriller, which was recorded by American singer Michael Jackson, is the best-selling album of all time: approximately how many copies has it sold? **a** 4.7 million **b** 47 million **c** 470 million

**2** Which city hosted the 1996 Olympic Games in which a record 197 nations took part? **a** Atlanta **b** Barcelona **c** Los Angeles

**3** Kazakhstan, which became independent in 1991, is the largest country without a coastline in the world. Which continent is it in?
**a** Africa **b** Asia **c** Europe

**4** During Lent, which takes place in the forty days before Easter, what were Christians traditionally supposed to do?
**a** stop eating chocolate **b** stop eating luxury foods such as butter and meat **c** stop smoking and drinking

**5** Which event, which is celebrated in cities throughout the world, takes place towards the end of January each year?
**a** Jewish New Year **b** Chinese New Year **c** Hindu New Year

**6** The Cannes Film Festival, which attracts the biggest names in the Hollywood film industry, takes place in which month?
**a** July **b** May **c** November

## Module 12: Exercise 1, page 133

①

### A NATION OF SHOPAHOLICS – ONE IN FIVE PEOPLE 'ARE ADDICTED TO BUYING'

It's the sort of thing men joke about in the pub. 'My wife's addicted to shopping,' they'll say, while their mates grin and nod sympathetically.
A study suggests, however, that the compulsion to buy may be a growing problem, affecting as many as one in five people, and in extreme cases leading to family break-up and financial ruin.
The number of people who confess to being shopaholics has grown from 15 to 22% of the population in five years. And while 29% of women admit to being addicted, so do 15% of men. Shopping is no longer simply a way of providing essentials for the family, say market researchers. To many women it is more like a hobby.
True, many people have more money to spend these days. Personal disposable income has risen by 75% in 20 years. However, what they buy is not necessarily what they can afford.
Over the same period, the number of people using credit cards has quadrupled, and consumer debt has trebled.
Spending sprees can be symptoms of serious personal problems, according to researchers who have studied the subject. There are 'revenge shoppers' who want to spite their husbands or boyfriends because they are unhappy with their relationships. There are those who need shopping trips to add excitement to their lives.
Dr Helga Dittma of the University of Sussex, believes habitual shopping – particularly for designer clothes and jewellery – is a symptom of a collapse of self-esteem. 'Addicts want not only the latest fashions, they want to be the sort of people who would normally own them, and to feel important, glamorous and loved,' she said.

## Module 9: Follow-up task, Exercise 2, page 103

# Isidor Fink

The story of Isidor Fink is a classic 'locked door' mystery. No one was ever arrested, and no motive was ever established, but it now seems clear how the crime happened. Fink can't have committed suicide since no gun was found in the room, and his murderer can't have escaped from inside the room because of the barred windows and locked doors. So Fink must have been shot at the door and somehow managed to lock the doors himself, before staggering across the room and collapsing on the floor. He might have been shot in the wrist as he was struggling with all those bolts and keys.

## Module 9: Exercise 3, page 106

● Booked holiday on Bondy Island. Tour operator promised dream holiday in five star hotel. Good weather guaranteed. But hotel far from sea, staff rude, rooms cold, food disgusting, foggy whole time. Write to complain and ask for compensation.

● Bought designer jacket at Nirvani clothes store. First time washed it, one of the sleeves fell off and the jacket shrank. Took it back — shop assistant rude, refused to change jacket or give refund. Write to manager and ask for refund or new jacket.

● Ordered some CDs by mail order. Two weeks later CDs not arrived and bill sent. Phoned mail order company. Week later CDs arrived, but not ones ordered. Sent back, received another bill, refused to pay. Write to complain and ask for correct CDs to be sent.

## Module 10: Exercise 2, page 111

**Student representative**
In previous years, the needs of the students and young people participating and spectating have not been considered enough. You are here to make sure that this does not happen again.

## Consolidation: A, page 139

• We're going somewhere completely different this year.
• I'll probably be riding on the back of a camel.

## Module 11: Practice, Exercise 2, page 125

*Imagine!* Questions for A
a Imagine if everyone could choose their children's appearance. How would the human race change?
b Imagine that we had no sense of smell. What difference would it make to our lives?
c Suppose cigarette smoking was made completely illegal. What would the effects be?
d Suppose that couples were banned from having more than one baby. What would the effects be?
e Suppose we discovered a way of communicating with other species (for example, cows). How would this change our attitudes?

## Module 12: Exercise 1, page 133

② Woman Banker stole £100,000 for clothes

A bank executive stole more than £100,000 from her employers and blew it on clothes and make-up to 'escape the stresses of being a working mother'. Lynne Harding hid her purchases from her husband who had no idea of what she was doing.
And she got away with it for four years, until Lloyds Bank became suspicious of the assistant branch manager and called in auditors.
Now the 31-year-old mother of two is facing a jail sentence. A court heard that Harding would open bank accounts using fictitious names and authorise loans of up to £10,000 a time. Harding went on huge sprees, sometimes spending thousands on designer make-up in one day. The only other luxury she allowed herself was a car, paid for with a cheque from a bogus account. 'It was a vicious circle, I couldn't stop spending,' she told police after her arrest in February. 'It all started as a way of escaping the demands of a full-time job, combined with looking after a home and two children,' she said. 'Although I had a boss, he did not take a very active part in running the bank. I dealt with almost everything and was finding it extremely difficult.'
She awaits sentence at Southwark Crown Court.

## Module 12: Exercise 3, page 138

Student A

1  If you have a very good opinion of someone and say good things about them you …
2  'Did anything important happen while I was away?' 'No …'
3  When you give your opinion about something, even though it is likely to upset people, you …
4  When you protest against something, even though it can be dangerous to do so, you …
5  If you want someone to speak louder, you say …
6  Never trust what people say: look at what they actually do. In other words …

## Module 11: Exercise 2, page 125

> *Imagine!* Questions for B
> a Imagine that a drug was invented so that we no longer needed to sleep. How would our lives change?
> b Suppose a cure was found for all colds and minor viruses. How would it affect our lives?
> c Imagine that the use of artificial lights was restricted to two hours a day. How would we have to change our lives?
> d Imagine that a harmless drug was invented which stopped people from ever feeling depressed or unhappy. How would life be different?
> e Imagine that pollution got so bad that the private ownership of cars had to be banned. How would life change?

## Module 12: Exercise 1, page 133

③

# Who's the weaker sex now?

**More women than men are becoming the main breadwinner. Is your partner coping with the sexual revolution?**

Every afternoon Hayden Eaton gets that awful three o'clock feeling when his baby son's taking a nap and he longs for conversation with another adult. But his partner, Georgina, won't be home for hours. Lonely, bored and unfulfilled, who can blame him for feeling sorry for himself?
Hayden is one of a new type of men who are taking a back seat to women with better jobs.
'I used to have a good social life and my own money in my pocket,' Hayden explains. 'But when Georgy became pregnant, it made financial sense for me to stay at home and care for Toby.' So he quit his job as a hospital porter, while Georgy, a highly-qualified nurse, became the breadwinner. 'I know Georgy is able to earn much more money than me,' admits Hayden, 29, 'but I just can't cope with the loneliness of staying at home. I don't just miss the wages, but all the laughs I used to have at the hospital. Most of my mates wonder how on earth I stand it.'
But some might soon find themselves in the same position, because for the first time since the Second World War, women outnumber men in the workplace. There are now 12,000 more women than men in paid employment in Britain, and experts predict the gap will continue to widen. 'In our economy, employers want the skills which women offer,' says Kiki Pade, from the Henley Centre, which monitors consumer trends. 'They believe they are better at managing their time, understanding people's problems, giving friendly service to customers, and adapting to changing working methods.'

## Consolidation: A, page 139

- I'll be travelling first class, as usual.
- Is your grandmother going with you again?

## Module 1: Exercise 3, page 7

Student B

> a How have houses changed in the last century?
> b How have clothes and hairstyles changed since you were younger?
> c How would you describe the problems of young people in your society today?
> d How will television in your country change in the future?

## Module 1: Exercise 3, page 13

Student B

> a If your hair was growing over your eyes, you'd …
> b If you remembered it was your sister's birthday tomorrow, you'd …
> c If you didn't know how to load some new software into your computer, you'd …
> d If you were sitting at home and someone phoned to invite you out, you'd quickly …
> e Before you apply for a passport, you have to …

## Module 4: Exercise 2, page 45

Student B

> **The English Centre**
> - Established in 1971.
> - Conveniently located in city-centre.
> - Business, general English and exam courses held all year round.
> - Groups limited to eight students with priority given to **spoken** English.
> - Well-equipped classrooms, recently refurbished.
> - Qualified native-speaker teachers.
> - Student coffee bar with special discount prices.
> - Study centre and language laboratory.

## Module 10: Exercise 2, page 111

> **Local mayor**
> You are here to look after the needs of local residents, and to make sure that the local area gets as much publicity as possible. You also want to become more well-known, as you are planning to stand in the national elections.

## Module 3: Practice, Exercise 2, page 37

### Student B

1 Write down what you were doing at 7.30 yesterday morning.
2 Write down how long you've been coming to this English class.
3 Write down where you think you'll be living in five years' time.
4 Write down how long you'd been waiting when your teacher arrived, or how long the lesson had been going when you arrived.

## Module 4: Exercise 2, page 45

### Student C

**OnLine English**
- Internet-based language school created in 1997.
- Classes (six students max.) taught by native-speakers, with emphasis on individual attention.
- Teaching via written text / one-to-one voice mail.
- Conversation groups established in many cities.
- New course in business English being developed.
- Low tuition fees.
- The flexibility to study when **you** want to!

## Module 5: Exercise 2, page 61

### Student B

a The company has invested a lot of money in the **latest** computer equipment.
b There's a light on in their window, so I assume they **haven't gone to bed yet**.
c I don't want to be critical, but did you realise that that ornament is **the wrong way up**?
d I wasn't sure if it was her or not, so I just **approached** her and said, 'Are you Marie?'
e If you make a mess, you should **clean it completely**.

## Module 10: Exercise 2, page 111

**International representative**
In previous years, the needs and interests of people from other countries have not been considered enough. You are here to make sure that people from all over the world enjoy the games.

## Module 7: Exercise 2, page 79

**Team B**

**1** Which sporting event, which is held every four years, took place in Nagano, Japan, in 1998?
**a** The Olympic Games **b** The World Cup **c** The Winter Olympics

**2** Which French leader, who was born on the island of Corsica in 1769, took the title Emperor of France in 1804?
**a** Louis XIV **b** Napoleon Bonaparte **c** Charles de Gaulle

**3** Tennis player Martina Hingis, who won her first major tournament at the age of sixteen, was born in which country?
**a** Slovakia **b** Sweden **c** Switzerland

**4** What is the name of the Islamic festival which takes place in the ninth month of the Muslim year when people do not eat or drink between dawn and dusk? **a** Diwali **b** Ramadan **c** Shawwal

**5** Which Spanish city holds a festival each year, in which a bull is let loose through the streets? **a** Barcelona **b** Seville **c** Pamplona

**6** The Palio, which is held annually in the Italian city of Siena, is famous for what? **a** horse racing **b** car racing **c** motorbike racing

## Module 11: Practice, Exercise 2, page 125

*Imagine!* Questions for C
a Suppose people had to pass an exam to become parents. How would this change society?
b Imagine that a law was passed banning people from eating meat. What would happen?
c Imagine that we all had the power to read each other's thoughts. What would the effects be?
d Suppose that men could give birth just like women. How would the roles of the two sexes change?
e Imagine that the sun became so strong that it burned us immediately. How would life change?

## Module 12: Exercise 3, page 138

### Student B

1 If you agree with someone's ideas and think they express sensible opinions, you can say they …
2 Polite, friendly conversation about unimportant topics is often called …
3 If you are in a difficult situation, but you manage to escape by giving excuses, you …
4 If someone talks to you in a patronising way, you can say they are …
5 People who talk about nothing but work in social situations are said to be …
6 If you persuade someone to do something even if they don't want to do it, you …

# Language summary

## Module 1

### Ⓐ Overview of verb forms

#### 1 Names of tenses

|         | Simple      | Continuous        | Perfect Simple    | Perfect Continuous          |
| ------- | ----------- | ----------------- | ----------------- | --------------------------- |
| Present | I work      | I'm working       | I've worked       | I've been working           |
| Past    | I worked    | I was working     | I had worked      | I had been working          |
| Future  | I will work | I will be working | I will have worked | I will have been working    |

#### 2 Present Simple versus Present Continuous

While the Present Simple is used for things that happen **regularly** or that we see as **permanent**, the Present Continuous is used for things that we see as **temporary** or are happening over a **limited period of time**. Compare:

*Normally I **take** the train to work ...* (= this is what I usually do)
*... but this week **I'm coming in** by bicycle.* (= for a limited period)

#### 3 Verbs not normally found in continuous forms

A number of verbs (state verbs) describe states rather than actions. They are rarely found in continuous forms. These include:
a   verbs that describe thought processes and opinions:
    *think, believe, remember, know, forget, agree, disagree*
b   verbs that describe emotions:
    *want, like, love, hate, adore, detest*
c   verbs that describe the five senses:
    *see, hear, taste, feel, smell*
d   others: *be, have, belong to,* etc.

#### 4 Verbs that can describe both states and actions

Some verbs can describe both states and actions, but there is a change of meaning. See page 150 D for more information on state versus action verbs.

*He's very unfriendly.* (= this is a permanent characteristic)
*He's **being** very unfriendly.* (= he is not usually like this)

#### 5 Past Simple and Past Continuous

a   The Past Simple is used to describe actions or states in the past that we see as **complete**. The time when the action happened is often stated, or understood.
    *Jane **went** to visit her aunt in hospital **yesterday**.*

b   The Past Continuous is used to describe actions or states that were **in progress** at a point of time in the past, or that we see as in some way **incomplete**.
    *I **was driving along** when suddenly I ran out of petrol.*

#### 6 Present Perfect and Past Simple

The Present Perfect is used when an action happened in the past, but is linked to the present. It is still relevant or important.

*She's **broken** her leg.* (= her leg is broken now)
*I **haven't seen** 'Titanic'.* (= I am unfamiliar with it now)

The Past Simple is used for actions or states which we see as being **completely in the past**.

#### 7 Present Perfect and Past Simple with periods of time

If an action continues over a period of time up to the present, we use the Present Perfect.
*I've **worked** in Singapore for two years.* (= I still work there now)

To describe a finished period of time in the past, we use the Past Simple. *I **worked** in Singapore for two years.* (= completely in the past: I don't work there now)

#### 8 Present Perfect and Past Perfect

The Present Perfect is used for things which continue **up to the moment of speaking**, or ended a short time before.
*They've **been** together for years.* (= and are still together)

The Past Perfect is used for things which continued **up to a point of time in the past**, or ended a short time before.
*We'd **been** there for over an hour when the taxi finally arrived.*

#### 9 Future forms

There are several ways of talking about the future in English. Often it is not a matter of one form being correct, but how the speaker sees the event. Three of the most useful future forms are:
*I'll **get** my coat ...* (= I have just decided this)
*I'm **going to** phone ...* (= it's my intention)
*They're **getting married** next June.* (= a definite arrangement)

#### 10 Future forms with *when, as soon as*

A number of words which refer to the future are followed by the Present Simple or Present Perfect: *when, if, unless, as soon as, before, after, until, the moment.*
*I'll phone you **as soon as** I **get** home.*
*Please do not stand up **until** the plane **has stopped**.*

#### 11 Past forms to express hypothetical meaning

We often use past forms to talk about situations which are hypothetical or imaginary. These verbs do not refer to past situations, but to the present.
*If only I **knew** the answer to your question!* (= but I don't know)

### Ⓑ Different uses of auxiliary verbs

Auxiliary verbs often emphasise things, show interest, or avoid repetition. If they are used alone, remember they must agree with the tense and person of the main sentence.

#### 1 To emphasise

A: *Are you hungry?*  B: *Yes, **I am**!*
A: *I don't think you want to go.*  B: *I **do** want to go, but ...*

#### 2 In questions

a   **Short questions**: you can show interest in what someone said by responding with a short question using an auxiliary verb.
    A: *Yes, I've got six grandchildren.*  B: ***Have you?** How lovely!*
    A: *We didn't like the film at all.*  B: *Really, **didn't** you, why not?*

**147**

# Language summary

Notice here that positive questions are used with positive sentences, and negative questions with negative sentences.

b **Question tags** at the end of a statement encourage the listener to respond. Here negative questions are used with positive sentences and positive questions with negative sentences.

*You've remembered (+) your keys, **haven't** (-) you?*
*It isn't (-) a very nice day, **is** (+) it?*

If there is no doubt about the statement, the voice goes down.

*It isn't a very nice day, **is** it?*

If there is an element of doubt, the voice goes up.

*You've remembered your keys, **haven't** you?*

## 3 To avoid repetition

We also use auxiliary verbs to avoid repeating whole phrases.
*I enjoyed the film very much, but most of my friends **didn't**.*
(= enjoy the film very much)
*The other students in the class don't understand Italian, but Alexandra **does**.* (= understand Italian)

This is common in answers to *yes / no* questions.
A: *Have you done your homework yet?*
B: *Yes, actually, I **have**.* (= done my homework)

# Module 2

## Ⓐ The gerund (-*ing* form)

### 1 Common uses

The gerund is the -*ing* form of the verb, but it is used in the same way as a noun either as the subject or object of the verb, or on its own. It is most commonly used in the following ways:

a to describe general activities or abstract ideas.
***Parking** is a nightmare in this city.*
*My favourite forms of exercise are **walking** and **swimming**.*
*I think **trusting your children** is very important.*

b when there is no single noun to describe that idea.
***Going to the dentist's** still makes me really nervous.*
***Feeling as if you are out of control** is very stressful.*

> **REMEMBER!**
> It is not correct to use an infinitive instead in these cases.
> ~~To go~~ to the dentist's makes me really nervous.

c when an idea or activities are not put into a complete sentence.
• in written lists

*Our priorities for next year are:*
*• expanding into new markets*
*• cutting costs*

• in conversation
A: *So what's your idea of relaxation?*
B: ***Having** a nice long bath and **reading** my book.*

### 2 More about the grammar of gerunds

a Negative gerunds
*It's great **not having to get up** early for work!*

b Passive gerunds
***Being followed** by a police car makes me very nervous.*

c Past gerunds
*You mentioned **having worked** in New York. – Tell me more.*

d Gerunds often have their own subject or object.
*I get really annoyed when I see **people throwing** litter around.*
*I really hate **buying presents** – I never know what to buy!*

e Gerunds are often used after prepositions.
***Without knowing** all the facts, it's difficult to comment.*
***After leaving** university she was unemployed for over a year.*

f Gerunds are also used after a large number of verbs (for example *admit, avoid, consider, deny, finish, imagine, involve, give up, feel like, mention, practise, suggest,* etc.).
*He **avoided paying** taxes for many years.*
***Imagine never seeing** your own children!*

These include verbs that express likes and dislikes (*like, dislike, don't mind, can't stand, love, enjoy, hate, adore,* etc.). Generally these constructions have to be remembered individually.
*I **can't stand getting up** early in the winter.*

## Ⓑ Other phrases for generalising

There are a number of other phrases for introducing generalisations or abstractions, usually followed by a clause.

1 For talking about ideas and feelings
***The idea that** anyone can come in here really worries me.*
*I don't like **the thought that** my friends are talking about me.*
***The feeling that** you don't have to do anything all day is great.*
***The sense that** everyone is being treated fairly is very important.*

2 For behaviour
*I hate **the way (that)** politicians never answer directly.*

3 For people
*I hate **people who** pretend to be really nice when they're not.*
*A friend should be **someone who** is always there to help you.*
*A good manager is the **kind of person** who listens to others.*

4 For abilities
***The ability to** delegate is very important for a successful manager.*

5 To describe the absence of a quality
*The murderer's **lack of emotion** was frightening.*
*The whole film showed a complete **lack of imagination**.*

## Ⓒ Common suffixes with nouns

| suffix | examples |
| --- | --- |
| -ness | happiness  nervousness  awareness  kindness |
| -ion | competition  depression  religion |
| -ation | imagination  population  qualification |
| -ment | involvement  improvement  unemployment |
| -ence / -ance | patience  violence  confidence  importance |
| -ety / -ity | society  anxiety  responsibility  hostility |
| -y | envy  hypocrisy  jealousy  fantasy  psychiatry |
| -ing | suffering  training  well-being  belonging |
| -ship | companionship  ownership  citizenship |
| -ology | psychology  biology  technology |
| -ism | communism  capitalism  racism |

## D Common suffixes with adjectives

| suffix | examples |
| --- | --- |
| -ous / -ious | anxious envious nervous religious famous |
| -al | psychological social physical mental |
| -ive | creative supportive imaginative |
| -able / -ible | miserable capable responsible incredible |
| -ed* | talented determined old-fashioned |
| -ing* | depressing surprising challenging |
| -ful | cheerful stressful careful successful |
| -ent / ant | confident violent pleasant relevant |
| -ic | genetic electronic tragic domestic |
| -y | happy healthy busy pretty sporty smelly |

*REMEMBER!*

*A large number of adjectives to describe feelings have both an -ing and an -ed form.*
amazed / amazing   annoyed / annoying
disappointed / disappointing   depressed / depressing
embarrassed / embarrassing   terrified / terrifying

*The -ed form describes how you feel.*
I'm always **terrified** when I drive with Tony.

*The -ing form describes what makes you feel that way.*
Tony's driving is **terrifying**!

*However, not all -ed / -ing adjectives have both forms.*
Agnes looks a bit **stressed**. Her job is very **stressful**.

## E Prefixes which alter meaning

| prefix | meaning | examples |
| --- | --- | --- |
| un- | | unknown unemployed |
| in- | the opposite of | inactive inexperienced |
| im- | | immoral impatient |
| dis- | | dislike disagree |
| il- | | illegal illegible illiterate |
| non- | not | non-alcoholic non-member |
| mis- | wrongly / badly | misunderstand mis-treat |
| re- | do again differently | reorganise rewrite |
| anti- | against | anti-abortion anti-drugs |
| pro- | on the side of | pro-European |
| pre- | before | pre-twentieth century |
| post- | after | post-Apartheid |
| over- | too much | overweight over-worked |

| prefix | meaning | examples |
| --- | --- | --- |
| under- | not enough | under-fed under-valued |
| well- | a lot / good | well known well-fed |
| badly- | badly / not enough | badly-written badly paid |
| ex- | former | ex-boyfriend ex-husband |
| multi- | many | a multi-cultural society |
| inter- | between | international |
| out- | more than | outnumber outlive |
| self- | relating to itself | self-confident self-esteem |

# Module 3

## A Narrative tenses

| Past Simple | I work**ed** | verb + -ed (regular verbs) |
| --- | --- | --- |
| Past Continuous | You **were** work**ing** | was / were + -ing |
| Past Perfect | She **had** work**ed** | had + past participle |
| Past Perfect Continuous | She **had been** work**ing** | had + been + -ing |

### 1 Past Simple and Continuous

The **Past Simple** describes the **main events** in a past narrative.
I **called** the police, and they **came** more or less straightaway.

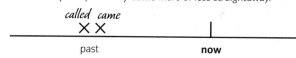

The **Past Continuous** describes **actions in progress** at the time that the main events happen.
When they **got** home, everyone **was waiting** to greet them.

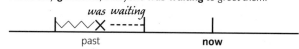

### 2 Past Perfect Simple and Continuous

Both these tenses describe events **before** the events in the main narrative. They are 'the past of the past'.
The suspects **had disappeared** when the police arrived.

The Past Perfect Continuous emphasises duration, and often describes actions that continue up until the main past events.
He **had been waiting** for hours when we got there.

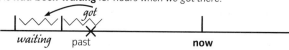

## B Continuous aspect

Continuous verb forms can:

1 emphasise that an action **lasts for some time** or is **repeated**. Compare:
*He looked at his watch.* (= he did this only once, quickly)
*He was looking at his watch.*
(= he did this several times, or for some time)

2 describe an action **in progress at a particular time**.
*I was just getting into bed when I heard a dreadful noise.*

3 describe a situation which is **temporary**.
*I'd been staying on a friend's floor for a few weeks, so I was very happy to find a flat of my own.*

## C Continuous aspect in other tenses

| Present Continuous | He **is working** | be + -ing |
|---|---|---|
| Present Perfect Continuous | She **has been** working | have / has + been + -ing |
| Future Continuous | We **will be working** | will + be + -ing |
| Future Perfect Continuous | We **will have been** working | will + have + been + -ing |

The points in B above are also true of continuous tenses with the Present Perfect and the future. Compare:
*I've cut my finger!* (= for a very short time)
*I've been cutting firewood.* (= for some time)

*She's been out with Charles.* (= once)
*She's been going out with Charles.* (= she's done this several times)

*We'll have dinner at eight.* (= the meal will begin then)
*We'll be having dinner at eight.* (= the meal will be in progress)

## D State versus action verbs

1 A number of state verbs are not normally found in continuous tenses. (See page 147 A for more information on state versus action verbs.) This is true of all continuous tenses.
*I have known him for years.* (not ~~I have been knowing~~)

2 Remember that most state verbs have other meanings where it may be possible to use continuous forms. For example:
STATE: *The city appears* (= seems) *to be returning to normal after last week's rioting.*
ACTION: *Liam Neeson is currently appearing* (= taking part in a play, film, etc.) *at the Playhouse Theatre.*

STATE: *These shoes fit* (= are the correct size) *perfectly, but I don't really like the colour.*
ACTION: *I've been fitting* (= installing) *a new radio in the car.*

STATE: *I weigh about five kilos less than when I started my diet!* (= how heavy you are)
ACTION: *I'm just weighing myself!* (= on the scales)

Notice that *taste* and *smell* can be used in the same way.

## E Use of present participle (-*ing* form) in descriptions

1 The -*ing* form is often used alone without an auxiliary verb, in narratives and descriptions. Like continuous verb forms, it often shows actions in progress at a particular moment.
*I looked out and noticed a man standing in the shadows.*

It can also emphasise **duration** or **repetition**:
*There were lots of people, running up and down, trying to help.*

2 We often use the -*ing* form after the complement with the verb *be*. We also use it after continuous verb forms, to avoid repetition of the pronoun and auxiliary.
*We had been standing there waiting for hours.*

3 After verbs of perception (*see / hear / notice,* etc.) two forms are possible. The -*ing* form emphasises duration / repetition.
*I heard someone knock.* (= once)
*I heard someone knocking.* (= several times / for some time)

# Module 4

## A The active and the passive

1 In active sentences the subject is the agent (or 'doer') of the verb.

*The two fire fighters* **rescued** *the child from the burning car.*
(subject) (verb) (object)

2 In passive sentences the subject is **not** the agent (or 'doer') of the verb.

*The child* **was rescued** *from the burning car by the two fire fighters.*
(subject) (verb) (object)

3 The passive is formed with *be* + participle.

| | Active | Passive |
|---|---|---|
| Present Simple | *It makes* | *It is made* |
| Present Continuous | *It is making* | *It is being made* |
| Present Perfect | *It has made* | *It has been made* |
| Past Simple | *It made* | *It was made* |
| Past Continuous | *It was making* | *It was being made* |
| Past Perfect | *It had made* | *It had been made* |
| Future Simple | *It will make* | *It will be made* |
| Modals (*must, can, may*, etc.) | *It must / can / may make* | *It must / can / may be made* |
| Infinitive (present) -*ing* form | *to make making* | *to be made being made* |

---

**REMEMBER!**
*Notice the passive form of modals, infinitives and gerunds.*

This report **must be finished** today.
I want **to be informed** of any new developments.
My brother hates **being told** what to do.

---

## B Reasons for using the passive

### 1 The agent is unknown, unimportant or obvious

*My bicycle's been stolen!* (= we don't know who did this)
*The mice are kept in cages.* (= it's not important who does this)
*A man has been arrested.* (= it's obvious the police did this)

### 2 The main topic of the sentence is not the agent

In English, the main topic of the sentence normally comes at the beginning, and new information about it comes at the end. If the agent is not the main topic, we use the passive. Compare:

> **David Branston founded** *Virgo Records in 1975, when he was still a teenager.*
> (In a profile of Branston, who is the main topic of the sentence.)
> **Virgo Records was founded** *by David Branston in 1975, when he was still a teenager.*
> (In a profile of Virgo Records, which is the main topic of the sentence.)

> **REMEMBER!**
> *You can still include the agent in the sentence, using by.*
>
> Virgo Records was founded **by David Branston** in 1975.

### 3 Formal texts

a In more formal texts, the passive is preferred because it sounds less personal. This is especially true in scientific, technical or academic writing.
> *The mice **are kept** in cages and **given** food twice a day.*
> (= in a report on a scientific experiment)

b The following passive constructions are particularly common in such formal contexts: *It is claimed that ..., It is believed that ..., It is agreed that ...*
> *It has been proved that the new drug has already saved hundreds of lives*

c Because of the emphasis on formality, the passive is more frequent in written English than spoken English (see below). However, the passive is still common in spoken English in more formal situations.

### C Alternatives to the passive

In informal speech, we can avoid the passive using a subject like *we, you, someone, they* or *people*. This sounds more personal and friendly. Compare:

> *The town centre **is going to be** closed to traffic.*
> (= from a newspaper)
> *Have you heard? **They're** going to close the town centre to cars!*
> (= in conversation)

> *The Gold Label credit card **can be used** worldwide.*
> **You can use** *a Gold Label credit card all over the place.*

> *More cars **are being bought** than ever before.*
> **People are buying** *more cars than ever before.*

### D Word order in English

#### 1 Basic word order

The basic word order for a statement in English is:

| *John* | *loves* | *Mary.* |
|--------|---------|---------|
| (subject) | (verb) | (object) |

This is only varied in specific cases (for example question forms).

#### 2 Indirect and direct objects

If we have two objects, the indirect object usually comes first.
> *She gave **me** the book.*

It is also possible to use to + a person at the end of the sentence.
> *She gave the book **to me**.*

#### 3 Adverbs of frequency

Adverbs of frequency usually come before the main verb and after auxiliaries, including modals.
> *I **sometimes** visit my grandmother at weekends.*
> *You must **never** do that again.*

Adverbs of frequency always go after the verb *be*:
> *He's **occasionally** a bit bad-tempered.*

### 4 Questions with prepositions

It is normal in modern English to put prepositions at the end of questions, not at the beginning. *Who were you talking **to**?*

### 5 Indirect questions

After phrases like *I don't know,* we do **not** use a question form.
> *I don't know **where he lives**. (not where does he live)*
> *I'm not sure **who they are**. (not who are they)*

After other phrases like this we do **not** use a question form either.
> *Could you tell me ...? Can I ask you ...? I was wondering if...*

### 6 Word order with adjectives

When there is more than one adjective before the noun, notice the following rules:

a adjectives which give an opinion (*nice, terrible,* etc.) come before adjectives which simply describe (*blue, French, plastic,* etc.).
> *a **stupid, old** man   a **nice, cold** drink   a **beautiful, black** dress*

b ordinal numbers (*first, second,* etc.) usually come before cardinal numbers (*one, two,* etc.)
> *The **first four** people to phone us will each receive a free ticket.*

c there are rarely more than two adjectives before a noun, but when this happens the order is:

| 1 opinion | 2 colour | 3 general description |
|-----------|----------|----------------------|
| *a **gorgeous*** | ***black*** | ***velvet** dress* |

### 7 The position of *enough*

*Enough* normally comes before a noun, but after an adjective / adverb.
> *Have we got **enough time** for lunch?*
> *It isn't **warm enough** to swim in the sea at the moment.*
> *If we do this **quickly enough** we can go home early.*

### 8 The position of *a / an* with *very, really, quite,* etc.

*A / an* comes before *very, really, completely, extremely,* etc. but after *quite.*
> *a **very** good meal   an **extremely** dangerous situation*
> *quite **a** good joke   quite **an** interesting story   quite **a** tall girl*

# Module 5

## A Overview of the perfect aspect

| | Positive | Negative | Question |
|---|---|---|---|
| **Present Perfect** **have** + past participle | I have left | I haven't left | Have I left? |
| | he has left | he hasn't left | Has he left? |
| **Past Perfect** **had** + past participle | I had left | I hadn't left | Had I left? |
| **Future Perfect** **will have** + past participle | I will have left | I won't have left | Will I have left? |

# Language summary

All perfect tenses link two points in time. They show events **before** a particular time either in the past, present or future.

## 1 Present Perfect

The Present Perfect links the present and the past. It shows events before the present: events in the past that are still linked to the present in some way.

Present Perfect
'before now'          **now**

a Verbs in the Present Perfect can be linked to the present in a number of different ways:
- they are not finished, but continue into the present.
  *My parents **have lived** here all their lives.*
  (= and they still live here)
- they take place in a period which continues to the present.
  *We**'ve** all **been** ill this week.*
  (= the week, and perhaps the illness, has not finished)
- the past action happened recently and is still 'news'.
  *They**'ve just bought** a new house.*
  (The speaker assumes that this is news to the listener.)
- the results of the past action are still important now.
  *My mum**'s gone** into hospital.* (= she's in hospital now)
- the past action may have happened a long time ago, but it is still important / relevant now for some reason.
  *I**'ve been** to Italy five or six times.* (= I know Italy well.)
b If you relate the action to a past time you cannot use the Present Perfect, you must use the Past Simple.
  *I first **went** to Italy **when I was a child / in 1979**.*
c The Present Perfect is often found with these time phrases:
  *for   since   all day / week*, etc.   *this week / month*, etc.
  *just   recently   already   yet   ever   never*
  *once / twice*, etc.   *it's the first / second / time that …*

## 2 Past Perfect

The Past Perfect links a point in the past with time further in the past: it describes events 'before the past'.

Past Perfect
'before the past'      past moment      **now**

We use the Past Perfect when we talk about a time in the past and we want to talk about something that happened before then.
  *She had been ill for many years before her death in 1992.*
  *When I got home (past time) I realised I had left my shopping on the bus. (before that)*

> **REMEMBER!**
> 1 Many of the same time words are used with the Past Perfect as with the Present Perfect.
>   Had you **ever** seen the man before the attack?
>   Mary hadn't seen her father **since** before the war.
>
> 2 Other common time words with the Past Perfect include:
> a by + past time phrase.
>   By eight o'clock yesterday morning I had been to the airport and back!
> b clauses with when, after, before, by the time, etc.
>   The party **had finished by the time** I left.
>   We went on holiday **after** our exams **had finished**.
>
>   *Notice that with before and after the order of events is clear, so the Past Perfect is not necessary. We can use the Past Simple instead.*
>   We went on holiday after our exams **finished**.

## 3 Future Perfect

The Future Perfect links two times in the future. It describes 'the past of the future'.

past   **now**   'the past of the future'   point in the future

We use the Future Perfect when we look forward to a time in the future and then think about what will have happened before that time. It is often introduced with *by* + future time phrase.
  *Phone me about nine. We**'ll have had** dinner **by** then.*
  ***By** the time I'm twenty-five, I hope I**'ll have finished** studying.*

Notice the word order of Future Perfect questions.
   1   2   3
  ***Will you have finished** it by tomorrow?*

## B More about the Present Perfect Simple and Continuous

### 1 What they have in common

Both the Present Perfect Simple and Present Perfect Continuous link the past and present as described above.
  *I**'ve written** my essay.* (= this is still news to the listener)
  *I**'ve been writing** my essay.* (= recently, so relevant now)

However there are certain differences of emphasis because, like all continuous forms, the Present Perfect Continuous emphasises **duration** (and sometimes repetition) while the simple form emphasises **completion** and is seen as '**instant**'.

### 2 'Long' / repeated versus 'instant' / complete actions

a If actions naturally have duration, the Present Perfect Continuous tends to be used, especially with *for* and *since*.
  *I**'ve been waiting** for ages.*
  *I**'ve been running** up and down these stairs all day!*

Notice the simple form sometimes sounds strange: *It's rained* sounds strange because it is not naturally an 'instant' action.

b If actions are naturally 'instant' (without duration), the simple form is used.
  *Oh no! I**'ve broken** a glass!*
  *I**'ve finished** my lunch, can I go and play?*

Notice that if the continuous form is used in cases like this, it has a very particular, sometimes strange meaning:
  *He**'s been finishing** his thesis.* (= it's taken a long time)
  *They**'ve been breaking** glasses.* (= repeatedly / deliberately)

> **REMEMBER!**
> Many 'long' actions are in fact states, which **cannot** go in the continuous form.
>
> I've known him all my life. (not I've been knowing)

### 3 Actions that continue into the present

Both the Present Perfect Simple and Continuous are used with actions that continue into the present, especially with *for* and *since*.
  *We**'ve lived / been living** here since we got married.*
  (= and perhaps we still live here)

But this is more common with the Present Perfect Continuous because it shows duration and not completion.
  *I**'ve been reading** the Bible.* (= perhaps I'm still reading it)
  *I**'ve read** the Bible.* (= completion)

### 4 For activities and results

a Because the continuous form shows duration, it is often used to describe activities. It answers the question, 'How has this person spent his time?'
  *What **have** you **been doing** today?*
  *I**'ve been cleaning** the house.*

b Because the simple form emphasises completion, it is often used to describe results. It answers the question, 'What has this person achieved?'
**I've cleaned** the bathroom, but I **haven't done** the bedrooms yet.
**I've written** five letters this morning.

> **REMEMBER!**
> *If you give a number, you always use the simple form because it emphasises completion / results.*
>
> I've been going to the gym a lot recently.
> (= the emphasis is on how I've spent my time)
> I've been to the gym **three times** this week.
> (= the emphasis is on what I've achieved)

# Module 6

## Ⓐ Use and non-use of articles

### 1 Basic rules you need to know

a **Indefinite article:** we use *a / an* when 'we don't know which one': it is **not unique** and it is has **not been mentioned before**. *He's studying for an important exam.*

b **Definite article:** we use *the* when 'we know which one' because:
• it has been mentioned before.
*The exam's at the end of May.*

• it is defined by a phrase or clause which follows.
*The car we had before was really old.*

• it is unique (or unique in that context).
*The engine was in a terrible state.*
(= it is the engine of this particular car and unique in this context)
*The Pope is going to visit next year.* (= there is only one Pope)

c **No article:** we don't normally use an article when we make **generalisations**.
*Cats are very independent creatures.*
*Overwork can cause stress and depression.*

> **REMEMBER!**
> *1 Nouns with an adjective in front of them are still general, and therefore no article is used.*
> My father doesn't really like **modern art**.
>
> *However if the noun is defined by a phrase that follows (or is part of a phrase), you need the.*
> **The** depression **you're talking about** is different.
>
> *2 More rarely (especially when talking about species and types) we can use both the definite and the indefinite article to make generalisations.*
> **The** great white shark is deadly.
> **A** small baby needs constant attention.
>
> *But the plural form can always be used instead.*
> Small babies need constant attention.
>
> *3 Notice that it is incorrect to use* the *+ plural noun or* the *+ uncountable nouns to make generalisations.*
> ~~The~~ small babies need constant attention.

d **Articles with names:** we **don't** normally use articles with the names of people or places, but there are many exceptions (see 2e).
*a book by **Professor Kretowicz***

e **Fixed phrases:** there are a large number of fixed phrases which have to be learned individually. These include:
• many phrases with *the* + noun + *of* + noun.
*the end of term    the Mayor of London*

• phrases of quantity with *a*.
*a few days    a number of problems*

• many other common phrases, especially with such adjectives as *the other, the same, the next, the last, the right, the wrong.*
*the other day    the same one    the next day    the wrong one*

### 2 Areas that often cause problems

a Institutions (*prison, college, church, home, hospital*, etc.). When you talk about the normal purpose of institutions, rather than a particular building, you don't use an article.
*to appear in court    to start school*

But when you talk about a specific building you use *the*.
*the prison is very old    the school is almost next door*

b *A / an* with jobs    *She's a nuclear physicist.*

c *The* in superlative phrases
*the biggest house in the street    one of the best meals I've had*

d Phrases of time
Usually there is no article with *years, seasons, months, days, parts of days, mealtimes,* etc. or in time phrases with *last, next, yesterday, tomorrow.*
*in 1990    at Christmas    on Wednesday mornings    at lunch time*
*last month    next time    tomorrow morning    yesterday afternoon*

Notice that we use an article if there is a **clause** or **adjective** to describe / define that time.
*a very cold winter    a fantastic lunch    the Christmas I broke my leg*

e Place names

| Without *the* | With *the* |
|---|---|
| countries, continents, islands, states, provinces, cities, towns, villages, suburbs<br>*to Romania  in Paris*<br>*near Corsica  from Florida* | • names with *republic, kingdom*, etc.<br>*the Czech Republic*<br>*the United Kingdom*<br>• names with *of*<br>*the Isle of Wight*<br>• plural names<br>*the Netherlands*<br>• other exceptions<br>*the Hague  the Bronx* |
| regions (with name of country, etc.)<br>*Central America*<br>*South-East Asia* | regions (without name of country)<br>*in the south  in the Balkans* |
| most roads, streets, parks, bridges, shops and restaurants<br>*Oxford Street  Hyde Park*<br>*Brooklyn Bridge  Harrods*<br>*Nico's* | • names with *of*<br>*the Palace of Versailles*<br>• names + adjectives<br>*the Science Museum*<br>• motorways    *the M6*<br>• names of theatres, cinemas, hotels, galleries and centres<br>*the National Theatre*<br>*the Odeon    the Guggenheim* |
| mountains<br>*Mount Kilimanjaro* | mountain ranges<br>*the Alps* |
| lakes<br>*Lake Geneva* | rivers, seas and canals<br>*the Danube    the Atlantic*<br>*the Suez Canal* |

**153**

## B Ways of giving emphasis

### 1 Intensifiers

a  *So, really, absolutely, completely*
We use these words with positive and negative adjectives.
*It's **so / really** annoying.*
*Her new book is **absolutely / completely** brilliant.*

*Absolutely* and *completely* are usually only used with ungradable adjectives (for example *fantastic, awful*, etc.) which already describe an extreme or absolute quality.
*The weather was **completely perfect**.*  (not ~~completely good~~)
*The holiday was **absolutely disastrous**.*  (not ~~absolutely bad~~)

b  *Far*
*Far* is used for emphasis with *too* + adjective, and in comparatives.
*Sonia's **far too young** to get married!*
*There are **far fewer** trees in the city than there used to be.*

### 2 Use of auxiliary verbs

We often insert an auxiliary verb into the positive form for emphasis.
*Your father **does** make me laugh.*

We use an auxiliary in the positive form to emphasise a contrast.
*Danuta is a vegetarian, but she **does** eat fish.*

We use *really* before the auxiliary verb to add further emphasis.
*I **really do** apologise for what happened.*

### 3 Emphatic constructions with *it* and *what*

The most common word order for a sentence in English is:
subject + verb + object      + adverbial phrase
*I*       *like   your sense of humour (most of all).*

However, if we want to emphasise that we like his sense of humour (more than anything else), we can use a cleft sentence that begins with a *what*-clause + verb *be*.
***What I like (most) about you** is your sense of humour.*
*His rudeness annoys me.  **What annoys me is** his rudeness.*

Similarly, if we want to emphasise a particular person (more than anyone else), we use a cleft sentence with *it* + *be* + *who*.
*Both my teenage children like fashion, but **it's** my son **who** spends the most money on clothes.*
***It was** Shakespeare **who** said that music is the food of love.*

### 4 Emphatic questions

Informally, we can use the phrase *on earth* after a *wh-* question word to emphasise surprise, annoyance, or the fact that we do not know the answer to a question.
*You're over two hours late – **where on earth** have you been?*
***What on earth** is she wearing?*

# Module 7

## A Revision of relative clauses

Relative clauses give us information about things, people, possessions, places and times using a relative pronoun.
a  Things (*which / that* or *nothing*)
*A stall is a kind of shop **which / that** sells things in the street.*

> **REMEMBER!**
> *It is incorrect to use* what *here.*
>                              *that*
> *A stall is a kind of shop* ~~what~~ *sells things in the street.*

b  People (*who / that* or *nothing*)
*A spectator is a person **who / that** watches a public event.*

> **REMEMBER!**
> *If the person or thing is the object of the relative clause, you can leave out* which, who *or* that.
> *a ring is a metal **thing** you <u>wear</u> on your finger*
> *(thing = object of verb underlined)*
> *Look there's the **man** I <u>met</u> at the party the other night.*
> *(man = object of verb underlined)*
>
> *This is not possible if the relative pronoun is the subject of the relative clause (see examples in a and b above).*

c  Possessions (*whose*)
*A widow is a woman **whose** husband has died.*

d  Places (*where, which, / that* + preposition)
*An auditorium is the place **where** the audience sits in a cinema.*

e  Times (*when*)
*A public holiday is a day **when** all the shops and offices shut down.*

## B Relative clauses with and without commas

### 1 Defining relative clauses (without commas)

Sometimes the relative clause is necessary to tell us which thing / person we are talking about (to define it).
In this case, there are no commas.
*Oh no! There's the woman **who shouted at me the other day!***
*(We need the relative clause to tell the listener which woman.)*
*I've just finished reading the book **you gave me for Christmas**!*
*(We need the relative clause to tell the listener which book.)*

### 2 Non-defining relative clauses (with commas)

Sometimes the relative clause is not necessary to define who / what we are talking about, it gives extra information. In this case, there are commas before, and if necessary, after the relative clause. Sometimes it comes at the end of the sentence.
*Christmas Day, **which is on a Thursday this year**, is always a public holiday.*
*(The relative clause gives extra information, it is not essential.)*
*When I was a child, my grandmother gave me a beautiful wooden box, **which I've always treasured**.*

> **REMEMBER!**
> *In non-defining relative clauses:*
> 1  *you cannot use* that.
>    *Christmas Day, ~~that~~ is on a Thursday this year, is always a public holiday.*
>
> 2  *you cannot leave out the relative pronoun.*
>    *When I was a child, my grandmother gave me a beautiful wooden box which I have always treasured.*
>
> 3  *prepositions can go either at the beginning, or the end of the clause.*
>    *Jan's hobby was motor racing, **on** which he spent all his money.*  (= *more formal*)
>    *Jan's hobby was motor racing, which he spent all his money **on**.*  (= *less formal*)

## C Shortened relative clauses

### 1 With the -ing form (present participle)

Sometimes we can omit the pronoun and auxiliary verb, and use just the present participle in the relative clause. This can happen with both past and present tenses.

*My sister was the one **wearing** the long grey dress.*
(= my sister was the one **who was wearing** the long grey dress)

### 2 With the past participle

We can do the same with the past participle, with passive relative clauses.

*Money **deposited** after four o'clock will not go into your account until the next day.* (= which is deposited)

## D Quantifiers

### 1 *Some* and *any*

a *Some* and *any* are used with countable and uncountable nouns, but not singular nouns.
*I've got **some** money with me. Have you got **any** children?*

b *Some* refers to **certain, but not all** of a group of things. It emphasises the positive, and so it is mostly used in positive sentences.
*I bought **some** clothes yesterday.* (= a certain quantity of clothes)

c *Any* refers to an **unlimited number** of things, and does not have a positive meaning. It is normally used in questions and negatives.
*He doesn't speak any foreign languages.* (= this is unlimited)
*Do you know any good restaurants near here?*
(= the number of restaurants referred to is unlimited)

d If we use *some* in a question, we expect the answer *yes* because *some* emphasises the positive. Compare:
*Can I have **some** milk, please?* (= I know the shop sells milk)
*Have you got **any** milk?* (= I don't know whether or not it does)

e We can even use *some* in negative sentences, but it has a special meaning.
*I **don't like some** types of jazz music.* (= not certain types)

f Similarly, if we use *any* in a positive sentence, it has a particular meaning.
*I **love any** chocolate.* (= it doesn't matter which: it's unlimited)
*My cousin is a brilliant mechanic – he **can** mend **any** car.*
(= it doesn't matter which: it's unlimited)

Notice that in *if* clauses it is quite common to use *any* with a positive verb form.
*If you need **any** help, call me.* (= it doesn't matter what kind of help)

### 2 Small quantities (*a few, several, quite a bit,* etc.)

a *A few / few* refer to countable nouns.
*Let's just make **a few sandwiches** for lunch.*

b *A little / little* (and *a bit of*) refer to uncountable nouns.
*We had **a little trouble** with the traffic.*
*Would you like **a bit of wine**?*

*A bit* is less formal than *a little*. It is much more common in spoken English than in written English.

c If we use *few* or *little* (without *a*), we emphasise the negative. We can increase the emphasis by adding *very*.
***(Very) Few** people remember the First World War, nowadays.*
*I speak **(very) little** German, unfortunately.*

d *A few / a little* put the emphasis on the positive.
*He's only been here a week, and he's met **a few** people already.*
*They say it's good for you to drink **a little** wine.*

e We emphasise this further by adding *quite*.
*I know **quite a few** Australians.* (= several / quite a lot)

Notice that we say *quite a bit* not *quite a little*.
*He's been learning English for a while and he knows **quite a bit**.*

f *Several* also means 'more than a few'. It is only used with countable nouns.
*She speaks **several** languages.* (= perhaps three, four or more)

### 3 Large quantities

There are a number of ways to talk about large quantities.
a *much / many*
These are mainly used in questions and negatives. *Much* is used with uncountable, and *many* with countable nouns.
*Hurry up, we haven't got **much** time!*
*Have **many** people phoned in reply to the advertisement?*

b *a lot of / lots of*
These mean the same. They are used with both countable and uncountable nouns, only in positive sentences.
*Don't buy anything else for the picnic — we've got **lots of** food.*

c *\*loads of, \*\*dozens of, \*\* hundreds of, \*\*\* a number of,* etc.
A number of phrases can be used instead of *lots of*.
*There were **loads of** people in the café. You couldn't move!*
*I'm fed up with the telephone today — I've had **dozens of** calls!*
*After his speech **a number of** people congratulated him.*

We can repeat these phrases to emphasise the quantity (except *a number of*).
*She's got **loads and loads** of clothes.*
*There were **hundreds and hundreds** of people out in the street.*

\* These phrases are informal.
\*\* These phrases are only used with countable nouns.
\*\*\* This is formal.

### 4 The right amount

a *too much* (uncountable) / *too many* (countable)
These phrases mean 'more than we need / than is good'.
*I feel sick. I've eaten **too much** dinner / **too many** cakes.*

With *slightly* it means 'only a little more than is good'.
*The meal was really good, but there was **slightly too much**.*

We show that it is 'a lot more than is good' by using *far*.
*Shall we go? There are **far too many** people here, you can't move!*

b *enough*
This means 'as much as we need'. It is used with both countable and uncountable nouns.
*Have we got **enough** cups for twenty people?*
*I've got **enough** money to pay the bill.*

Notice the negative forms, *not enough* and *not nearly enough* (= a lot less than we need).
*He's only bought one loaf – **not nearly enough** for eight people.*

c *plenty (of)*
This means 'more than we need'. It is used with both countable and uncountable nouns.
*Don't bring any wine, we've got **plenty**.*

d *just the right amount (of)* (uncountable) /
*just the right number (of)* (countable)
These phrases mean 'not too many and not too few'.
*The party was great. There were **just the right number of** people there, and there was **just the right amount of** food and drink.*

## Language summary

### Summary of quantifiers

Notice which phrases are used with uncountable nouns, which are used with countable nouns, and which are used with both. Notice also which phrases take *of* before nouns and which do not.

| Uncountable |
| --- |
| *some any a little a bit (of) a lot (of) / lots (of) loads (of) tons (of) too much enough plenty (of) just the right amount (of)* |

| Countable |
| --- |
| *some any a few several a lot (of) / lots (of) loads (of) tons (of) hundreds (of) dozens (of) too many enough plenty (of) just the right amount (of)* |

# Module 8

## Ⓐ Infinitive forms

| | With *to* | Without *to* |
| --- | --- | --- |
| Infinitive | **to do** | **do** |
| Perfect infinitive | **to have done** | **have done** |
| Continuous infinitive | **to be doing** | **be doing** |
| Passive infinitive (present) | **to be done** | **be done** |

### 1 Negative infinitives

Negative infinitives are formed with **not** + *(to) do*, etc.
> I told you **not to do** that.

### 2 Continuous infinitives

We use the continuous infinitive instead of the Present Continuous in infinitive constructions.
> I think the weather **is getting better**. > The weather seems **to be getting better**.

### 3 Perfect infinitives

We use the perfect infinitive when the infinitive clause refers to a time before the main clause. Compare:
> I'd like **to visit** Rome while I'm in Europe. (The speaker wants to visit Rome and is in Europe now.)
> I'd like **to have visited** Rome while I was in Europe, but unfortunately I ran out of money. (The speaker wishes he had visited Rome, but is no longer in Europe.)

This construction is very common after phrases such as *is said to have, is believed to have, is thought to have*.
> It **is believed to have happened** shortly after midnight.

### 4 Infinitives without *to*

Infinitives without *to* are used:
a after modal verbs. *I **can't wait** for the weekend.*
   **You must have been waiting** a long time.
b after *I'd better*, and *I'd rather*.
   **We'd better** go home now: it's getting late.
   **I'd rather watch** a video than go out to the cinema.
c after *make, let*, and *help*.
   She's the kind of person who really **makes you laugh**.
   When I was a teenager, my parents **let me stay out**.
   Can you **help me carry** the suitcases to the car?*
   (*In this construction, the infinitive with *to* is also possible.)

## Ⓑ Patterns using infinitives (with *to*)

### 1 Verb + infinitive

Certain verbs are followed by the infinitive with *to*. Some of the most important are: *agree, hope, offer, promise, tend, decide, intend, plan, refuse, threaten, expect, manage, pretend, seem, want.*
> The prince has agreed **to give** us an interview.
> Claire pretended **not to know** who I was.

### 2 Adjective + infinitive

A number of adjectives are followed by an infinitive with *to*.
> I was very **sorry to hear** about your accident.
> He isn't **old enough to vote** yet.
> It's **too late (for us) to go** out now.
> He was **the first person to win** three successive elections.

A common construction with adjective + infinitive is *too ... to ...*
> He's **too** old **to behave** like that.

### 3 Noun + infinitive

The following nouns take infinitive constructions: *chance, decision, effort, opportunity, time.*
> I don't agree with the **decision to postpone** elections.
> It's not every day you get the **opportunity to visit** India.

### 4 Infinitive of purpose

We use an infinitive with *to* to explain why someone does something (to express purpose).
> Helen's gone out **to buy** a newspaper.

In more formal English, we use *in order to*.
> Taxes have been increased **in order to** reduce inflation.

### 5 *Something / nowhere*, etc. + infinitive

We often use infinitive constructions after words like *something, somewhere, nothing, nowhere* and *what, where*, etc.
> I never go on a long journey without **something to read**.
> I really don't know **what to do** about this.

## Ⓒ Constructions with the gerund

1 Certain verbs are followed by the gerund (*-ing* form of the verb). For example *admit, like / dislike, (don't) mind, love, practise, consider, enjoy, miss, can't stand, mention, deny, hate, imagine, suggest, risk.*
   He **admits breaking** into the house, but **denies stealing** the television.

2 There are also a number of useful patterns with *it* + gerund.
   It's worth **visiting**, the garden is absolutely fantastic.
   It's no use **leaving** yet, the traffic's too bad at the moment.

3 Prepositions are always followed by the gerund.
   We're thinking **of buying** a new car.
   **Without being** rude, can I ask you how old you are?

Notice that *to* is a preposition (not an infinitive) in the following constructions, and is therefore followed by an *-ing* form.
   *be / get used to*   It's hard to **get used to living** away from home.
   *look forward to -ing*   I'm **looking forward to seeing** my friends.

See page 148 A for more information on other uses of the gerund.

## D Different types of linking words

Two types of phrase are used to link together ideas / arguments.

### 1 Conjunctions (*although, even though, whereas, while, despite, in spite of*)

These conjunctions link two ideas (clauses) in the same sentence. *Although, even though* and *whereas* can go before either clause. The emphasis is on the clause without the conjunction.

> **Although** *he's terribly famous, he lives a very ordinary lifestyle.*
> *He's terribly famous* **although** *he lives a very ordinary lifestyle.*

> **(Whereas)** *in the olden days, people believed that politicians' private lives were their own business,* **(whereas)** *these days the newspapers are full of their affairs and other private matters.*

> **REMEMBER!**
> *Despite* and *in spite of* are prepositions and are therefore not followed by a subject and verb. They are followed by a noun, a pronoun or a gerund (-ing form).
>
> **Despite** all their **achievements**, they feel insecure.
> They feel insecure, **in spite of this**.
> **In spite of being** a millionaire, he never spends any money.

### 2 Adverbial phrases (*however, nevertheless, therefore, on the other hand, for this reason, what is more, furthermore, besides*)

These adverbial phrases link ideas in two different sentences (or even different paragraphs). The adverbial phrases always go in the second sentence, usually at the beginning.

> *Wealth cannot buy happiness.* **However**, *it can make life much more comfortable.*

They can go at the end or in the middle of the second sentence and are separated from the rest of the sentence by commas.

> *Wealth cannot buy happiness. It can make life much more comfortable,* **however**.
> *Wealth cannot buy happiness. It can,* **however**, *make life much more comfortable.*

# Module 9

## A Revision of modals

### 1 Should / shouldn't

*Should* is used for obligations which are not strong. It is not necessary, but it is 'a good idea' or 'the right / correct thing'.

> *The children* **should be** *in bed by now.* (= this is the right thing)
> *You* **shouldn't eat** *too much fat.* (= it's not a good idea)

> **REMEMBER!**
> 1 You can use should *in the continuous form.*
>   You **shouldn't be carrying** that heavy suitcase, you'll hurt your back. (= now)
> 2 Ought to *means the same as* should.
>   The children **ought to be** in bed by now.

### 2 Must / mustn't

*Must* expresses necessity. There are two types of necessity:
a obligation.

> *I* **must go** *home now. I've got to be at work early tomorrow.*

> **REMEMBER!**
> Have to *and* have got to *also express obligation.* Must *often expresses an obligation that comes from the speaker while* have to / have got to *express an external obligation.*
>
> I **must go** home. (= I have decided this)
> I've **got to** be at work early tomorrow morning.
> (= my boss says / I've got an early meeting, etc.)

b logical necessity.
   Here *must* means 'from the evidence, I am sure this is true'.

> *This bill* **must be** *wrong. We haven't spent that much!*
> *Apparently Karina's father's ill again. She* **must be** *very worried.*

> **REMEMBER!**
> Mustn't *is used for obligation and it means 'obliged not to' or 'not allowed'.*
> You **mustn't smoke** in here, or we'll be sent out!
>
> *If you want to say that logically you think something is impossible, you use* can't.
> This bill **can't be** right. We haven't spent that much!
> Surely he **can't be** sixty, he only looks about forty!

### 3 Can

*Can* expresses possibility in three ways:
a ability (negative form *can't*). *He can (can't) speak Russian fluently.*

b permission. *Can I interrupt you for a second?*

c theoretical or general probability.
> *It's very hot here in summer, but it* **can** *be freezing cold in winter.*
> *Polar bears look cuddly, but in fact they* **can** *be very dangerous.*

Notice that *can* is not used to express specific possibilities, either in the present or future.
*Look in that cupboard, the umbrella might / may / could be in there.*

### 4 Could

*Could* also expresses possibility in three ways:
a like *might* and *may* it expresses present / future probability.
> *Of course, I* **could** *be wrong. You should decide for yourself!*

> **REMEMBER!**
> *You cannot use the negative form here. (Instead, use* may not *or* might not.)

b to ask for permission. **Could** *I borrow your lighter?*

c it is the past of *can*.
> *Queen Elizabeth I* **could** *speak six languages.*

### 5 May

Generally, *may (not)* expresses possibility in two different ways:
a present / future probability.
> *He* **may (not)** *be at home now, try him and see.*
> *Apparently, there* **may** *be thunderstorms tomorrow.*

b permission. This is mostly in the first person and is formal.
> **May** *I come in?*

### 6 Might

*Might (not)* also expresses possibility. It is used:
a to express probability.
> *We* **might (not)** *come to the party tonight. We'll see how we feel.*

Many people believe that *might* sounds more probable than *may*, but the intonation you use with modal verbs is more important in showing how probable you think the action is.

b to express permission. It is old-fashioned and rarely used.
*Might I ask you a favour?*

c in reported speech. *Might* is the past of *may*.
*It **may** rain. > The weather forecast said it **might** rain.*

> **REMEMBER!**
> 1 The different degrees of probability expressed by modal verbs can be summarised like this:
>
> | sure / logically certain | must |
> |---|---|
> | probable, but not sure | may (not) might (not) could |
> | sure / logically certain not to happen | can't |
>
> 2 These modal verbs can be used in the continuous form to talk about actions happening now.
> I won't phone now, they **might / may / could be having** lunch.
> The house looks empty. They **can't be living** there.

## B Past modals

Modals sometimes have different past forms according to the meaning.

### 1 *Had to*

When *must* expresses obligation, the past form is *had to* and the negative *didn't have to.*
*When I was at school, I **had to / didn't have to** wear a uniform.*

### 2 *Could*

The past of *can* is *could* or *was able to.*
*He **could / was able to** read before he **could** walk!*

> **REMEMBER!**
> *Could is only used to express general abilities.*
> Although he was badly injured he **could** still walk.
> (= general ability)
> *If we wanted to express the idea that the person actually did the action, we can only use was able to.*
> Although he was very badly injured he **was able to** ~~could~~ walk several hundred metres to safety.
> (= he actually did this)
> *The verb manage to is often used to express this idea too.*
> Although he was badly injured, he **managed to** walk several hundred metres to safety.

### 3 *Must have, might (not) have, may (not) have, could have, can't have*

All these modals of probability have equivalent past forms (modal + *have* + past participle).
*You **must have been** worried when you heard about the accident.*
*Someone phoned earlier on, it **may have been** Rachel.*
*You **can't have locked** the door. It was open when I got home!*

### 4 *Should have* and *ought to have*

The past of *should* is *should have* + past participle.
*You **should have put** it somewhere safe, so you'd be able to find it!*

The past of *ought to* is *ought to have* + past participle.
*You **ought to have** booked – there are no tables left.*

# Module 10

## A Plans and decisions in the future

1 *Going to*
We use *going to* to express present intentions for the future. The action may be in the distant or the near future.
*I'm never **going to get** married.*

2 *Will*
We use *will* to express a decision made at the moment of speaking. (Telephone rings) *Don't worry, **I'll** answer it.*

3 Present Continuous
We use the Present Continuous to talk about an arrangement for the future. *I'm meeting Henri this afternoon.*

> **REMEMBER!**
> 1 The use of going to and the Present Continuous is very similar. You can always use going to instead of the Present Continuous in the future meaning.
> I'm going to meet Henri this afternoon.
>
> The use of the Present Continuous is more limited. You only use it to talk about definite arrangements.
> I'm going to get married when I grow up. (= general intention)
> They're getting married. (= they're engaged / it's arranged, etc.)
>
> 2 Notice that when the main verb with going to is go, it is commonly omitted.
> We're **going** (~~to go~~) to France for our holidays this year.

4 Present Simple
When an action in the future is part of a regular timetable, we use the Present Simple. *The game **starts** at 7.30.*

## B Predictions

1 We use both *going to* and *will* to make predictions about the future. When the prediction is based on some evidence in the present, we usually use *going to*.
**You're going to drop** those plates if you're not careful!
(= I can see you're not carrying them properly)
*All the polls suggest that the government **is going to win** the election with a large majority.*

2 When the prediction is based on our own beliefs and expectations, rather than present evidence, we use *will*.
A: *I wonder where Anna is?*
B: *Oh, I'm sure **she'll get** here soon.*

3 In many cases, however, there is no important difference in meaning and either form is possible.
*Who do you think **is going to / 'll win** the next World Cup?*

> **REMEMBER!**
> There are many other ways of making predictions using modal verbs, adverbs and phrases such as likely to, certain to, there's a good chance that, I bet, etc.
>
> Economists say that inflation **may (well)** rise.
> She will **almost certainly** buy me socks for Christmas.
> In this heat, **it's likely to be** an uncomfortable journey.
> **There's a good chance that** our team will win.

## C Future clauses with *if*, *when*, *in case*, etc.

1 We use a present tense in many future subordinate clauses. Notice that the main clause uses a future form.
*Will there be anyone to meet me **when I get** to the airport?*

2 Words that introduce such clauses are: *if, when, in case, until, after, before, as soon as, once, unless, next time.*
*I'm taking my warm clothes **in case** the weather **gets** cold.*
*I'll pay you back **next time** I **see** you.*
***Unless** we **hurry up**, all the shops will be shut!*

## D Other ways of talking about the future

### 1 Verbs + infinitive with *to*

We use a number of verbs followed by the infinitive with *to* to talk about the future: *aim, arrange, expect, hope, intend, plan, prepare,* etc.
*We**'re aiming to get** this work finished by six o'clock this evening.*
*I'm sorry, I**'ve** already **arranged to go out** on Thursday.*

### 2 *about to*, *due to* and *is / are to*

We use *about to* to talk about something we expect to happen in the very near future.
*Ladies and gentlemen, the show **is about to start**.*

We use *due to* to talk about something which is expected to happen at a particular time.
*Flight BA502 from Miami **is due to** arrive in a few minutes.*

We use *is / are to* to talk about official future arrangements. This form is commonly found in newspaper reports.
*The Prime Minister **is to** visit Washington next month.*

## E Future Continuous and Future Perfect

### 1 Future Continuous

| Positive form | Negative form | Question form |
|---|---|---|
| I 'll (= will) + be + -ing | I won't + be + -ing | Will I be + -ing? |
| *I'll be working.* | *I won't be working.* | *Will you be working?* |

a As with all continuous tenses, we use the Future Continuous to talk about an action in progress at a particular time.

*I**'ll be driving** home at 7.30 this evening.*

Compare:
*We**'re having** dinner at eight o'clock this evening.*
(= the meal will start at that time)
*We**'ll be having** dinner at eight o'clock this evening.*
(= the meal will be in progress at that time)

b We also use the Future Continuous for something that will happen as a result of other arrangements or normal routine.
*... and after his speech the President **will be having** dinner with local VIPs.* (This is part of the arrangements for his visit.)
*I**'ll be seeing** Eva at the gym tonight: we always go on Tuesdays.* (This is the result of their normal routine.)

---

> **REMEMBER!**
> *The Future Continuous question form is often used with polite requests because it expresses the idea 'if you are doing it anyway, then I am not causing you any trouble'.*
>
> **Will** you **be passing** my house on your way to the gym? If so, could you drop in the book I want to borrow? (= have you already arranged to do this because I don't want to give you any trouble)
> **Will** you **be using** the computer this afternoon? If not, could I use it? (= have you already decided because I don't want to borrow it if you need it)

### 2 Future Perfect

| Positive form | Negative form | Question form |
|---|---|---|
| I 'll (= will) + have + past participle | I won't + have + past participle | Will I have + past |
| *I'll have done it.* | *I won't have done it.* | *Will you have done it?* |

a We use the Future Perfect to talk about an action which will be completed **before** a point of time in the near future.

*We**'ll have had** our dinner by the time you arrive.*

Compare:
*We**'ll have finished** painting the ceiling in a few hours.*
(= we will finish work **before** then)
*We**'ll finish** painting in a few hours.* (= we will finish work then)

b There are many phrases commonly used with the Future Perfect with *by* and *by the time*.
***by** one o'clock / dinner time*
***by this time** tomorrow / next week / next month / next year*
***by the end of the** week / month / year / century*
***by the time** we get home / I'm thirty / I retire / I go to bed*

# Module 11

## A Hypothetical or imaginary situations in the present

### 1 Imaginary situations with *if*

When talking about hypothetical or imaginary situations in the present, we go back one tense into the past.
*I **don't have** time, but if I **had** more time, I would go to the gym.*
*It**'s raining**, but if it **wasn't raining**, we could go to the park.*

This is sometimes called the 'unreal past'. The unreal past is most often used after *if* (in conditional sentences) as above.

# Language summary

## 2 Imaginary situations with *wish* and *if only*

We also use the unreal past after *if only* and *wish* because they also describe imaginary situations.

| | |
|---|---|
| **I wish I could** speak Spanish. | (= I can't speak Spanish) |
| **I wish it wasn't** raining. | (= but it is raining) |
| **If only** you were here with me now! | (= but you aren't) |

## 3 Other phrases to describe imaginary situations

a  *Suppose* and *imagine* are also followed by an unreal past as they describe imaginary situations.
   **Suppose we lived** in a big house ...
   **Imagine you were** a famous Hollywood star ...

b  *It's time* also takes an unreal past. It means 'I / you / he, etc. should do this now'.
   **It's time** you **went** out and **looked** for a job.

The same idea can be expressed using an infinitive construction.
   It's time **for you to go out** and look for a job.

## B Talking hypothetically about the past

1  When we talk hypothetically with *if, if only* and *I wish* the Past Simple becomes the Past Perfect.
   **If you'd told** me about the problem earlier, I would have done something about it. (= you didn't tell me about it)
   If only I **had thought** about it more! (= I didn't think about it)
   I wish I **hadn't listened** to him. (= I did listen to him)

2  In conditional sentences, if the main clause also refers to the past, *would have* + past participle is used.
   We **wouldn't have lost** if our best player hadn't been sent off.

3  Notice that in the sentences in 2 above, **both** the *if* clause and the main clause refer to the past. It is also possible to have a sentence where the *if* clause refers to the **past** and the main clause refers to the **present**.

       Past                      Present
**If we'd set off** earlier this morning, **we'd be** at the hotel now.

Alternatively, the *if* clause may refer to the **present**, and the main clause to the **past**.

       Present                     Past
If his father **wasn't** the boss, he **wouldn't have got** the job.

# Module 12

## A Reporting the exact words people use

### 1 Change of tense

When we report what someone said, the verb forms often move one tense into the past.
   '*I **believe** that what I **am doing is** right,*' she said, '*I **will** continue to fight for justice.*'
   *She said she **believed** that what she **was doing was** right, and that she **would** continue to fight for justice.*

Verb forms change in the following way:

| Direct speech (the actual words) | | Reported speech (indirect speech) |
|---|---|---|
| Present Simple (do) | > | Past Simple (did) |
| Present Continuous (is doing) | > | Past Continuous (was doing) |
| Present Perfect (has done) | > | Past Perfect (had done) |
| Past Simple (did) | > | Past Perfect (had done) |
| Past Continuous (was doing)* | > | Past Perfect Continuous (had been doing) |
| Past Perfect (had done) | > | no change possible |
| Past Perfect Continuous (had been doing) | > | no change possible |
| will | > | would |
| is going to | > | was going to |
| can | > | could |
| must | > | had to |

* This frequently does not change in reported speech.

> **REMEMBER!**
> 1 The change of tense often happens because what the person said is now in the past.
> His teachers at school said he **would** end up in trouble, but today he is a successful businessman.
>
> 2 If what the person says is still true / relevant now, we often don't change tenses.
> 'I**'m** probably **going to** be late for the meeting.'
> Pippa said she**'s** probably **going to** be late.
>
> It is possible to change tenses in such cases, but it is often done in more formal contexts.
> 'Today's agreement **is** a historic opportunity,' the Prime Minister said.
> The Prime Minister said that today's agreement **was** a historic opportunity.
> (Probably in a newspaper or on the news.)
>
> 3 Notice that if the reporting verb is in the present tense, then there is no tense change.
> Mum **says** I **can** borrow the car tonight.

## 2 Reported questions

Because reported questions are not real questions, the word order is the same as in statements.

　　　1　　2
'**Will you** continue to fight this case,' the journalists asked.

　　　　　　　　　　1　　　2
The journalists asked if **they would** continue to fight the case.

## 3 Some common reporting verbs and the constructions used after them

a　Statements

| | |
|---|---|
| **say** | He **said (that)** he was enjoying his new job. |
| **tell** | He **told me (that)** he was enjoying his new job. |
| **answer** | She **answered that** she had no intention of resigning. |
| **reply** | She **replied that** she had no intention of resigning. |
| **add** | She **added that** she wanted to thank her supporters. |

b　Questions

The verb *ask* is most commonly used to report questions, but *wonder* and *want to know* are sometimes used too. After *wh-* questions, the question word is used as a conjunction.

The police **asked (him) where** he had been.
They **wanted to know what time** he arrived home.

With *yes / no* questions *if* or *whether* are used.
Ben **wondered if / whether** you wanted to come round for dinner.

## B Verbs which summarise what people say

There are a large number of verbs which summarise what people say, without reporting every word.

*Please, let me go. I'll do what you say, just let me go, please.*
He **begged** them to let him go.

The constructions with these verbs vary and have to be learned separately. With some verbs several constructions are possible. Here are some of the most important ones:

### 1 Verb + *that*

**deny**　He **denied that** he had done anything illegal.
**agree**　We **agreed that** we would meet again soon.
(Also: *decide, conclude, threaten, complain, imply.*)

### 2 Verb + object + *that*

**warn**　We **warned you that** the building was dangerous.
(Also: *promise, persuade, assure.*)

### 3 Verb + gerund

**suggest**　Molly **suggested meeting** for a coffee first.
**deny**　He **denied seeing** her on the evening of the murder.

### 4 Verb + preposition + gerund

**insist**　The children **insisted on coming** with us.

### 5 Verb + object + preposition + gerund

**accuse**　You **accused me of lying**!
(Also: *blame, congratulate.*)

### 6 Verb + infinitive

**refuse**　She **refused to tell** me where she had been.
(Also: *offer, promise, decide, agree, threaten.*)

### 7 Verb + object + infinitive

**order**　The police **ordered them to put up** their hands.
**warn**　Her parents **warned her not to speak** to strangers.
(Also: *persuade, urge.*)

> **REMEMBER!**
> Negative gerunds and infinitives can also be used.
>
> I decided **not to accept** the new job.
> She blamed her mother for **not helping** her.

# Irregular verbs

| Verb | Past Simple | Past Participle |
|---|---|---|
| be | was / were | been |
| beat | beat | beaten |
| become | became | become |
| begin | began | begun |
| bend | bent | bent |
| bite | bit | bitten |
| blow | blew | blown |
| break | broke | broken |
| bring | brought | brought |
| build | built | built |
| burn | burned / burnt | burned / burnt |
| burst | burst | burst |
| buy | bought | bought |
| can | could | been able |
| catch | caught | caught |
| choose | chose | chosen |
| come | came | come |
| cost | cost | cost |
| cut | cut | cut |
| dig | dug | dug |
| do | did | done |
| draw | drew | drawn |
| dream | dreamed / dreamt | dreamed / dreamt |
| drink | drank | drunk |
| drive | drove | driven |
| eat | ate | eaten |
| fall | fell | fallen |
| feed | fed | fed |
| feel | felt | felt |
| fight | fought | fought |
| find | found | found |
| fly | flew | flown |
| forget | forgot | forgotten |
| forgive | forgave | forgiven |
| freeze | froze | frozen |
| get | got | got |
| give | gave | given |
| go | went | gone / been |
| grow | grew | grown |
| hang | hung | hanged / hung |
| have | had | had |
| hear | heard | heard |
| hide | hid | hidden |
| hit | hit | hit |
| hold | held | held |
| hurt | hurt | hurt |
| keep | kept | kept |
| kneel | knelt | knelt |
| know | knew | known |
| lay | laid | laid |
| lead | led | led |
| learn | learned / learnt | learned / learnt |
| leave | left | left |
| lend | lent | lent |

| Verb | Past Simple | Past Participle |
|---|---|---|
| let | let | let |
| lie | lay | lain |
| light | lit | lit |
| lose | lost | lost |
| make | made | made |
| mean | meant | meant |
| meet | met | met |
| must | had to | had to |
| pay | paid | paid |
| put | put | put |
| read / riːd / | read / red / | read / red / |
| ride | rode | ridden |
| ring | rang | rung |
| rise | rose | risen |
| run | ran | run |
| say | said | said |
| see | saw | seen |
| sell | sold | sold |
| send | sent | sent |
| set | set | set |
| shake | shook | shaken |
| shine | shone | shone |
| shoot | shot | shot |
| show | showed | shown |
| shut | shut | shut |
| sing | sang | sung |
| sink | sank | sunk |
| sit | sat | sat |
| sleep | slept | slept |
| slide | slid | slid |
| smell | smelled / smelt | smelled / smelt |
| speak | spoke | spoken |
| spend | spent | spent |
| spill | spilled / spilt | spilled / spilt |
| spoil | spoiled / spoilt | spoiled / spoilt |
| stand | stood | stood |
| steal | stole | stolen |
| stick | stuck | stuck |
| swim | swam | swum |
| take | took | taken |
| teach | taught | taught |
| tear | tore | torn |
| tell | told | told |
| think | thought | thought |
| throw | threw | thrown |
| understand | understood | understood |
| wake | woke | woken |
| wear | wore | worn |
| win | won | won |
| write | wrote | written |

# Tapescripts

## Module 1

### Recording 1

E = Eric        D = Debbie        J = Joel

E: Well, at one time I had a job on the railways, British Railways as it was then. I used to be a driver and then ... well, 1972 was a very important year because I was made redundant, I lost my job which as you can imagine was a bit of a disaster with four young children, so we decided, my wife and I, to emigrate to Australia ...

D: Wollongong is the place where I first went to school in Australia, I grew up there from the age of twelve. We lived there for about six years. It's a town about eighty kilometres from Sydney. The thing I remember most is the way the other kids there used to tease me because of my accent. It was awful at first ...

J: My mum and dad met in Australia, but when they got married, they decided to come back to England, and they moved to Folkestone, which is the place where I was born. It's a smallish town on the south coast ...

E: To be honest, I don't have that many ambitions left nowadays, though I must say I still have high hopes of becoming a great grandfather. I'm very lucky, I have eleven grandchildren, but no great grandchildren, not yet anyway. The eldest granddaughter is sixteen, that's Christina, so we'll see what happens. I'm in no hurry ...

D: I'd love to go back to Australia one day, not necessarily to live, but just to see my old friends and also to show Joel where we used to live and things like that ... I'd especially like to take him to the Palm Beach Café, which is where his father took me on our first date, but I don't suppose he'd be very interested!

J: Tiffany is the name of our family dog. She's got no sense at all, completely stupid. We all love her dearly.

E: Now I'm retired, I think it's important to take up new interests in life. I always felt I missed out on my education when I was younger, so I'm trying to make up for it now. I'm doing some evening classes, learning Spanish, or trying to, anyway!

D: Yes, I am working at the moment. I'm involved in careers advice for young people. At the moment I'm doing a lot of work with school-leavers, sixteen to eighteen-year-olds, advising them on what kind of courses are available to them. I find it very rewarding ...

J: Oh yeah, I play in a band, there are five of us ... I play the guitar ... we've been rehearsing for a few weeks now ... the band's called 'Objects of Desire' ... pretty good name, huh? Our biggest ambition is to be rich and famous. We're actually playing our first-ever gig next week, Friday I think it is ...

### Recording 2 *(missing words / phrases only)*

b is it    c isn't    d does    e she has

### Recording 3

1  Oh, what's the use. I can see you don't believe me.
2  ... that I didn't want to have anything to do with it, and then he told me that ... you're not listening to me, are you?
3  I bet things have changed a lot since you were a child, ...
4  It's just not fair. All my friends are allowed to have friends to stay, but ...
5  Oh that's just great, we've missed the last train. Why didn't you tell me there were no trains after midnight?
6  So this year we thought we'd go somewhere really original for our holiday, somewhere no one else goes, so we're going to Iceland.
7  Do you want any of this ice cream or not?

8  Have you heard about Carmen and Roger? They're going to have another baby!
9  Well, in those days all my brothers were really keen on sports, but ...
10 When we first met it was such a romantic occasion ...

### Recording 4

1  A: Oh, what's the use. I can see you don't believe me.
   B: I do believe you, it's just that what I don't understand is how you managed to ...
2  A: ... that I didn't want to have anything to do with it, and then he told me that ... you're not listening to me, are you?
   B: Yes, I am!  I was just thinking about something else, that's all.
3  I bet things have changed a lot since you were a child, haven't they?
4  It's just not fair. All my friends are allowed to have friends to stay, but I'm not. It's so unfair!
5  A: Oh that's just great, we've missed the last train. Why didn't you tell me there were no trains after midnight?
   B: I did tell you, actually. You just didn't listen.
6  A: So this year we thought we'd go somewhere really original for our holiday, somewhere no one else goes, so we're going to Iceland.
   B: Are you? What a coincidence. That's where we went last year.
7  A: Do you want any of this ice cream or not?
   B: Of course I do!
8  A: Have you heard about Carmen and Roger?  They're going to have another baby!
   B: Are they?
9  Well, in those days all my brothers were really keen on sports, but I wasn't.
10 When we first met it was such a romantic occasion, wasn't it, darling?

### Recording 5

1  Things have changed a lot since you were a child, haven't they?
2  A: We're going to Iceland for our holiday this year.
   B: Are you?
3  A: Do you want any ice cream or not?
   B: Of course I do!
4  A: Carmen and Roger are going to have another baby!
   B: Are they?

### Recording 6

S = Sean        F = Fiona        R = Hotel Receptionist

F: ... right ... so I'll pick that up in the morning then.
R: Right, madam.
F: Okay, thank you.
S: Hi, excuse me, I couldn't help overhearing ... is that a Scottish accent there? I thought I noticed ...
F: Um, yes. It is. I am Scottish, yes.
S: Oh, that's great.
F: Yes. Well ...
S: Mm ... Which part of Scotland are you from? I haven't actually been there myself, but ...
F: I'm from a place called Dunoon. It's just outside Glasgow.
S: Right. So are you over here for long?
F: No, I just arrived, in fact ... just come from the airport.
S: I see. So have you had any chance to look around yet?
F: No, not really.
S: So are you here on holiday?

**163**

F: No, I'm here for work actually ... just for a couple of days ... then I'm off back home ...

S: Oh, right. So what kind of work do you do?

F: I'm a researcher ... I work in television research. We're doing a programme about the elections here.

S: Oh, sounds interesting. You must get to travel a lot ...

F: Well, not all that often, actually. Well, if you'll excuse me ... I have to er ...

S: Oh, right, don't let me keep you.

F: Okay.

S: My name's Sean, by the way.

F: Hello, nice to meet you, Sean.

S: Nice to meet you. Sorry, I don't know your name.

F: Er ... Fiona.

S: Fiona, right. That's a nice name.

F: Thank you. So, I must be getting on, really. I've got to unpack. It's been nice talking to you.

# Module 2

## Recording 1

| noun | verb | adjective | person |
|---|---|---|---|
| | | psychological | psychologist |
| psychology | | | |
| a anxiety | | anxious | |
| b awareness | | aware | |
| c depression | to depress | depressed / depressing | |
| d science | | scientific | scientist |
| e suffering | to suffer | | sufferer |
| f support | to support | supportive | supporter |
| g involvement | to involve | involved | |

## Recording 2

B = Beth     M = Martin     D = Denise     P = Philip

### Section A

B: Trash on the street ... people not sharing sidewalk space or pavement space ... sort of muscling or elbowing me out of the way.

M: The thing that gets me is when you hold a door open for someone and they don't say 'thank you' and they just treat you like you're not there, yeah? And you can be left there for about half an hour while there's a stream of people walk past.

D: When people are sitting in their cars in traffic jams and they throw litter out of the car window ... and big things quite often ...

P: And for me there are two things: meanness, like my sister who never gives anything away, and hypocrisy – the people who pretend to be so nice, but they're just being dishonest ...

### Section B

M: Spontaneous niceness ... I hate it when people give me presents, or give me a compliment. I just cannot handle it and I colour up bright red ... luckily it doesn't happen too often ...

P: Um, yes, people telling me that I'm good at something – I just never believe them.

B: I find it really emb ... really difficult ... to find I've told a little white lie, I'm in a social situation and someone finds out ... I find that really difficult to deal with.

D: Also when somebody knows your name and it's past the point of you being able to ask them their name, you're just supposed to know, that's really, really awful.

### Section C

B: A large dog running toward me that I don't know ... leaves me breathless ... I always have to find an escape route ...

D: My house is ... quite old and very quiet and I'm terrified when I'm there on my own ... I'm terrified at the slightest noise...

M: Um, I'm not very good with bugs and insects ... anything with more than four legs or less than two ... and I'm terrible ...

P: I'm not frightened of anything at all! *(laughing)*

B: I also get incredibly nervous driving with some people. Either I ... I always have the feeling I need to lie down in the back seat of the car so that I can't see either how fast we're going or how close we are to the edge of the cliff or ... bad or reckless driving terrifies me ...

D: When I'm driving and there's a police car behind me and it's terrible! And I haven't done anything wrong although I always feel as though I have ...

### Section D

B: Meeting deadlines, because I tend to procrastinate, I tend to put things off and then I'm two or three days toward a deadline and it's going to take me more than two or three days to actually do what it is I have to do ...

D: Traffic jams and the thought that I'm going to be late, I can't cope with that ...

B: Yes, getting stuck in a tube tunnel on my way somewhere I have to be there at a certain time, or ... I've just ... it's the end of the day, I want to get home, ... very stressful.

D: ... a situation where you're completely out of control, you have no power over your destiny.

## Recording 3

a Never mind, these things happen!

b Don't take any notice of them!

c Don't worry, it doesn't matter at all!

d It sounds really awful.

e You must be really worried.

f Try not to worry about it too much!

g What a shame!

h Come on, pull yourself together!

i Just try and ignore it!

j There's no point in getting upset about it!

k Calm down!

l How awful!

## Recording 4

M = Man     W = Woman

W: ... so anyway, how's your new job going?

M: Oh, okay. The work's really interesting ... really different from my old job ... you know there's lots of planning projects and going out and meeting different people, and researching markets and things ... and most of the people in the office seem very friendly ... so, yeah, all that side of things is fine ...

W: Oh, good ...

M: Yeah, it's just ... well, I don't want to sound as if I'm moaning already or anything, but I've got a bit of a problem with my boss somehow. It's a bit hard to explain ... when you first meet her, she seems perfectly nice ... you know, quite sort of jolly and good fun, and young and everything, but I don't know, she's got this way of kind of ignoring whatever I say ... she doesn't actually criticise me, not openly, but she just doesn't seem to take any suggestions I make very seriously. It's as if she just knows better and she's not really listening to what I've got to say. It's very undermining ... you know I'm supposed to be her deputy manager, and she treats me like some junior who doesn't know anything about the job, do you know what I mean?

W: Yeah, I do. It must be really difficult knowing how to respond, especially when you're new to the job ...

M: Yeah, and another thing, in meetings she'll just kind of cut straight in and interrupt what I'm saying or completely contradict what I've just said, like I'm an idiot or something!

W: She sounds awful! The boss from hell!

M: Yeah, and then afterwards, she'll be all smiles and sweety-sweety and making jokes again as if nothing's happened. It's really getting on my nerves, I tell you ...

w: It's really difficult isn't it. Have you tried talking to anyone else about it? I mean, maybe she's like that with everyone?

m: I don't know. I don't really feel as if I know any of them well enough yet.

w: No. And I don't suppose it's worth trying to say something to her about it, I mean, I suppose it is possible that she doesn't realise she's doing it?

m: Can you imagine! No, ugh! I don't think that would work. I think she knows exactly what she's doing ...

w: Oh dear, poor old you, it's such a shame when everything else is going so well ...

m: Yeah ...

w: Still, maybe things'll get better when she gets to know you a bit better, and realises how deeply and fantastically brilliant you are! Try not to worry about it too much, eh ... have another drink, what do you want?


# Module 3

## Recording 1

BILL: It was about midnight, I guess. I was coming home from a Christmas party with Frank, a Hungarian friend of mine. It was very, very cold, all the puddles had frozen over, and there was thick ice everywhere ... and on top of that it had been snowing for several hours. Actually, I think it was still snowing because we couldn't really see very well where we were going. The road we were walking down was on this really steep hill too, so you could imagine it was terribly, terribly slippery ... and as I say, we couldn't see a thing so we kept falling over. We'd get up and two seconds later we fell over again, not because we were drunk or anything, we'd only had a couple of glasses of wine at the party, but just because it was so slippery. Anyway, for some reason it all seemed terribly funny, and we were laughing our heads off, and calling to each other for help because we didn't really know how we were going to get down the hill ... we weren't making any progress at all. Eventually we realised that the only way we could move at all was if we held onto the cars that were parked in the street so that's what we did, and slowly we were managing to move along ... except suddenly this police car drew up and two policemen got out and started shouting at us. I couldn't understand a word they were saying. Frank tried to talk to them and find out what was going on, but they wouldn't listen to him. They just pushed us in the back and drove us to the nearest police station. To be honest, I can't remember much after that, but a few hours later, I woke up in a police cell, wearing only my underwear, and feeling absolutely terrified, not to mention freezing cold ...


## Recording 2

OLD LADY: It all happened at about one in the morning, I would say ... I went to bed at ten as usual, but I had to get up to go to the toilet, and as I was getting back into bed I heard this dreadful noise outside in the street ... men shouting ... so, of course, I went to the window to find out what was going on. Anyway, I looked out and saw these two young men just outside my house: they were swaying all over the place, shouting and swearing to each other. They'd obviously been drinking, you could see they were drunk – very aggressive and nasty ... very suspicious-looking types – then I noticed that they were doing something to the cars. The weather was very clear, so I got a good view of what they were doing – they were banging on all the car windows trying to break into them! Obviously, as soon as I realised what was going on, I called the police straightaway, and thank God they came more or less immediately and arrested them, before they could do any more damage. It was very lucky that I happened to wake up and catch them, otherwise I'm sure half the cars in the neighbourhood would have been robbed, perhaps even stolen. This is a nice neighbourhood, quite a few people have expensive cars, with radios and stereos and all sorts in them. As I say, it was very lucky that I saw it at all ...


## Recording 3 (answers only)

a had just left / happened    b had been snowing / were falling
c went / swaying / falling    d had obviously been drinking
e shouting / swearing    f were laughing / were calling
g decided    h banging / were obviously trying
i arrived / arrested


## Recordings 4 and 5

Some years ago, Denis Thatcher, husband of the then Prime Minister, Margaret Thatcher, was on a train, travelling back to London. The train stopped, and Mr Thatcher looked up from his papers to see a group of inmates from a psychiatric institution getting into his carriage, their supervisor following them. They all sat down and the supervisor began to count them. 'One, two, three, four, five,' she counted, stopping when she got to Mr Thatcher. 'Who are you?' she asked, frowning. 'I'm the Prime Minister's husband, actually,' he replied, looking surprised. 'Oh, right,' she continued, smiling kindly now, 'six, seven, eight, nine ...'


## Recording 6 (answers only)

1 It's been raining / I haven't been    2 We'll be having
3 I've been waiting / broken down / we've lost    4 you'll break it


## Recording 7

a A: Excuse me, can you tell me which stop to get off at for the National Museum of Film?
   B: Sorry, I'm not going that far, you need to get on another bus.

b A: Er ... we'd both like the chicken in mushroom sauce, please.
   B: I'm afraid we've only got enough of that left for one portion, sir.

c A: I'd like to book two tickets for the performance on Wednesday evening, please. Can you tell me what tickets there are available?
   B: Sorry, I'm only dealing with today's performance at this desk. You want the advance booking office over there, but it's not open at the moment.

d A: Can I change these dollars into Turkish lira, please?
   B: I'm sorry we don't keep Turkish lira in stock, you'll have to order them. It takes about forty-eight hours.

e A: Can I have a packet of Mellow cigarettes, please?
   B: Have you got proof of your age, please. You know we're not allowed to sell to under-sixteens.


## Recording 8

a A: Excuse me, can you tell me which stop to get off at for the National Museum of Film?
   B: Sorry, I'm not going that far, you need to get on another bus.
   A: Oh, right. Which one do I need to change to?
   B: If you just get off this one and wait for another number nineteen behind, and then check that it says Clerk Street on the front ...
   A: Okay, thank you.

b A: Er ... we'd both like the chicken in mushroom sauce, please.
   B: I'm afraid we've only got enough of that left for one portion, sir.
   A: Oh dear, that's a shame ... er, perhaps I'll have the roast lamb then.
   C: Are you sure? I don't mind changing.
   A: No, no, no, you have the chicken. I couldn't decide between the chicken and the lamb anyway, so that's fine.
   B: So one chicken and mushroom, and one roast lamb. Any wine?

c A: I'd like to book two tickets for the performance on Wednesday evening, please. Can you tell me what tickets there are available?
   B: Sorry, I'm only dealing with today's performance at this desk. You want the advance booking office over there, but it's not open at the moment. It doesn't open again until tomorrow morning at ten I'm afraid.

A: Oh, no. It's really difficult for me to come in again tomorrow. Can I phone up and book?

B: Yes, sure. If you take one of those leaflets over there, you'll find the credit card hotline number on the back. You can phone any time after ten.

A: Right, thanks.

d A: Can I change these dollars into Turkish lira, please?

B: I'm sorry we don't keep Turkish lira in stock, you'll have to order them. It takes about forty-eight hours.

A: Oh, dear. I'm flying to Turkey tomorrow morning. Do you know anywhere that I can get them a bit quicker?

B: There's a bureau de change across the road, you could try there. Otherwise your best bet is at the airport, I would say.

e A: Can I have a packet of Mellow cigarettes, please?

B: Have you got proof of your age, please. You know we're not allowed to sell to under-sixteens.

A: I haven't got anything with me. This is ridiculous. I'm twenty. I've never been asked my age before!

B: Okay then, if you say so. How many did you want?

A: Twenty, please.

## Recording 9

| | | | |
|---|---|---|---|
| a | What a pity ... | f | This is ridiculous! |
| b | Oh dear. | g | Oh, for goodness sake! |
| c | You must be joking! | h | Oh dear, that's a shame ... |
| d | What a nuisance! | i | Oh, right ... |
| e | Right, I see ... | j | Oh, no! |

## Recording 10

a A: Is it okay if I pay for this book by visa? I haven't got much cash on me.

B: We can't really take cards for amounts under five pounds. That one's only £3.99, isn't it?

b A: Can I have three tickets at the special student price, please?

B: I'm sorry we don't do the student reduction on Saturday mornings.

c B: Hello, Justin and Toni, Angela speaking, how may I help?

A: I'd like an appointment for a trim tomorrow afternoon if that's possible.

B: I'm afraid we're shut all day tomorrow, is Wednesday any good?

d A: Can I have five photocopies of this, please. How much is it a copy?

B: It's ten 'p' a copy, but I'm afraid the machine's out of order at the moment.

e B: Good morning, Morgan and Webb.

A: Oh hello, I need to speak to Kathy Parker, please.

B: I'm afraid she's not in today. She's working at home.

# Module 4

## Recording 1

IQ – or 'Intelligence Quotient' tests have been around for nearly a hundred years now, although their usefulness is still much debated. The first tests were devised in France in the early part of the twentieth century, but their use was limited to children until World War I, when the tests were given to two million American military recruits. The tests measured both general knowledge and the ability to reason logically, and the results were used to decide who should get which job, and to identify the most intelligent recruits for training as future army officers. Their use was greatly expanded when the war ended ...

... the vast majority of people fall somewhere in between ... the chances are that you have something around the average IQ of about a hundred. Only two per cent of people are at the 'genius' level of 130 or more. Interestingly, more women tend to score around the average. There are fewer women than men at genius level, but fewer at the bottom as well, a fact from which any number of conclusions could be drawn! It's also a matter of controversy that East Asians consistently perform better on IQ tests than Europeans ... although no one has so far been able to explain exactly why! The bad news if you're over twenty-three is that, although people's knowledge increases as they get older, the average score on IQ tests goes down steadily, so that by the time people reach the age of ...

... and if you do find yourself tackling an IQ test – either when applying for a job or just out of curiosity – here are a couple of handy tips to help you do better. Firstly, do two or three practice tests first. Research suggests that, with practice, your score will increase by between ten and fifteen per cent. Also, it helps to keep your mind clear. A survey of American businessmen revealed that they often made mistakes because they wore their neckties too tight – it cuts off some of the vital blood supply to the brain! And finally, have a good breakfast! Recent research reveals that people do better on IQ tests if they've had a healthy breakfast: cereal, coffee and orange juice are particularly recommended!

## Recording 2

### Question 1

This question is designed to test artistic or visual intelligence. The correct answers are: Figure A ten sides, Figure B eight sides, Figure C thirty sides. To do this type of test well, you need to be able to visualise an object – that is imagine it in your mind's eye, pick it up and move it around. Tests show that many highly intelligent people simply cannot do this.

### Question 2

This is a memory test. The ten items were: a pair of scissors, a rubber, a ruler, some drawing pins, felt-tip pens, a pencil, glue, a paintbrush, a wastepaper bin and a door handle – all items you might expect to find in a normal classroom. The average number of items remembered was eight. If you got more than eight, you have a better than average memory. If you got less than five, you probably need to write your address on the back of your hand before you go out in the morning!

Although memory is not directly linked to intelligence, it is a very useful function, and one that can be improved by doing regular memory exercises, or by using memory aids such as remembering the first letters of items, making them into a mental picture or story or repeating them over and over again.

### Question 3

This question is designed to test your emotional intelligence. If you decided to kindly tell the child not to cry, tried to distract her, or thought you should tell the children to sort it out for themselves ... I'm afraid you score no points! According to experts, the best answer is to talk to the child and help her find ways to get the other children to play with her. Emotionally intelligent parents use their children's moments of upset to help them understand what it was that made them upset, what they are feeling, and the alternatives the child can try.

### Question 4

This question is designed to test creativity. There is no correct answer, but the average number of uses people thought of in two minutes was eleven.

The most popular uses were: to read, for news or information, to cover the floor while painting, and to make a fire. Some unusual uses were: to sleep under, to wrap up a baby and to write a blackmail letter!

### Question 5

This question tests practical problem-solving skills and logic. Some people are able to solve the problem in twenty or thirty seconds, whereas others pore over it for ages without seeing the answer. It's best to start with the people who have to be in particular rooms: Mr E in room two; the A children in room four (because it's the only one overlooking the pool) and their parents, Mr and Mrs A, in room three because it's the only one next door to the children. That leaves room one for Miss C who wants a view of the sea, and if Mr F, Mr and Mrs G, and Miss H all want adjoining rooms, they can take rooms six, seven and eight at the back of the hotel, leaving room five for Mr and Mrs D – the quietest room because it's away from the swimming pool. Did you get that?

### Question 6

As you'll probably have guessed, this is also an emotional intelligence question. The commonest answers are: to apologise (and ask your partner to do so!), go silent, or to stop for a moment and state your side of the argument as calmly as possible. According to the experts, however, the best thing is to take a twenty-minute break and then continue the conversation. Apparently, it takes this long to clear the body of the physical effects of anger. Once both people have been given some time to calm down, a more amicable discussion can be expected!

## Recording 3 *(missing words / phrases only)*

a  you can improve    b  They've discovered    c  they feed
d  bring them up    e  they keep    f  some people are saying

## Recording 4

**I hated languages** at school. I just wasn't interested in learning, so **I never did** my homework  and **I was always** bottom of the class when it came to exams! Maybe it wasn't her fault, but I really didn't get on with my teacher. She seemed to think I was a **stupid young girl** just because I didn't know a past participle from an auxiliary verb (I still don't, actually). And even if I did learn English, there were no English-speaking people in my town, so who would I ever **speak English to**? Things started to change when I got my first job, though. I spent my **first two years** in the Sales Department, and I had to speak English on the phone almost every day, which wasn't easy. I didn't really **have enough time** to go to classes, so at first I tried to study on my own. I also persuaded an English-speaking friend to **give me some** private lessons and I started to make progress. I don't know **when it was** exactly that I realised my English **was good enough** to do First Certificate, but I did ... and I passed! So, I don't hate English any more. In fact it's made **quite a big** difference to my life!

## Recording 5

A: Okay, so I haven't actually used one of these things before so I'm a bit unsure of how to use it.
B: First of all, take it out of the case ... carefully.
A: Yeah.
B: Put it on your knee.
A: All right.
B: Right, can you see ...
A: It's quite heavy, isn't it?
B: It is heavy, yeah.
A: Uh-huh, okay.
B: Now can you see a red button that says 'operate'?
A: This one?
B: Right, you need to press that and the red light'll come on ...
A: All right, okay.
B: Okay, great. The next thing is to take the lens cap off ... which is at the front ...
A: Right, that's this thing here, yeah?
B: Yeah, it just hangs down, it's attached.
A: Right.
B: Fine. Take the viewfinder ...
A: Viewfinder ...
B: ... which is on the right side ... pull it out at right angles.

A: What just ... oh ... okay ... right?
B: Now look through the viewfinder. Turn round so you're looking at me ... and press the record button which is the one at the top.
A: Where is it?
B: That one. Okay, okay. Now can you see through the viewfinder that it says R-E-C?
A: Yeah, it's flashing on and off ...
B: R-E-C ... that means you're recording me.
A: Right.
B: Now, if you want to do anything ... if you want to get close-up then you press the zoom button, if you press it at the top ... that's it.
A: This one?
B: Yeah ... no, no ... no... the other one.
A: Okay, oh sorry. Okay?
B: Yeah. Can you see I'm getting bigger?
A: Right, yeah.
B: Sort of close-up? If you press it at the bottom, I'll recede again, I'll go back ...
A: Back to normal.
B: Yeah, that's right.
A: That's back to normal, yeah. Okay, okay, right ... well, that looks simple enough. Thanks!
B: Okay!

## Recording 6

a  take off the cap      b  pull it out at right angles
c  rest it against your shoulder      d  press it at the top
e  switch it on      f  hold it by the handle      g  turn it round

# Consolidation
# Modules 1–4 *(missing words only)*

a  1 sentence    2 was forced
b  3 lost    4 has been refused
c  5 have decided    6 had never met
d  7 has been trying    8 had answered
e  9 has passed    10 is caught    11 will be sent
f  12 lay    13 had been arranging    14 was demonstrating
    15 looked    16 was lying
g  17 floating    18 was turned down    19 swept
    20 have just passed    21 flying

# Module 5

## Recording 1

For me, the greatest achievement of the last 150 years has definitely been the invention of the car. They've completely changed our lives, if you think about it. Before everyone had their own cars, people had to walk everywhere, or catch the bus, which was time-consuming and inconvenient. Things like getting home from work or going shopping took much longer so people had less time for other things, for having fun. Cars have meant that we have more time for leisure and that we can go further, to more interesting places. You can easily go to the theatre in another town in the evening, for example, or spend the weekend in a nice village in the countryside a hundred miles away. In the olden days, people travelled much less, they had fewer holidays, and they couldn't go to so many exciting places ... maybe they just went a few miles away to visit relatives or whatever. Nowadays, thanks to the car, they can go all over the place and have a much wider experience of life. In the olden days, if you weren't born near the sea then probably you'd never seen the sea, if you weren't born near the mountains, then probably you'd never seen mountains, and people who lived in remote places were very isolated, they had much less contact with the outside world, so society was less mixed and open, and people were more limited in their jobs. These days, with cars, you can drive quite a long way to work – you can work in the city and live in the countryside, for example – and because people travel from town to town more, it's more common for people to go and live and work in different towns, so people have more opportunities, and have more contact with people from other places. And because these days cars are relatively cheap, they have affected almost everyone's lives. It's something everyone can benefit from, not just a few people. Although people complain about traffic and pollution, and things like that, would anyone really want to give up their car, and go back to the days when you had to walk or cycle everywhere, when people didn't often even visit other towns, let alone other countries?

## Recording 2

a  Look outside: it's been snowing.
b  Oh no! I've left my credit card at home!
c  I'm exhausted! I've been rushing around all day!
d  Ow! I've cut myself!
e  Sorry, but I've changed my mind. Could I have the chicken instead, please?
f  Has Sam spoken to you about babysitting on Saturday night?
g  Hi! I haven't seen you for ages. How are you? What have you been doing?
h  My sister's made a lovely chocolate cake. Would you like a piece?

## Recording 3

P = Paul    MR J = Mr Jones

P:  It's very interesting. How long have you been living here?
MR. J:  Over sixty years. My wife and I have been very happy here.
P:  So why have you decided to move?
MR. J:  My wife's been rather unwell ... she hasn't been sleeping, she's been behaving strangely. We've decided to move somewhere quieter.
P:  I understand. You said there were three bedrooms. I've only seen two. Can I see the other one?

J = Jayne    C = Cindy

J:  Hi! What's happened, Cindy! Have you been crying?
C:  I'm fine. I've just been watching a really sad film, that's all.
J:  Have you heard from Nick today?
C:  I don't care about Nick anymore. I haven't thought about him all day. I've forgotten what he looks like.
J:  That's good ...
C:  Actually, that's not the truth. I've been phoning him all day. I've left about six messages on his answerphone, but he hasn't phoned me back ...

## Recording 4 *(missing words / phrases only)*

1  take up
2  used up
3  upside down
4  turned up / warm up
5  What's up
6  It's up to you
7  up?
8  eat up
9  broken up

# Module 6

## Recording 1

**1  Answer:** He / she is suffering from **amnesia**. Insomnia is the inability to sleep; influenza – or 'flu' – is a virus; and anorexia is an eating disorder.

**2  Answer:** Delhi is in fact in the **north east of India**, so the best answer is **a**.

**3  Answer:** When you are discharged from hospital, it means that the doctors say you are **ready to go home**.

**4  Answer:** This is a trick question – Lake Victoria is **not in North America** at all. It is, in fact, the largest lake in Africa, so the correct answer is **d**.

**5  Answer:** The answer is **d**. Ladybirds are **red and black insects**.

**6  Answer:** If you are a pastor, you are a type of **minister or priest**, so the correct answer is **a**.

**7  Answer:** Thanksgiving Day is **in November**, so the correct answer is **d**.

**8  Answer:** The answer is **d, the River Shannon**, which is in the Republic of Ireland. Since the UK includes both Scotland and Wales, Glasgow is obviously in the UK, as are the Scilly Isles and the Isle of Wight, both of which are off the south coast of England.

**9  Answer:** Prague is now the capital of **the Czech Republic** so **a** is the correct answer. Prague was formerly the capital of the whole of Czechoslovakia, but Slovakia has its own capital now – Bratislava.

**10  Answer:** **c** is the correct answer. Lizards are **reptiles**.

**11  Answer:** The answer is **d, none of these**.

**12  Answer:** It is the distance from **the Sun to the Earth**, so **a** is the correct answer.

## Recording 2

**1**  an insect    an animal    an exotic plant    an African bird    an attractive young woman

**2**  the Earth    the East    the Alps    the Atlantic    the end of October

## Recording 3

Okay, so on to step two. Now I guess we all know the feeling when we're trying to get down to some work and ... what happens? Of course, the phone rings – yeah? Or just when you're sitting down, a friend drops by – you know that kind of problem, that kind of interruption? I'm sure you do. So step two is dealing with interruptions.

Now the person who is in control of their own time – and that means you from now on – that person needs to have two skills, two very special skills. Number one is preventing interruptions before they happen and number two is managing those interruptions when they do happen – and they will happen, you can be sure of that.

Let's talk about number one first, about avoiding interruptions. How can we make sure we don't get interrupted? There are three very simple things you can do, and I promise you they will really help you not get interrupted constantly. Okay, number one, make a list of people who you think may interrupt you – family, friends, whoever – and before you start your work, ask them not to phone or visit until after the time you're working because, after all, how can people know that you don't want to be interrupted if you don't tell them?

Okay. Second thing ... you've got an answering machine for your telephone? Use it. Try to work someplace where the phone is out of reach, and just let the answering machine do its work. Don't check your messages until after you've finished what you have to do. That's something to look forward to when you're through with what you're doing. Or if there's someone else around, let them be your answering machine. And third thing is the simplest of all ... just two letters ... N-O. What does that spell? Okay, no ... N-O ... the second most important word in the English language. You've got to learn to say that, nicely but firmly. It can be tough to say no sometimes, yeah? A girlfriend says to you, 'So how about going for lunch Friday?' and you say, 'Yeah, that sounds good, I'd like that,' and then you remember, 'Oh, but I've got that work to do. Maybe I can work Saturday instead,' but you've got to say, 'No'. You have your work to do, you can fix lunch for another day. So these are three ways to avoid being interrupted: warning your interrupters you're not to be disturbed, learning not to answer that telephone and learning to say no. Sounds easy, huh? Well you try it, see how it works.

Now we all know that we will get interrupted at times ... this is gonna happen ... there are a number of things we can all do here. Set a time limit for interruptions. The doorbell rings. It's your neighbour. Just tell yourself, 'Okay I will allow this interruption one minute no more.' And when that time limit is up, you go right back to work – immediately. Okay? So that's the first thing. This'll save you a lot of time, believe me. And second ... okay, I want you all to learn this phrase ... by heart if necessary. It will save you more time than you can imagine. 'That sounds interesting. Can we discuss it once I've finished this?' That's important, I'm gonna say it once more for you, 'That sounds interesting. Can we discuss it once I've finished this?' This will prove very, very useful when you're ...

## Recording 4

It's one of the great inventions of this century, but what we have to learn is how to control the telephone so the telephone doesn't control us. I talked earlier about how to prevent interruptions from the telephone, now I'd like to share with you four ways, four 'hot tips' if you like, which will help manage your telephone time efficiently, this is step three. The first thing you gotta do is organise your telephone area efficiently. So, first of all, let me ask you ... what are the four things you should always keep next to the phone, four things ...

Yes? This will save you a lot of time ... Okay, this is my list. Before you sit down to make that phone call, check you have these four things in a place where you can reach them easily ... they are paper of course, pen, yes, diary of course, you need to have your diary with you, and ... okay ... your personal address book or the phone book. Yeah, it sounds like a little thing, but you should always have those things right by you ...

Okay now I'm going to mention three telephone habits which'll help you stop wasting valuable time. First, have a 'telephone time'. This is the time you set aside for making all those important calls. If you make all your calls in one go, you're more likely to stay with the task in hand rather than stopping to chat for hours so make sure you dedicate that time, and make sure you use it. Secondly, make notes before and after each phone call. Now you might think this is gonna take longer, but you'll find that if you plan your calls in advance ... if you plan what information you need, what questions you're going to ask, you won't find yourself ringing back an hour later saying, 'I forgot to ask you ...' And finally, just as I gave you a useful phrase for cutting short interruptions, you need one for ending conversations. This one's a real honey, I use this one every day particularly with talkative people who you can't get to shut up. 'It's been good to talk with you. I'm sure you have other things to do, so I'll go now.' Yeah? D'you like that one? That's my favourite phrase, and I'll tell you why ...

## Recording 5

H = Hannah    D = Dan

H: Oh this is **so annoying**. Where **on earth** did I put my car keys?

D: Not **again**! Have you looked on the kitchen table?

H: I've looked everywhere.

D: Hannah you **really are** hopeless!

H: Hmm, thank you. Oh look, here they are under this magazine.

D: Well, that just shows ... **what you need is** some kind of system for where you put things. You're **always** losing things, it's **ridiculous**!

H: You've got a nerve! **It was you who** lost all your credit cards the other day, and **it was me** who found them for you!

D: Yes, I know, and I'm **extremely** grateful to you, but you **do** need to get yourself organised with keys.

## Recording 6

1  A: They should have been here <u>hours</u> ago!
   B: Where on <u>earth</u> can they be?

2  A: Was it <u>you</u> who invited Linda's ex-boyfriend to the party?
   B: Yes, but how on <u>earth</u> was I to know that he'd behave like <u>that</u>?

3  A: Could you wait till this afternoon?
   B: No, I <u>can't</u>, it's ex<u>treme</u>ly important that I speak to her <u>right</u> a<u>way</u>.

4  A: He's a <u>typical</u> politician!
   B: Oh, I don't know. He does <u>seem</u> to believe in what he's saying.

5  A: What on <u>earth</u> have you been <u>doing</u>?
   B: <u>Nothing</u>! It wasn't <u>me</u> who made the mess!

6  A: Promise you'll <u>never</u> do it again!
   B: I <u>pro</u>mise, and I do mean it this time.

7  A: You look absolutely ex<u>hausted</u>! Would you like a nice cup of coffee?
   B: Actually, what I need is a nice <u>cold</u> drink.

8  A: I just <u>can't</u> get this computer to do what I <u>want</u>!
   B: You <u>really</u> need to <u>buy</u> a more up-to-date <u>mo</u>del.

9  A: I suppose you've come to see <u>Liz</u>?
   B: No, in fact it was <u>you</u> I wanted to see ...

# Module 7

## Recording 1, Part A

B = Beth    P = Pete

P: So Beth, when is Thanksgiving exactly?

B: The last Thursday of November.

P: Right, and what does it celebrate? What is it about?

B: It celebrates the survival of a group of settlers. They survived their first year, and basically the celebration was for that reason.

P: Right, so what actually happens on the day? How does your normal American spend Thanksgiving Day?

B: Preparing dinner, eating dinner and then recovering from it. That's basically it. It is entirely a food-oriented holiday. The settlers celebrated the first Thanksgiving with the Native Americans and there was a huge amount of food that they shared, and that tradition continues. So basically, you sit down at the table and there is turkey and ham ... usually a couple of different kinds of meat, sweet potatoes and regular potatoes, green stuff, but not a lot, it is not a green vegetable holiday. Other traditional things are things like cranberry relish and pumpkin pie. So all those things that are normally harvested in sort of September, October, November, that time ...

P: And do people give presents or send cards?

B: No presents. I think that people send cards, especially family members if they can't get together ... But it is, in general, a family holiday. Family or friends, it is not a holiday to spend alone.

P: And does anything public happen then? Are there any kind of special processions or firework displays, or anything like that?

B: No, not a thing. It's a very inside holiday. People spend the day inside, and once they finish eating, there is always at least one American Football game and people then sit with their poor, groaning stomachs watching the game.

P: So would you say it is still ... it's still important for most people in the States?

B: Very. Very, very important. It's always interesting, there is a bit of a down time in work right around Thanksgiving time, so people start their holiday on Tuesday or Wednesday. Actually, only the Thursday is a formal holiday. It's ... there are no businesses open or anything except, you know, your usual 7 – 11, or something of that sort. But then, it sort of carries over into the Friday and people don't go into work. So it's a holiday before Christmas.

P: But it's not as commercialised, would you say, as Christmas, which is so commercial nowadays ...

B: No, it isn't.

P: Right. An how about you? Do you have any special memories of Thanksgiving Day? What are your associations with it?

B: I have very happy memories of Thanksgiving. I like the food that is cooked at that time anyway and I love eating. So, for me, it's heaven to have so much food on the table. And besides, it's because it's so family-oriented or friend-oriented, it's a very happy holiday. It's people spending time together enjoying food, enjoying each other, so I have very happy memories of it.

## Recording 1, Part B

The Notting Hill Carnival happens at the bank holiday weekend every August. The carnival is really a religious festival, but our carnival is a celebration of our ancestors' freedom from slavery. We commemorate that in the carnival activity. We brought that with us from Trinidad, where it is a huge pre-Lenten festival that would normally take place in February, or March, but the reason why we have it at August bank holiday here in England is because, one, it's a bank holiday weekend, and two, it is the only time of the year you can guarantee warm weather. Approximately two million people attend the carnival from all walks of life, all races, all creeds. We have the English, the Irish, the Greeks, the Spanish, the Caribbean people, the Africans, and all of them contribute towards making the carnival what it is today, a great multi-cultural festival that takes place in the streets of Notting Hill. There are five main artistic disciplines in carnival. They are the mas, short for masquerade, the costume bands in carnival; then we have the pan which are the steel bands; and then we have the static sound systems. These are like steel bands to be found on street corners and they cater for more contemporary forms of celebration, so you'll find jazz music, pop music, rap music, reggae music, whatever, being played on those static sound systems, and then there are the calypsonians who are the reporters or raconteurs of carnival who will make up calypsos on any theme that affects us in society, like the senior citizens, like the crime rate, like the interest rate, whatever, they will make a song or calypso about it. These disciplines are found in the main in carnival, added to that there are three live stages of carnival where very high quality music goes on.

Nothing is charged for in carnival, except of course the food you eat, and the food is provided by 250 food stalls that are scattered across the carnival area, and those food stalls represent a range of different cuisines. So for a tourist coming to carnival, the experience isn't necessarily a planned one, you just have to go with the flow of the crowd and you know, we have a saying in carnival, 'You do not come to carnival just to spectate, every spectator is a participant.' So you, as a spectator, you're expected to dance, jig a little and add to the general atmosphere and the culture of carnival. Freeing up your spirit to celebrate your freedom as an individual.

We have over seventy costume bands in carnival, each one with over a hundred players in them. Each band is allowed to choose their own theme for the particular carnival and then they have to make costumes that reflect that theme. The bands are made up of, I would say, seventy per cent women, because it is the women who tend to be able to make the costumes, because they can sew, and who tend to take costume-wearing certainly more seriously than the men do. There is no embarrassment, whereas the men feel embarrassed about prancing around in a leotard.

What makes the Notting Hill Carnival special is that it is, by and large, spontaneous and it includes everybody. No spectator stands and spectates. Every spectator is expected to contribute and in contributing you express yourself, you find yourself. You can be as creative as possible and that makes it different.

## Recording 2 *(missing words / phrases only)*

**Surprise, surprise!**
which are elaborately decorated with Christmas paper and bows
are concealed in a series of much larger Chinese-style boxes

**Easter soaking**
is sometimes known in Hungary as 'Water Drench Monday'
brings good health

**Feasting with the dead**
the dead are supposed to return to life
are made of chocolate
are made of sugar
made from fancy bread!

## Recording 3

1 Halloween, which takes place on 31st October, is a night when witches and wizards are supposed to come out.

2 A witch is a woman who can cast magic spells.

3 A wizard is a man who can do the same.

4 Children, dressed up as witches or wizards, go round knocking on people's doors, asking for a 'trick or treat'.

5 This means that if you don't give them a treat, which usually consists of sweets or money, they will play a trick on you.

6 Guy Fawkes' night, which takes place a few days after Halloween, celebrates a time 400 years ago when the British Houses of Parliament were nearly blown up.

7 People build bonfires and burn 'guys', which are models made of old clothes and stuffed with newspapers.

8 The guy represents a man called Guy Fawkes who was responsible for trying blow up the Houses of Parliament.

9 In the days before Guy Fawkes' night, you often see children walking around with guys that they have made, shouting, 'Penny for the guy'.

## Recording 4

a A: Go on, have a bit more. It'll do you good!
  B: Thank you, it was lovely, but just a tiny portion, I'm rather full …
  A: Go on, I insist. Have the last piece, Bella!
  B: No really, I'm really fine thank you. It was lovely but I couldn't possibly manage any more!

b A: Oh dear, how clumsy of me! I'm really sorry, let me get a cloth.
  B: Don't worry, it doesn't matter in the slightest!

c A: You know Vera, don't you, Bella?
  C: Hi there, Bella. Of course she knows me. How are things with you then?
  B: Hello, Vera, how lovely to see you again. It seems ages since we last met. Let me see, when was it …

d A: You must try some of this spinach salad, Bella. It's their speciality!
  B: Actually, I'm afraid I can't eat spinach. It doesn't agree with me, unfortunately. It brings me out in a rash!
  A: Oh dear …

e A: It's been lovely to see you again, Bella. You must come and spend a day with us some time, mustn't she, Mary? I tell you what, how about the weekend after next for Sunday lunch?
  B: Oh that's really sweet of you, Uncle Geoff. It's really nice of you to think of me. I'd love to come, but I don't think I'll be able to make it then – I've got some really important exams starting that week. Perhaps some other time, when I'm not so busy?

## Recordings 5 and 6

1  a / b  No, really, I'm fine thank you. It was lovely, but I couldn't possibly manage any more!
2  a / b  Don't worry, it doesn't matter in the slightest!
3  a / b  How lovely to see you again. It seems ages since we last met!
4  a / b  Actually, I'm afraid I can't eat spinach. It doesn't agree with me.
5  a / b  I'd love to come, but I don't think I'll be able to make it.

# Module 8

## Recording 1, Part A

At Manchester, the protest was against the building of the second runway, but erm primarily that protest was about the destruction of the Bollen Valley that the building of the second runway necessitated and the wiping out of the wild animals and the multitude of different kinds of trees. It was said that we had nearly almost every British tree in that valley and it's been completely annihilated, and we were there protesting against the runway, not because we don't want a second runway, but because we didn't want the Bollen Valley trashed and neither did the people that lived there. It was a tunnel campaign, it was a tree campaign we were there to protect the trees so we lived in the trees, we were there to protect the earth so we lived in the earth, and to do that you have to dig into it and build tunnels, you have to build defences in the trees which are 'lock-ons' in order to lock yourself to, so that the bailiffs can't get you out too quickly. The idea is that the longer it can go on the more money it will cost the company, the more money it costs the company the less effective they're going to be in the long run.

Living underground is frightening. I've done it less than many other people, but erm my experience of closing a door down and being fifteen, maybe twenty feet underground in an unshored tunnel for the whole night is a bit frightening. Erm, I've been through some quite frightening situations, but what happens is, when you close the doors and there er ... of a night time, when you ... you go into the tunnels you have to make sure everything's locked up just in case they decide to come and evict that night. So when you go in the last thing at night you close the doors, you sneak off into the depths of the tunnels and go to a chamber, and then you close a secondary door, or third or fourth door down and ... and try and get to sleep. You get into your sleeping bag and within an hour erm you're panting for air because the oxygen level in there's been used up and it's dropping, and erm you start to sweat a lot and that becomes very uncomfortable because you can't move about in your clothes as well as you want to, and you feel restricted and you feel claustrophobic and er all your senses, er your human education, tells you to leave the place but erm, because of what you're doing, and because you've made a commitment to ... to the cause that you're fighting, you, you tend to stay there ...

## Recording 1, Part B

The reason that I campaign so vigorously for the environment and for the animals is I look at the, the history of the world, this country and mankind and erm I see in the past it's been a pretty beautiful place, the world, and what we have and what we've been given and it seems to me that erm with every passing year we seem to be destroying more and more and more of what we have been given naturally, and we cannot go on sustaining life, we cannot sustain the the the quality of life that we have had, that we no longer have (ha) erm with with the way that we're going about doing things, manufacturing, pol... erm driving cars, erm. The way we spray our hair, the way we do lots and lots of things, the way we abuse animals to try new products ourselves, which aren't necessarily any good, and er I think we've, we've just got everything sort of like back to front and we need to stop and go back to basics and say, look this is the world, this is where we live, if we kill it we're not going to have another one and erm we've got to think of our children, we've got to think of the future of the world, it's not ours to destroy and that's it really.

## Recording 2

Mr Tony Valentino, leader of the New Democratic Party, shocked his followers earlier today by **announcing** his resignation. He said he was retiring in order **to spend** more time with his family, and refused **to comment** on recent newspaper reports about his financial affairs. Mr Valentino is accused of **avoiding** up to $10 million in taxes over the last five years, but has always denied **doing** anything illegal. Mr Valentino said he was happy for his financial affairs **to be investigated** and was willing **to co-operate** fully with the tax authorities as soon as he returns from a four-week **skiing** holiday at a secret location abroad.

Mr Valentino seems **to have begun** his holiday already, as his private helicopter was seen flying away from his luxury villa this afternoon. 'We are very sorry indeed **to lose** Mr Valentino as our leader and are confident that he will be able **to prove** his innocence', said Deputy Leader, Jayne Belowski. 'It is far too early **to talk** about **choosing** a successor, although of course, if I am asked **to stand** as leader, it would be foolish **not to do** so, I have a duty **to serve** the party as best I can.'

## Recording 3 *(missing words / phrases only)*

1  What about    2  round about    3  Just about.
4  It's about / worried about / tell me all about it
5  do something about it    6  I'm about to    7  walk about

# Consolidation Modules 5–8

Toddler Aruw Ibirum, **who lives in Bradford, Yorkshire**, miraculously survived after a thirty-eight ton lorry ran her over, as she lay in her pushchair. The lorry driver, **who was unaware of what was happening**, pulled up after he heard an unusual scraping noise. Aruw, **whose pushchair had been dragged along for nearly a kilometre**, was discovered with just a few cuts and bruises. An astonished elderly woman, **who saw the whole thing happen**, told reporters, 'You wouldn't have believed a child could have come out of that alive.'

An Australian man, **who has been suffering for years**, finally discovered the cause of his acute backache last week. It was due to a shark's tooth **which had been stuck in his spine for almost forty-eight years**.
Leo Ryan, sixty-six, **who will be having an operation to remove the tooth**, had been attacked by the shark as a teenager. In the accident, **which happened off the Gold Coast where he had been swimming**, he also lost three fingers and part of his arm. 'That shark was determined to hang onto me!' he told reporters.

# Module 9

## Recording 1

Well, it's quite a strange picture, quite unusual. It gives you a strange sort of feeling. It's like a desert scene, but it's not all desert, there are some things which would obviously be impossible in the desert ... like in the corner, in the top-right hand corner of the picture, it looks quite windy and stormy. There's a woman walking along with what looks like an umbrella, to protect her from the wind and rain I guess, but it's blown inside out so it's not much use. There's a **stone wall** which is broken down, there's a big kind of hole in the wall as well. In the distance there are some trees and **a chimney**. One strange thing is that there's smoke coming out of the chimney but it's sort of going

# Tapescripts

the wrong way, the opposite direction to the trees, it's going **left to right rather than right to left** ... which it should be, logically ...

Then in the foreground there's a man sitting down ... almost as if he's sitting on a terrace ... in the middle of the desert. He's reading something, a book, I can't actually read the title, it's written **back-to-front**. His clothes are a bit strange, he's wearing a white suit, looks a bit shabby ... as if it's seen better days. There's a big stain on one side, looks like coffee or blood or something ... and **it's torn on the same side**. There's a clock on the table. The clock face is missing and one of the hands of the clock isn't there. There's a candle as well, **it hasn't been lit**, it's completely new ...

On the other side, there's a sort of desert convoy ... a group of vehicles trying to cross the desert ... but they're having quite a lot of trouble by the looks of things. One of them has broken down ... there's a group of people looking at the engine, trying to find out what's wrong, I suppose. One of the other cars seems to have had an accident ... **people are trying to move it,** but it's got stuck in the sand, they can't move it.

## Recording 2

**A**  This enormous egg, with a circumference of 81.78 cm, was found on a Western Australian beach in 1993 by three children who initially mistook it for a very large, smooth rock. What makes the egg even more extraordinary is that the bird that laid it – a monstrously large flightless bird called the Aepyornis Maximus or 'elephant bird' – became extinct about 400 years ago and lived only on the island of Madagascar, at least 6,500 kilometres from the Australian coastline. Scientists believe that the egg must have been transported from Madagascar on the prevailing ocean currents: the Indian and Southern Oceans actually converge at the exact point where the egg was found. The egg is now kept in the Western Australian Museum, which paid AUS $25,000 to the children's families in recognition of the egg's importance to scientists.

**B**  On September 21st and 22nd 1995, thousands rushed to Hindu temples throughout India after reports of a miracle: marble statues of the elephant-headed god Ganesha were drinking the traditional spoonfuls of milk offered by worshippers. News of the miracle spread throughout the world. Ten thousand Hindus flocked to the Vishwa temple in London, and one small statue in Hong Kong apparently consumed twenty litres of milk! While scientists claimed that the milk had been drawn up from the spoons and absorbed by the texture of the statues and then trickled down the outside of the statue in an invisible film, millions believed they had witnessed a miracle. 'I feel that the gods are showing their power, specially to the younger generation, who will now start believing,' said one priest.

**C**  The photograph claims to show the huge prehistoric monster, supposedly seen in Loch Ness in Scotland. The photograph was published in 1934 in the English newspaper, *The Daily Mail*, and immediately caused a sensation. It was widely accepted as genuine, and began a craze for monster-hunting which has continued to this day. In 1994, however, the photo was revealed as a fake. Duke Whetherill – wishing to play a trick on the press – sent his children to a toyshop to buy a toy submarine and some plastic wood. From these things they made a 'monster' which they floated on the lake and photographed. Sixty years later, one of Weatherill's children (now an old man) decided it was time to confess to the deception he and his father had played on the world. Whether or not the Loch Ness Monster really exists is still a mystery, however.

## Recording 3

1   This is false. Over a period of time, shock or stress can turn your hair white, but it can't happen overnight.
2   This is also false. You only have to count your ribs to check this – it's a myth from the Bible which people have tended to take literally.
3   This is true. Babies do have more bones than adults, they join together as the baby develops.
4   This is false. People don't normally die from tarantula bites.
5   This is also false. Elephants can't even <u>see</u> mice, apparently, let

alone be afraid of them! It is not clear where this myth comes from – possibly the children's film *Dumbo*!
6   This is again false. In fact, only a quarter of all people struck by lightning actually die.
7   This is true. Although they have wings, turkeys are indeed unable to fly.
8   This is also true. It is due to the different gravitational forces in the two hemispheres.
9   This is again a well-known myth, but there is no evidence in fact to support it – it's also false.

## Recording 4

### Conversation 1

A = shop assistant        B = customer

A:  Yes, can I help you?
B:  Yes, I bought this in the sale here ... a couple of weeks ago, I think it was ...
A:  I see, yes ...
B:  And I've only worn it a couple of times, but when I looked at it the other day I just thought, no, I don't like it. I don't think it suits me ... the colour's not really right for me, do you know what I mean?
A:  Well ... um, do you have any receipt, or proof of purchase?
B:  No, no, I didn't keep the receipt, sorry ... does that mean that I can't change it? Because I've seen another one I like ...
A:  Well, we can't normally exchange goods without proof of purchase, you see ...
B:  Oh no!
A:  I can speak to the manageress if you like, see what she says.
B:  Well yes, if you would ... because I would like to change it ...

### Conversation 2

A = customer        B = waiter

A:  Excuse me, what is this, please?
B:  That's your pizza, madam.
A:  Yeah, I can see that ...
B:  It's pizza Napoletana – mozzarrella cheese, tomato, garlic ...
A:  Yes, I know what it is, but it's not what I ordered ...
B:  Oh, I'm sorry.
A:  I ordered the lasagne with green salad. I think you must have the wrong order ...
B:  I'll just go back and check, sorry about that.
A:  Okay, you go check, I think you'll find I'm the lasagne ...

### Conversation 3

... yeah, I've got the delivery okay ... yes everything seems to be here, there's just one slight problem ... well I've got it all set up according to the instructions, and I managed that all right, but when I switch it on, nothing happens, the screen's just completely blank ... no, nothing at all. Yes, I've tried that ... yes, it is plugged in. Well, I don't know, that's why I'm ringing you. Well is there anyone there who can help me? ... I see, right. Well, if I leave my number, can you ask that person to ring me back as soon as possible, yeah? Okay, it's 0-1-3-5 ...

### Conversation 4

A = teenage male customer        B = female shop assistant

A:  I'd like to change this CD, please.
B:  You'd like to change it. What exactly is the problem?
A:  It was a Christmas present, I asked my mum to buy me a CD for Christmas, but this isn't the one I wanted. I wanted the new CD by Chaos Theory, and she bought me this ... it's the wrong one, my mum bought it by mistake ... it's their first CD, not the latest one ...
B:  I see, so you'd like to exchange it for the right CD, is that right?
A:  Well no, not really, you see I don't like Chaos Theory any more. I'd like a computer game instead ...
B:  I see, well if you'd like to choose which computer game you'd like, then we can probably take the price of the CD off the price of the computer game ... if you have the receipt with you. Do you have

the receipt?

A: Yeah, it's here.

B: Okay then ... so if you'd like to choose the computer game, then we'll try to sort it out for you, okay?

# Module 10

## Recording 1

J = James    R = Richard

J: Hello?

R: Hi James, it's Richard.

J: Richard, hi, how are things with you? What's new?

R: Oh, nothing much. Listen, the reason I'm calling is that **I'm going to take** Sam, my nephew, to the hockey game on Saturday. **Are you going**?

J: I want to, the only problem is that we **are having** lunch at my mom's this Saturday, but if the game **starts** later on, I'll probably go.

R: It **starts** at five – I've just phoned to check. Do you think your mother**'ll mind** you leaving a bit early?

J: I don't think so – not if I tell her it's something really important!

R: Well, what could be more important than a hockey game?

J: Yeah, **it's going to be** one of the biggest games of the season. Apparently they've already sold over 10,000 tickets.

R: Yeah, I know. So who do you think**'ll win**?

J: Well, Buffaloes **aren't going to win**, not with all the injuries they've had this season, and the way they've been playing! Saints are definitely the favourites!

R: Mmm, I really hope you're right! By the way, do you want me to collect you? **I've decided to drive** there, it'll be easier with Sam.

J: Yeah, that would be great if it's no trouble.

R: No, no problem. Let me think, what time do we need to be there?

J: About half four to buy the tickets?

R: Yeah. Okay then, **I'll collect you** at four – we'd better leave plenty of time in case the traffic**'s** bad. Is that okay?

J: Yeah, great. See you on Saturday, then.

R: Yeah, see you then.

## Recording 2

D = Diane Alberry    R = Robert Emsworth

D: Welcome back, this is Diane Alberry on LBR 95.9, and I'm joined in the studio by Robert Emsworth, author of the book *Getting in Touch: What the Communication Revolution is Really About*. We're talking about the so-called communication revolution. What exactly is meant by that?

R: Well, when we talk about the communication revolution, what we're talking about is the availability of high-speed systems of communication: electronic mail, communication via computers, and more familiar things like telephones ... and this is something which is changing our lives ... not for all of us, though, because it's important to remember that, although there are about half a billion telephone lines worldwide, ninety-six per cent of those telephone lines are in the developed world, Europe, America, parts of Asia. Many people in the less developed countries have no access to even a telephone, never mind e-mail. Another statistic: there are twice as many telephones in Italy as there are in the whole of China which has a population 200 times bigger!

D: Really? So perhaps this communication revolution doesn't go quite as deep as some of us might think?

R: Exactly. Also, just because you've got the technology, doesn't mean you are always going to use it effectively. If you take e-mail, for example, the wonderful thing about e-mail is that you can send a message electronically to another computer anywhere in the world – instantly. But that doesn't mean that the person who receives it

will actually bother to read it or answer it. There's every chance that your message will still be sitting there days, weeks later, waiting to be answered.

D: It's like with answering machines – you ring someone up and all you get is the recorded message and you ring again and again and keep getting the same message, and you never get to talk to the actual person.

R: Yes, it can be very frustrating, can't it?

D: So when would you say it all started, all this communication age business?

R: Well of course people have been writing letters for hundreds, thousands of years but, in fact, we only start to see more instant communication about 150 years ago with the invention of the telegraph. This allowed messages to be sent down a wire almost instantly. This was actually rather bad news for one man, John Tawell was his name, he was a suspected murderer and Tawell was seen getting on a train to London, obviously convinced that the police would never catch him. Unfortunately for Mr Tawell, the railway company had just installed a telegraph system and so a message was sent to the police in London, who were calmly waiting for a rather surprised Mr Tawell when he got off the train at the other end ...

D: The first victim of the communication revolution, you might say.

R: Indeed, yes.

D: So what about the future? What changes do you foresee?

R: Well, when people make predictions they're usually wrong. For example, about twenty years ago, everyone was saying, 'Of course, in twenty years ordinary telephones will have become a thing of the past, we'll all be using videophones.' ... and well, they haven't really caught on ... they're still not all that popular.

D: Well, I know I certainly don't want anyone knowing how I look first thing in the morning.

R: Exactly. Just because the technology is there, it doesn't mean that people necessarily want to use it.

D: So what do you see as the changes that ...

## Recording 3

1 A: So when can I speak to Mr Hammond?

   B: If you try again about half past two, he'll have come back from his lunch by then.

2 A: Debbie said you can't come to the party on Friday.

   B: No. I'm on late shifts, so I'll be working, I'm afraid.

3 A: I'm just going out to get some lunch. I won't be long.

   B: Could you just post this for me? You'll be passing the post box, won't you?

4 A: So what time do you want us for dinner tomorrow night?

   B: Say about half past eight? The kids'll have gone to bed by then, so it'll be a bit more peaceful.

5 A: So see you in about half an hour. I've just got to go out and buy some coffee.

   B: Oh don't bother, I'll get it. I'll be driving right past the supermarket. What sort do you want?

6 A: So, same time, same place next week?

   B: I won't be here next week, I'm off on holiday! Hopefully, this time next week I'll be lying by the pool in the sunshine!

7 A: Is it okay if I have the car tomorrow ?

   B: Yeah, no problem. Matt's giving me a lift to work this week, so I won't be using it.

## Recording 4

### Conversation 1

A: 78461?

B: Hello is that Stephen Hyder, please?

A: Sorry?

B: Is that Stephen Hyder?

A: Yes, this is Stephen Hyder, yeah.

B: Hello, this is Adriana Simonescu, I'm calling from Romania.

A: I'm sorry, could you speak up a bit please? This is a really bad line – I can hardly hear you.

B: Is that better?

A: Sorry? Your voice is very, very faint.

B: I said is that better?

A: Oh yes, yes. I can hear you perfectly now, that's fine.

B: Good. Yes, this is Adriana Simonescu. I'm ringing about your visit here on the 22nd.

A: Yes ...

B: Well, something quite important has come up which I felt you ought to know about.

A: Oh dear, is there a problem?

B: Well, I hope it won't be such a problem, you see what's happened is that ...

A: Oh no. Hello, hello? Sorry the line's got really bad again. Could you ring me back, please? I can't hear you! Oh no, we've been cut off!

### Conversation 2

B: Hello, Teletron International, how may I help you?

A: Hello, my name's Christine Ford, I'm phoning about a letter I received from you today saying ...

B: Can you give me your customer reference number, please?

A: Yes ... just a second ... it's V-2-0-6-P ...

B: Okay, I'll put you through.

C: Hello, Customer Services?

A: Hello, my name's Christine Ford, I'm phoning about a letter I received from you today regarding ...

C: Can I take your customer reference number, please?

A: V206P.

C: V206P. Just a moment while I get your file up on screen ... yes, what can I do for you?

A: It's about a letter I got from you this morning saying that I haven't paid my bill, and actually I sent you a cheque over three weeks ago, I ...

C: Right, you actually need to speak to the Invoice and Finance Department, I'll just transfer you ...

'You are through to Teletron International Invoice and Finance Department. I'm afraid all our operators are busy at the moment but we'll deal with your inquiry as soon as we can. Thank you for waiting.'

D: Hello, Mark speaking, how can I help?

A: Yes, I'm phoning about a letter I got from you this morning – the reference number's V206P – you say in the letter that I haven't paid my bill, when in fact I sent you a cheque three weeks ago ...

D: Okay ... I think you actually need to speak to our Customer Services Department ...

A: I've just spoken to them and they told me I needed to speak to you – I'm getting a bit fed up with being put through from one department to another. Do you think someone could just deal with it, please!

D: Okay, yes, I quite understand. Perhaps if I can just take your name and number, then I can look into it and call you back in ten minutes?

A: Thank you – it's Christine Ford, and the number is 5700770.

D: And the reference number is?

A: V206P.

D: Okay, I'll call you back in ten minutes Mrs Ford.

A: Okay.

### Conversation 3

A: Yes, hello, Linda Bates speaking ...

B: Hi, Linda, it's Jane Markham from Adonis Travel, it's regarding your flights to Rome – I've just got a couple of queries ...

A: Oh, yes - hello, oh sorry ... just a second ... NO! NOT THERE! WHERE I TOLD YOU, BY THE BOOKCASE – sorry ...

B: Yes, I just wanted to know if you mind flying late at night, I've got ...

C: Mummy, Alex says he won't play with me any more.

A: I've told you, don't interrupt me when I'm speaking on the phone.

Yes, sorry, you were saying?

B: Don't worry, listen, am I ringing at a bad time? I'll ring back a bit later if it's easier for you.

A: Do you mind, it's just that I've got some delivery men here and – NO! NOT THAT ONE THE OTHER ONE – sorry ...

B: Look, I'll ring you back in about half an hour when things have calmed down a bit. Is that okay?

A: Yes fine, I'll speak to you later.

B: Bye.

A: Bye.

## Recording 5

1 Am I ringing at a bad time?

2 Could you speak up a bit, please? This is a really bad line.

3 I'll put you through.

4 Oh no, we've been cut off!

5 I'll just transfer you.

6 I'll ring you back in about half an hour when things have calmed down a bit.

7 What can I do for you?

8 It's regarding your flights to Rome – I've just got a couple of queries.

9 Perhaps if I can just take your name and number then I can look into it and call you back in ten minutes.

10 Sorry, you were saying?

# Module 11

## Recording 1

**1** Treatments now exist which can decide the sex of a baby according to the parents' wishes, but most doctors continue to feel that whether the child is a boy or a girl is a decision best left to nature. Mr and Mrs Schwarz are a married couple **in their late thirties**. They have five healthy children – all **boys** – and are a happy, unified family. They are now planning a sixth child, but they are desperate to have a **girl** this time. Mrs Schwarz says she would rather have an abortion than have **another son**; Mr Schwarz is equally insistent, 'What possible harm can there be in granting us our dearest wish to have **a daughter**?' he asks. However, allowing parents to choose the sex of their children could affect the delicate balance of the sexes. It's estimated that **sixty-five per cent** of parents in the West would prefer a **girl,** with serious social consequences.

**2** Scientists at the University of Texas (USA) believe they have discovered the key to stopping the ageing process – a simple chemical called telomerase – which is produced naturally by **the human body**. Telomerase enables human cells to divide and replace themselves, but after a certain age the body stops producing it and begins to age. An American drug company has now applied for a licence to produce Telozan, a drug containing large quantities of telomerase which, it is claimed, will enable takers to live for up to **150** years. No harmful side effects have been identified after **five** years of laboratory tests, though some scientists are concerned that there may be a small risk of **cancer**. With **sixteen per cent** of the population of the USA already over sixty years old, the implications for the worlds of health and work are enormous.

**3** In 1996, the papers were full of the story of L., an **eighteen-year-old** girl paid by a Mr and Mrs R., a **childless** couple, to be a surrogate mother for their baby, using **L's** eggs and sperm donated by Mr R. In return for bearing it and then handing it over to its new parents, L. received **$30,000**. All seemed well until **two days** after the birth of baby M., when L. refused to hand over the child, claiming that Mr and Mrs R. were not suitable parents and that, as the child's natural mother, she had the right to keep her. Although she had no **job or means of support**, L. claimed she would work to repay the money (which she had spent) rather than hand the baby back. The R's said they had no interest in the money, but only wanted their baby, and took L. to court to get the child back. The judge ruled in their favour and, at the age of **three months,** baby M. went to live with the R's. L. was not allowed to have any contact with the child which was legally not hers.

## Recording 2

D = Denise       P = Philip       K = Karen

D: Well, I think in view of the fact that they have five children already, all of the same sex, I think it's fair enough that if they've made that decision that they want a sixth child, then I think it's fair enough that they should be able to have access to information which allows them to know the sex of the child and in fact determine the sex of the child if they're desperate for a girl. I think that's fair enough.

K: I don't know, I think the idea of actually treatment being made available is actually quite a dangerous thing because in view of the statistics, the possibility of sways in population swaying towards one gender or the other is actually not unreasonable, is not unlikely and I actually think even although scientists have actually, I don't know, invented the treatment or have produced the treatment, I don't know that actually making it available is such a good idea.

P: You're worried about there being too many women and not enough men in the world?

K: Or vice versa, depending on the society.

P: ... but it wouldn't really matter because that might be a problem over a period of five or even twenty years, but the balance would change fairly quickly afterwards, I can't see that's a problem.

D: I suppose it's always in terms of people finding partners, isn't it? Because left to its own devices, nature tends to go like fifty-three to forty-seven per cent, it's always hovering around the fifty per cent mark in terms of the balance of the sexes ... so I suppose it's a reluctance to interfere with the balance of nature ...

P: Yeah ... for me, this is not a problem, I just don't think it's significant ... I just find – and I have no arguments about it at all – that there's something wrong about going to the supermarket and choosing the sex of the child. I can't explain it intellectually or anything like that, it just seems wrong.

D: I think I can understand that maybe if it was your first or second or third, but I suppose that if you've got five children, y'know, we're coming up to the millenium, I think, well, if the science is ... if the technology is available to enable people to create the family that they want to create, well, why not, really?

P: Because, well ... I don't know, it just seems to be too much like playing God, having that kind of power seems to me wrong. I don't know why.

K: Yes, I'm with you on that one because I think this idea of, if you have five boys already, choosing another one, choosing the sex, and having that child only if you can have a child of that sex, it is ... it's like going to the supermarket for a child, it's not allowing nature to take its course.

P: Perhaps it's irresponsible in any case to have six children in the first place, I mean what are they doing having five children and then asking for another one after that, ... um .... nah!

## Recording 3

1  Mm ... it is a difficult one. I think as long as everyone knows exactly what they're letting themselves in for, everyone knows exactly what the situation is, then okay, as far as I'm concerned, people should be allowed to do it. I know that many people would say that it's wrong, but if it gives parents who can't have children the opportunity to do so, and no one suffers because of it, then to me ... I can't see why not, frankly. I don't have any objection.

2  Definitely. Absolutely, definitely, yes. I'm absolutely convinced that it should be stopped, yeah. Personally, I find smoke really repulsive, really horrible and I really don't see why I should have to endure other people's smoke when I'm at work. It just makes me yeuch,

really. It seems that most places have some kind of ban on smoking nowadays, and I think it's to everyone's benefit. It's often said that eighty per cent or something of smokers want to give up anyway, so this seems a good way of helping them to do it.

3  Well, I must say I haven't really thought about it. I think if it's just for unimportant things like cosmetics, they do a lot of testing on animals to see if cosmetics are safe, don't they, I don't think that should be allowed, no, that seems wrong to me, but as for medical research ... there might be some real benefit that comes out of it. I haven't really made up my mind about it, to be honest.

4  Actually, I think it can be justified in many cases, but I'd say that it has to be clear that there is some benefit, or possible benefit. I've read that most experiments on animals don't actually have that clear a purpose. I think they should be allowed, but there has to be very strict control over exactly what experiments are permitted. I know some people believe that all experiments should be banned, but I don't completely go along with that.

5  I think you have a really tricky moral issue here. I know that apparently in the States, there are special agencies that can fix this up for you ... if you have the money, of course, and, actually, when you think of it ... I don't think that's right, it's like you're treating babies as a commodity, something you can buy, like a new washing machine or something ... frankly, no, I don't agree with it.

6  Erm ... it doesn't really bother me. I mean everybody says that smoking's bad for you, and the experts all say that other people's smoke can make you ill, but I don't know really ... I don't smoke myself, but I don't have any real objection to other people doing it.

## Recording 4

a   I'm <u>absolutely</u> convinced       b   To be <u>honest,</u>
c   As far as <u>I'm</u> concerned       d   I've <u>no</u> doubt       e   To <u>me</u>

# Module 12

## Recording 1

1   Well the things I don't really look at usually are the financial pages, sports pages, things like editorials, because they tend to be very long and quite boring, unless it's a topic that I'm really, really interested in. The things that I do actually read a lot of are things like the arts pages, and reviews of new films, new books, and that's why I like reading on a Sunday, because the papers that you get on a Sunday are usually full of the reviews of the week, and I find that quite interesting, but things like the financial pages just bore me, I just don't understand them and I'm not interested, and sport, I'm just not interested, so I just don't bother.

2   We turn it on at 5.45 in the morning, and stay in bed and drink our tea and listen to the news then more news and more news, and, basically, we listen to it until we leave the house and that's a good hour and forty-five minutes later. When I come home at night, I turn on the radio, sort of one of the first things I do is turn on the radio, I find it so relaxing to have that noise in the background, and then I hear the news at the end of the day, so I don't miss out on what's happened all day long. I turn it off by about ten past seven, because I'm not interested in the programmes after that, but I love having it on when I'm working, doing either schoolwork or housework in the house, I like listening to music, just to have it on.

3   Yeah the best stuff is on cable and satellite, which I don't have, so I've got to go to the pub to watch it, which is all right, I don't mind, that's a good excuse. But on what I've got at home it's just division two, division three, stuff like that, games which aren't very interesting, and then sports which only people who are not really interested in

sport like watching – like cricket and darts and bowls and things like that. So I just go out on Wednesdays and Saturdays and Sundays, and watch it down the pub.

**4** Sometimes I think it's almost impossible to turn on the television without seeing violence, and I never thought I'd feel like that, but maybe it's just because now I've got a little child I feel like that, but I turn it on and adverts seem to be quite violent, and there is cartoons, and it seems to be from seven o'clock in the morning until you turn the TV off at night on one of the five channels, you're bound to find something which shows people being aggressive towards each other. I think it's something I've become more aware of since I've had a child of my own, but it's not the kind of thing I'd write to the paper about, but it bothers me quietly, I suppose.

**5** Well the ones I really, really hate are for perfume, above all others I absolutely detest them, usually around about Christmas time, you're completely bombarded by these things for perfume, and they usually have women in the most ludicrous clothes, doing something really stupid – like, I don't know, wearing an evening dress and stepping out of a shell. They're just absolutely dreadful, they're absolutely dreadful – they're supposed to be really, really sophisticated, and I don't know, the women who are on them are supposed to be really beautiful, but they just look absolutely ridiculous and I loathe them!

## Recording 2

... this article describes a study that has been done which claims to 'prove' that TV advertising works.  Basically, what the researchers did was to attach a machine to people's TVs and monitor which adverts they'd watched, then check this with what they bought in the supermarket ... and they found that – surprise, surprise – people did buy the products that they had seen in advertisements, especially if they'd seen the advert several times, just a few days before they went shopping. Apparently, the most effective adverts were in the middle of soaps and other very popular programmes, when, according to the article, people concentrate a lot more on the television.
Two questions struck me, really – which I'd like to know other people's opinions about. Firstly, do you feel as if TV adverts influence you personally – and if so, which ones do you think influence you and why?
And secondly, if it's really been proved that TV adverts influence what people buy, then should the government ban adverts for anything that might be bad for you like alcohol, or cigarettes, for example?

## Recording 3

1  A:  Tammy, can you tell us if there's any truth in the rumour that you're pregnant?
   B:  I haven't got any plans to start a family at the moment – at present I'm just concentrating on my career.
   C:  Okay, that's enough ... thank you very much everyone.
2  A:  ... so I'm afraid Rachel isn't here at the moment, Sheila ...
   B:  Well can you tell her to call me back as soon as she gets in – it's something quite important I need to discuss with her. You won't forget, will you?
   A:  Of course I won't.
3  A:  Zoe, have you borrowed any money from my purse – I thought I had a lot more than £20.
   B:  No, I haven't. I haven't touched it! You always think everything's my fault!
4  A:  A group of us are going out for a meal tonight after work, would you like to come with us?
   B:  I'm not sure what I'm doing ... but thank you ... I'll let you know later.
5  A:  I want to go first!
   B:  Okay, Alex, you can have the first turn, but only for about ten minutes, then it's Rosie's turn, is that clear?
   A:  Okay.

# Consolidation Modules 9–12

## Recording 1 *(missing words / phrases only)*

1   a  may have thought   b  should have done   c  must have been
2   d  must have been   e  would get   f  might go
3   g  must have been   h  could have been   i  would have been
4   j  must be   k  would feel   l  would change   m  might start
     n  might lose   o  could end up
5   p  I'd been   q  would have been   r  would feel
6   s  happened   t  would be   u  might get   v  might feel

## Recording 2

**Conversation 1**
A:  Your bill for room 603, madam. How will you be paying – cash or credit card?
B:  Cre ... just one moment, what's this?
A:  What is what, exactly, madam?
B:  This ... $120 ... here.
A:  That is for your telephone calls, madam. Just here it says 'Telefon', that means 'telephone', madam.
B:  Are you laughing at me?
A:  No, madam, of course not.
B:  Well, you'd better not be, that's all I can say because, listen, I am not going to pay this $120, do you hear me?
A:  But madam ...
B:  I phone my husband for two minutes and it costs me $120. It's crazy.
A:  I'm afraid the calls were made from your room, madam, you are obliged to pay for them.
B:  Listen, I'm not paying anything until I see the manager.
A:  I'm afraid the manager is not available at the moment, madam.
B:  I said I want to see the manager and I want to see him NOW, you hear RIGHT NOW.
A:  Well, he's having his lunch at the moment.
B:  He's having WHAT?
A:  Perhaps you might like to make an appointment to see the manager when he comes back from his lunch. Would two thirty be okay?

**Conversation 2**
A:  You idiot! What do you think you're doing? You did that on purpose, didn't you? You deliberately backed into me! It's all your fault, you shouldn't be on the road ...
B:  Oh no, no – it wasn't on purpose ... it was an accident. I didn't see you coming, I honestly didn't mean it!
A:  Look at the damage you've done to my car! That'll cost a fortune to get fixed. You're going to pay for this ...
B:  Well, I think you'll find ...
A:  Just a moment, don't I know you?
B:  Well, you might do, I am quite well-known ...
A:  You're Andrew whatsitsname ... Andrew, er ...
B:  Clark. Yes, that's me, I'm Andrew Clark, yes.
A:  I've seen you on the television ... my wife thinks you're wonderful. ... I wonder if you'd mind giving me your autograph?
B:  Well, I don't normally ...
A:  Oh, go on ... just write 'To Lenora' ... she's my wife ... she thinks you're fantastic.
B:  Well, okay, if you insist ... 'To Leonora, best wishes Andrew Clark'.
A:  Thanks, oh – and sorry I lost my temper just now ... it's just that it's not my car. It belongs to my wife, you see ...